Payday Lending in Canada in a Global Context

Jerry Buckland • Chris Robinson
Brenda Spotton Visano
Editors

Payday Lending in Canada in a Global Context

A Mature Industry with Chronic Challenges

palgrave
macmillan

Editors
Jerry Buckland
Menno Simons College
Canadian Mennonite University
Affiliated with the
University of Winnipeg
Winnipeg, MB, Canada

Chris Robinson
Faculty of Liberal Arts
and Professional Studies
School of Administrative Studies
York University
Toronto, ON, Canada

Brenda Spotton Visano
Faculty of Liberal Arts
and Professional Studies
Department of Economics
School of Public Policy and
Administration
York University
Toronto, ON, Canada

ISBN 978-3-030-10028-5 ISBN 978-3-319-71213-0 (eBook)
https://doi.org/10.1007/978-3-319-71213-0

Printed on acid-free paper

This Palgrave Macmillan imprint is published by Springer Nature
The registered company is Springer International Publishing AG
The registered company address is: Gewerbestrasse 11, 6330 Cham, Switzerland

Dedicated to Financially Challenged Consumers Who Use Payday Lending but Deserve Better Options

Foreword

Few things have been debated as passionately or for as long as has the question of what constitutes usury. The Merriam-Webster Dictionary (website) defines usury as an unconscionable or exorbitant rate or amount of interest, or interest in excess of a legal rate charged to a borrower for the use of money. The usury question is at the heart of this timely and important book, where it is explored unlike ever before, and with a focus on a recent phenomenon: the rise of high-cost credit providers, with payday lending being the most well known.

The writers in this book have been shining a light on this important issue long before most wanted to, knew we needed to, or knew how to. This book provides new evidence, context, and analysis regarding an issue that is relatively new in the Canadian context, and growing in reach and concern across the country.

I work for Momentum, Calgary, Canada, a non-profit community economic development organization that offers financial empowerment programs, including financial literacy workshops and asset-building programs, for people living on a low income. We have been doing our work for more than 25 years, yet it was only five years ago that we started to take notice that so many of our program participants were drowning in payday loan debt. We began to listen and look for stories of people's experiences with payday loans and other harmful high-cost lenders, and what we heard was astounding. People revealed that they had multiple loans from multiple lenders across the city at one time, and that once they paid off a loan they were bombarded with advertising, phone calls, and reminders to come and borrow again. We also learned that most only paid off their loan in order to borrow again, because they could not make ends meet. Participants shared with us that when they needed the money, they needed it right away, but in the end, they wished they had never gotten a loan. The short-term relief of immediate cash turned into long-term grief and an endless debt cycle.

In Momentum's most recent public consultations on high-cost credit, participants shared the following wise words, many of which were similar sentiments shared by the group:

- "I probably spent more on interest than on the actual loan."
- "We felt powerless to negotiate a lower interest rate. It felt like kidnapping."
- "Insurance payments cost more than car payments."
- "The fine print should be the big print."
- "We need better options. They are often the only option. Not even the last option."
- "Banks need to offer credit building products."
- "We use banks, but this has a limit. Banks are very protective, and their practices are not flexible. You are treated well at a [payday] lender, but not treated well at the bank."
- "I would change the regular banks. I would make them friendlier, more understanding, and make them provide services that are similar, but a lower cost."

One participant shared with us that she got a payday loan to finance payments for a rent-to-own computer, which her kids needed for their schoolwork. Soon after, she decided to pawn the computer to cover basic living expenses. This series of decisions left her indebted to three different lenders at annual interest rates of 60–300%, and owing two places a computer. She later learned in our money management workshops that there were a few alternatives that she could have used to prevent this level of debt. However, at the time she had no idea and was left wondering how on earth she could legally end up in such financial turmoil.

Momentum works directly with people to grow their financial literacy and assets, but we also work with government to change the system and to identify the root causes of poverty and financial exclusion. High-cost credit contributes to a two-tiered banking system, where the poor pay more for far inferior services. Often referred to as having a poverty premium, and often likened to throwing someone an anchor when they are drowning, high-cost credit services appear to help when an individual is strapped for cash and already in debt. They are also an easy place to turn when the banks say "no." However, they hurt people's financial well-being and are targeted at people with no other choice. Their neon signs and slogans dot the landscape online and on the street.

- "We say yes when banks aren't an option."
- "Welcoming all cash- and credit-constrained consumers."
- "Instantly borrow the money you need today—no credit checks, no delay!"
- "Good, poor, or bad credit? No problem! ... We don't do credit checks."

Some view these lenders as pernicious, insidious, and extremely harmful. Others see them as providing a vital service to a population long ignored by the mainstream financial institutions. What is sometimes forgotten is their impact on whole communities. These retailers drive away more desirable business and diminish residents' capacity to invest in other businesses and their community. In the words of a resident of Calgary's Greater Forest Lawn area, the clustering of high-cost lenders has a significant impact on how the community is perceived. High-cost lenders reinforce narratives about the area as undesirable to live or start a business in, dangerous, crime-ridden, poor, and so on and greatly limit the community's ability to present an alternative, positive narrative.

Improving access to safe and affordable credit requires the careful attention of academics, policymakers, economists, urban planners, politicians, community leaders, and community members. This book is for these leaders. This book provides a careful, thorough, and forward-thinking analysis of this complex issue in the context of an ever-changing market. It equips you with the knowledge and know-how to effect change, particularly regulatory change. In a time when most literature and analysis on this issue is from the United States, this Canada-specific research is necessary and appreciated. This book is a must-read for anyone interested in gaining a better understanding of financial inequality and wondering what we can do about it.

Read it and join us in advocating for fairer and more responsible lending in Canada.

Public Policy Manager, Momentum — Courtney Hare
www.momentum.org

Acknowledgments

This book relies upon a large amount of research completed over the last 13 years. Many people assisted us in this research including respondents, research assistants, research associates, academic colleagues, and organizational leaders. We are grateful to all of them and are able to mention some names here: Marilyn Brennan, Tom Carter, John Osborne, Brian McGregor, and Evan Sinclair. We thank Zoe St-Aubin and Anita Friesen for particularly important insights they shared with us from their research.

We are very grateful for the long-standing support provided to our research by Gloria Desorcy, Executive Director of the Consumer Council of Canada (Manitoba) Inc.; John Silver, Executive Director of Community Financial Counselling Services; and Louise Simbandumwe, Co-director of SEED Winnipeg. We are most appreciative of the collaborations with and support from the staff at Public Interest Law Centre, Winnipeg Harvest, ACORN Canada, and our Toronto community partners convened under the auspices of the Black Creek Financial Action Network.

We are indebted to the editorial staff at Palgrave Macmillan for the support that we received from them including Sarah Lawrence, Elizabeth Graber, and Allison Neuburger. The idea for the project began with a conversation with Ms. Lawrence who set the process in motion, and we are indebted to her for that. We are thankful for the ongoing assistance of Ms. Graber and particularly grateful for all the support that Allison Neuburger provided us. Thank you! We would like to thank Mr. G. Nirmal Kumar and his team for his careful copy editing of this volume.

The co-editors would like to thank their respective universities for continued research support. Brenda Spotton Visano acknowledges the

Department of Economics, the School of Public Policy and Administration, and the Faculty of Liberal Arts and Professional Studies, York University. Chris Robinson acknowledges the School of Administrative Studies and Faculty of Liberal Arts and Professional Studies, York University. Jerry Buckland is grateful to Canadian Mennonite University, its thoughtful programming and engaged faculty members in (International) Development and Conflict Resolution Studies, and its Menno Simons College campus.

Contents

Notes on Editors and Contributors

Editors

Jerry Buckland is Professor of International Development Studies at Menno Simons College, Canadian Mennonite University, University of Winnipeg affiliate, in Winnipeg, Canada. His research and teaching areas include research and evaluation methods, financial empowerment (microfinance/financial inclusion/financial literacy), community-based development, and rural and Indigenous Peoples' development.

Chris Robinson PhD, CFP®, CPA, CA, is a Professor of Finance at York University and a Fellow of the Financial Planning Standards Council. He has been researching and teaching personal finance for 30 years and researching and testifying in public hearings about payday lending since 2004.

Brenda Spotton Visano is a Professor of Economics and Public Policy at York University, a steering committee member of both the Black Creek Microcredit Program and the Canadian Progressive Economists Network. She has written books, scholarly articles, and several reports for various government ministries and agencies in Canada, UNESCO, and NGOs related to her research in financial crises, financial inclusion and microfinance.

Contributors

Katrine Dilay joined the Public Interest Law Centre as an articling student in 2015 and remained as a lawyer after her call to the bar in 2016. Katrine practices mostly in the area of human rights and consumer rights and has appeared before the Public Utilities Board, including representing Manitoba consumers in the hearing on payday lending in 2016, and the Canadian Radio-television and Telecommunications Commission. In 2016, Katrine received the Law Society of Manitoba's Montague Israels, Q.C. Prize.

Khan Islam has completed his PhD in Economics from the Department of Economics at the University of Manitoba. Khan started teaching as a sessional/contract instructor at the University of Manitoba in 2011 and the University of Winnipeg in 2013, before his appointment as a lecturer at UBC Okanagan in August 2016. His major fields of research are economic development and personal finance. Khan has published scholarly articles in peer-reviewed journals and another article has been accepted in the Journal of International Development.

Denys Robinson has a BA in Philosophy from the University of Toronto, an MA in Philosophy from Queen's University, and is currently a student in the Master of Public Policy program at Ryerson University.

Wayne Simpson is Professor of Economics, University of Manitoba, and Research Fellow, School of Public Policy, University of Calgary. His areas of specialization include labor economics, applied microeconomics, quantitative methods, income distribution, and social policy. He is the author of three books and more than 60 refereed journal articles.

Byron Williams is the Director of the Public Interest Law Centre of Legal Aid Manitoba. Focusing on consumer, human rights, and environmental matters, he has appeared before all levels of Manitoba Courts, the Federal Court of Appeal, and various provincial and federal administrative tribunals. Byron acted as lead counsel for Manitoba consumers in payday lending proceedings in 2008, 2013, and 2016. In 2013, Byron was the first recipient of the Law Society of Manitoba's Richard J. Scott Award, and in June 2017 he received an honorary doctor of laws from the University of Winnipeg.

List of Figures

List of Tables

CHAPTER 1

Introduction

Jerry Buckland and Brenda Spotton Visano

Overview of the Book

Customers of payday lenders and other providers of Fringe Financial Services (FFS)[1] are people who can least afford to pay the higher cost of these alternative loans, check cashing, and payment services; those with less income are paying considerably more than the non-poor for basic banking services. A growing number of Canadians have been turning to higher-cost financial services from these non-deposit-taking firms despite the widespread availability of mainstream banking services in Canada. Recent surveys suggest that users of payday loans turn to these services because they are denied adequate credit services from traditional banks (see Box 1.1).

[1] "Fringe financial services" is one of many terms used to describe this category of business. Other common terms include alternative financial services, fringe banking, and high-cost/interest financial services.

J. Buckland
Menno Simons College, Canadian Mennonite University,
Affiliated with the University of Winnipeg, Winnipeg, MB, Canada

B. Spotton Visano (✉)
Department of Economics, School of Public Policy and Administration,
York University, Toronto, ON, Canada

J. Buckland et al. (eds.), *Payday Lending in Canada in a Global Context*,
https://doi.org/10.1007/978-3-319-71213-0_1

Box 1.1 Targeted surveys of Canadian payday loan users

In the spring of 2016, the Association of Community Organizations for Reform Now (ACORN) Canada (an independent national organization of low- and moderate-income families) undertook a survey of Canadian payday loan users (Fantauzzi 2016).

> The survey finds that the majority of the 268 respondents turn to high interest financial services such as payday loans as a last resort because they are denied adequate credit services from traditional banks.
>
> According to the respondents, payday loans and cheque cashing services are the most in-demand alternative financial services:
>
> - A little more than half (52.3 per cent) say they have used an alternative financial service to obtain a payday loan;
> - Half (50 per cent) of those who used an alternative financial service told ACORN they did so to cash a cheque…
>
> Just under half (45.3 per cent) of respondents said they visited a high interest financial service provider because they had no overdraft protection available on their bank accounts.

The results of the ACORN survey differ, in some cases considerably, from the Financial Consumer Agency of Canada's (FCAC) recent survey of payday loan users (2016). Where 43–45% of the respondents to the ACORN survey had no access to a credit card or to a line of credit, of the respondents to the FCAC survey, 65% had no credit card and 88% had no line of credit. ACORN respondents used payday loans that were conveniently located (12.5%), and 90% FCAC respondents reported using payday loans because they were the "fastest or most convenient" option. Many respondents to both surveys used these loans to pay for expected, necessary expenses of housing and utilities (33% of ACORN respondents, 41% of FCAC respondents). When food is included, 63% of the ACORN respondents were borrowing just to cover basic living expenses.

The growth of the FFS sector has been remarkable in terms of both its geographic scope and the variety of products and services on offer through storefronts and online. This growth is one manifestation of "financialization"—a process that sees a marked increase in the value of financial services and financial products relative to the non-financial output of an economy. In this particular dimension, financialization is prima facie evidence of a form of financial exclusion. The existence of a large group of Canadians financially excluded by virtue of using FFS and thus being "underbanked" raises serious social justice concerns.

In the first seven chapters of this book, we provide a wealth of evidence about how the payday loan industry functions in Canada and its effects on its customers. We tell you who the customers are and how they feel about their situation. We show the financial and operational nature of the payday loan companies, both storefront and internet lenders. We explain the options to payday lending that exist in the mainstream financial services and show what they lack. We summarize other research work, particularly from the United States. We explain how the legal and regulatory environment operates and analyze the ethics of regulation.

In Chap. 8 we summarize our findings and argue for regulators, banks, and credit unions to implement strong actions to reduce financial exclusion in general and the harm that payday loans in particular can cause. We recommend an outright ban on payday loans accompanied by the mainstream offering an expanded menu of short-term loans at more reasonable rates and other services to ensure Canadians are receiving the basic financial services they need to manage in the modern economy. If the political will to ban payday lending is lacking, we offer alternatives including a limit on fees to $15 per $100 borrowed and options for installment loans instead of payday loans that require full repayment on the due date.[2]

The Payday Loan Industry in Canada

There are over 1400 payday loan outlets in Canada today, and there were virtually none in the mid-1990s. Prior to the mid-1990s, there were check cashers. Once check cashers, including National Money Mart, added payday lending to their services, this became their principal product and even led them to being renamed payday lender from check casher. We estimate the national payday loan market to be $2.3 to 2.7 billion face value of

[2] All references to dollars ($) are in the currency of the country in the context. References to US companies, statistics and regulations are in US$ unless stated otherwise. References to Canadian companies, statistics and regulations are in CD$.

loans per year. The majority of payday loan outlets are located in Ontario, with 800, and it is estimated that they issue $1.1–1.5 billion in loans each year in that province (Deloitte 2014, p. 1).

Data on the Canadian payday loan industry are, however, limited. There is little by way of official data, and private sources have dried up. Until recently the two largest payday lenders, National Money Mart through its parent company DFC Global Corporation and Cash Store Financial,[3] owner of the Cash Store and Instaloans, were publicly traded so that there were some data on their size and trends. Dijkema and McKendry (2016) reinforce a common narrative that based on outlet numbers, the industry grew rapidly in the early and mid-2000s and growth slowed by the early 2010s (p. 27).

Surveying the limited data available on payday lender financial performance, Buckland (2012) concluded, "[t]he data ... demonstrate the strong, if somewhat bumpy financial performance of the larger fringe banks" (Buckland 2012, p. 139). The bankruptcy of Cash Store Financial and DFC Global Corp sale to private equity firm Lone Star Funds mean that there are very limited data available to analyze this industry in Canada. The last date for which there are data available for DFC Global Corp and hence for Money Mart is March 31, 2014. These data demonstrate growth in total revenues and payday lending, a decline in check-cashing revenue, and a small rise in revenue from other sources, from 2009 to 2014. Although many payday lenders offer other financial services like preloaded debit cards, money transfers, gold purchases, advances on tax refunds, currency exchange, and more recently pawnbroking, these contribute only a small portion of total revenue, more than half of which comes from payday loans and most of the rest from check cashing.

A consolidation process, or process of "corporatization," has been occurring among payday lenders in Canada as evidenced in the early 2000s beginning with the rapid expansion of National Money Mart Inc. and Cash Store Financial, and somewhat more recently Cash Money and Cash4You. Cash Store Financial has since gone out of business, but Money Mart has at least half the market and the top five chains have 65% of the outlets and a greater percentage of the loan volume. Chapter 4 provides a more detailed history of the industry and its present status: corporate concentration, stores by province, and financial performance.

[3] Cash Store Financial was originally called Rentcash and included also a rent-to-own division. The rent-to-own division was spun off as a separate company, Easyhome, and the payday lender was renamed.

The Payday Loan Product and Its Usage

As a very short-term (2–3 week) consumer loan, payday loans offer consumers convenient access to cash advance against their next paycheck. The costs of these loans are considerably higher than the costs of similar credit from a mainstream bank or credit union. In the past decade, regulations have imposed rate caps that have, in most sub-federal (provincial and territorial) jurisdictions, constrained the fees payday lenders can charge, but the cost of a payday loan remains more than ten times the cost of these same funds obtained from a line of credit or a credit card cash advance.

Data on payday lending in general, and repeat loans in particular, for Canada are more limited than in the United States because of fewer national surveys that include relevant questions and a lack of data available from government regulators. Using the 2005 results of an FCAC-sponsored survey undertaken by Ipsos-Reid, it was found that 52.4% of respondents who reported taking out a payday loan at least 12 times per year had household incomes of less than $30,000. This proportion declined as income rose: just over 40% of respondents with household incomes between $30,000 and $50,000 and around 5% for respondents with household income over $50,000 (Buckland et al. 2007, p. 33). Drawing on more limited data from the 2009 Canadian Financial Capability Survey, Simpson and Bazarkulova (2013) find evidence that repeat borrowing is more common among poor- and modest-income and asset-holding Canadians as compared to the non-poor (Box 1.2).

Box 1.2 Vignette

Judy ran into serious family financial problems and lost her ability to get regular credit. She turned to the local branch of a payday loan chain and handled her first loans successfully. Then she borrowed $1300 and was unable to repay all of it on the due date. The branch cashier accepted a small repayment, and for a while Judy repaid $100–200 per payday. Twice the payday lender debited her bank account unexpectedly; since there were insufficient funds to cover the debits, the debit was NSF (non-sufficient funds), for which Judy was charged substantial NSF fees. Then one payday she arrived at the branch, and in her words: "I made $100 payment, was supposed to be $200 but could not afford this; teller called manager to approve this and manager approved if entire remaining balance was paid next pay day; I informed teller that I would not be able to afford that and she stated 'You can only pay what you can pay so agree to it and pay whatever you can next time you come in.'" Up to this point, Judy had repaid $1100 on this loan. The next payday she was unable to pay anything. The payday after that she arrived at the branch to make another payment and the branch denied it unless she promised to repay the entire loan the next day. At this point Judy still did not have a loan statement from the payday lender to determine what had been charged on the loan.

In subsequent attempts to pay, the branch refused to accept anything, refused to give her a statement of the loan, and gave her a phone number which she discovered was the number of the lender's law firm. Judy tried calling the payday lender's head office instead, but no one answered the phone and no one answered the messages she left. Two days later she received a threatening letter from the law firm that demanded payment of almost $3000, inclusive of "legal and administrative fees." The letter stated that the amount owing on the loan itself was $1687.90. Through a friend, Judy contacted one of the authors of this book and received some information, including a link to the legislation governing payday loans in her province. She was finally able to get the loan record from the store and discovered the actual amount owing on the loan was $722.63, which means she had been charged $522.63 in fees on the original loan of $1300, plus an additional $952.27 that the law firm claimed on the loan itself before adding its own charges. She wrote to the law firm and enclosed a check for $722.63. She cited the legislation and insisted on her rights and refused to pay anything more than that. She has not heard from them again, and her personal affairs have improved as she has been able to avoid payday lenders since this experience.

British Columbia's payday loan regulator, Consumer Protection BC (2016), finds in the 2016 reporting year that the average customer took out five loans and over 57,000 customers borrowed six or more times in the year. Over 4000 customers took over 15 loans in the year. The average loan size was $460, and the percentage of loans the lenders wrote off was 4.4% (see Chap. 4, Appendix 4.3). Nova Scotia's regulator noted that, for Nova Scotia in 2013–14, 52% of all payday loans were repeat loans of some type, and, of those, 30% received eight or more loans: "It is estimated that these borrowers, which total about 5000 individuals, received an average of 13 loans each in addition to initial loans" (Service Nova Scotia 2015).[4]

Privacy Issues

Ensuring that client information remains private is an important consumer protection issue in Canada. If client information is shared with others it might be used for other purposes including compromising the client's identity and/or finances.

Generally speaking, a feature that fringe banks have accented in their services, as compared to mainstream banks, is client anonymity. To open a mainstream bank account clients are required to submit personal information such as two forms of acceptable personal identification, and to access certain types of loan products, a credit bureau check will be undertaken. Fringe banks have lower standards, are more flexible regarding personal identification requirements, and they do not undertake credit checks for a payday loan. Clients of fringe banks have more anonymity than do clients of mainstream banks. Indeed, greater anonymity is one factor that explains some people's use of fringe banks.

Nevertheless, privacy issues arise with payday lenders and in particular with online payday lending. Payday lenders require information such as the client's bank account number and sample statements, employment payroll statements, and in some cases the client's Social Insurance Number.

Some of the risks that the consumer faces involve lenders, lead generators, or others gaining unconstrained access to the client's bank account; use of the client's references for harassment purposes; use of client data as one point in creating a database to target consumers for other products (Denise Barrett Consulting 2015). A recent Canadian report highlights the complexity of protecting one's privacy in regards to online payday lending:

[4] No other provinces have reported data on payday lending and it does not appear that they are collecting the information that Nova Scotia and BC collect.

> [A] customer cannot be sure she is dealing with the same company if she returns to a web site. Domain names become available to be sold to new owners, making it difficult for consumers to know if they are dealing with the same entity. Besides not knowing who or where the lender is located, difficulty in enforcing consumer protection laws or compliance with state licensing requirements, these financial transactions expose consumers to identity theft and loss of privacy and control over personal financial information. All Internet payday loans involve transmitting bank account numbers, social security numbers, name and address, and extensive other personal information to a distant lender. (Fox and Petrini 2014, p. 12, cited in Consumers' Association of Canada (Manitoba) 2015, p. 9)

In its review of privacy concerns related to payday lending, CAC Manitoba found evidence of abuse on the part of some web-based lenders and noted that the majority of online payday loan consumers it surveyed did not read the lender's privacy policies (Consumers' Association of Canada (Manitoba) 2015, p. 20). Respondents noted that privacy policies were long, difficult to understand, and repetitive.

In addition to interviewing online payday loan clients, this study examined seven online payday loan websites and assessed them vis-à-vis requirements associated with the Canadian Personal Information Protection and Electronic Documents Act (PIPEDA). The examination found compliance with the guidelines varied across lenders and a number of concerns were identified including not requesting client consent to use personal information; ambiguity regarding how lead generators share information; requiring clients to provide Social Insurance Numbers when this may be contravening PIPEDA; and using client information to promote other products when this is not allowed in Manitoba regulations.

Regulation of Payday Lending

Regulation of payday lending involves benefits and costs to businesses, consumers, and government. In the case of potentially harmful products, a minimum level of regulation is justified to protect consumers from harm. This is the route that has been taken by most Canadian provinces as well as many US states. The purpose of this regulatory approach is to enable payday lending to operate within certain accepted standards, for example, disallowing rollovers, outlawing fees above certain caps. The state of

Colorado has been more prescriptive by requiring the payday loan industry to move toward a more traditional longer-term and installment loan product. The province of Québec and some US states have regulations that disallow payday lending, basing the justification presumably on the argument that regulations cannot modify the product sufficiently to prevent social harm. Each of these approaches have strengths and weaknesses and the evidence is mixed about which approach is superior but arguably the strongest evidence supports at least a moderate regulatory approach associated with the approach in Canada with the exception of Québec or the approach taken by the state of Colorado. The more restrictive model in Québec may be justified but without more data and analysis it is hard to make a conclusion.

A Roadmap to the Book

The question of why financial consumers turn to these fringe financial services has been the subject of recent study. In the latter part of this first chapter, we survey the existing literature, much of it from the United States but increasingly from other countries including the United Kingdom, South Africa, Australia, and Poland, in addition to Canada. While the US banking system is considerably different from that of Canada, many of the social justice issues in the American research hold important lessons for other countries, or at least point to some of the questions that need to be asked.

Surveys of users on the reason for their use of payday loans differentiate between why users need access to immediate cash and why, when they need that cash, they turn to a payday loan. As Wayne Simpson and Khan Islam (Chap. 2) note, however, surveys such as the Financial Consumer Agency of Canada's 2016 survey of a non-random sample of payday loan borrowers recruited respondents from among payday loan clients and so did not allow for a comparison of payday loan consumers with non-consumers. Simpson and Islam draw instead on data from two iterations of the Canadian National Survey of Financial Capability to present information about the characteristics of the payday loan customer and their use of payday loans. Simpson and Islam present a "big picture" perspective on who uses payday loans in Canada. Investigating such questions as what is the income and asset position of the typical borrower, how many payday loans per year are commonly taken out, and why do people take out payday loans, Simpson and Islam find that payday loan clients tend to be concentrated near the bottom of middle-income and the top of low-income Canadian households, relatively asset-poor, younger, unmarried, are often repeat borrowers with the average number of loans per year having increased between 2009 and 2014.

Interestingly, Simpson and Islam find evidence to suggest that while payday loan clients are financially vulnerable they are not from the poorest quarters of society and unexpectedly, employment status is not a significant factor affecting payday loan use. Simpson and Islam note that, in terms of income, between 2009 and 2014 the payday loan client now resembles more closely the income characteristics of the non-payday loan client. The level of assets and liabilities of payday loan clients is lower than that of non-clients, but now one-quarter of payday loan clients fall into the highest asset category, households having more than $100,000 in assets. They also find that more payday loan clients were relying on a payday loan not from a paycheck but rather from other income sources such as social assistance.

Exploring consumer characteristics more closely, Jerry Buckland (Chap. 3) analyzes the results of a small-scale survey, a semi-structured interview, and a focus group completed with payday loan clients. Buckland's in-depth small-scale analysis complements the analysis of national surveys undertaken by Simpson and Islam. Buckland's survey revealed reasons why people use payday loans including "push" factors such as deteriorating income and employment status, lack of small loan product available at mainstream financial institutions, and poor credit record and "pull" factors including convenience of payday loan services and familiarity with them from one's friends and family members. Buckland's participants demonstrated an awareness of the relatively high fees of payday loans, but two-thirds of them did not know the annual interest rate associated with their payday loans.

In a focus group, participants provided mixed reactions to a comparison of the common Manitoba payday loan with two other similar products: Vancity Credit Union's Fair and Fast Loan and the common installment loan available from payday lenders in the state of Colorado, United States. When considering the choice between a one-time only payment of the higher cost of Manitoba payday loan and the alternative lower-cost (in terms of Annual Percentage Rate), longer-term, installment repayment options of the Vancity and Colorado options, most participants preferred the lower fees of the alternatives, but the group was split in terms of their preference for a one-time two-week repayment contract versus longer-term and installment repayment option with some also concerned that a larger loan such as Vancity's Fair and Fast Loan could put them further into debt.

Repeat borrowing was quite common (one-quarter of Buckland's survey respondents took out ten and more loans per year) and associated with chronically or acutely low or negative net income. Buckland's evidence supports the concern that the considerably higher cost of the payday loan risks creates a financial dependency that can spiral down into a debt trap especially for those on a low income. The pressure to borrow again, often to repay the previous loan, increases with each new payday loan taken. Via this rollover loan process and the resulting higher threat of a debt trap, those financially excluded by virtue of being underbanked become increasingly so.

Indeed, from his analysis of the firm's side of payday lending, Chris Robinson (Chap. 4) argues that for the payday lender to succeed, firms need these customers who take out many loans per year. Examining the industrial organization, revenues, costs, profitability, and the effects on the payday lender's finances of regulation to date, Robinson makes a strong financial argument for capping lending rates at $15 per $100 loaned (for a term of less than 1 month). While the business of payday lending as it currently operates in the storefront segment of the industry is an inefficient way to deliver small loans, Robinson argues that the rate ceilings are high enough for the larger chains to still earn a considerable profit. Robinson examines the internet segment of the payday lending industry but the lack of publicly available information prevents any in-depth analysis. His meticulous financial investigation and calculations do suggest that there is virtually zero contribution to profits from the internet lending side of the business of at least one large retail chain.

The social justice concerns raised by our examination of the consumers combined with the excess profits exposed by the analysis of the businesses raise critical ethical questions. Chris Robinson and Denys Robinson (Chap. 5) examine ethical issues in the delivery of payday loans and the implication this has for justifying government regulation of the industry. Focusing on the consequences for the borrower as the criterion against which they will assess exploitation, they conclude the business is exploitative in its effects despite not intending to be so. They argue that the harmful consequences of the payday lending business model justify state intervention to reduce that harm and appeal to a broader corporate social responsibility argument for additional justification for regulation of the industry.

The significant presence of payday lenders in a country with as well developed a banking system as Canada begs the question as to why FFS consumers are not using mainstream banking services. Where Buckland's research suggested there may be some "push" factors barring access to mainstream services, Brenda Spotton Visano (Chap. 6) examines this question in more detail. While bank account ownership in Canada is very high, there are some vulnerable Canadians who do not have a bank account and many more who do not use the one they have. Spotton Visano argues that there are six general barriers to mainstream banking and that these barriers partly explain the use of payday loans. These barriers are limited financial literacy, attitudinal barriers, difficulty in opening a bank account, the high cost of using a bank account, distance from mainstream banking services, and lack of trust. Spotton Visano then examines the regulations that have been put in place to build financial inclusion that includes, among other things, the requirement that banks publish annual public accountability statements and that they provide bank accounts for anyone with adequate personal identification. Other initiatives to address financial exclusion include the use of prepaid benefits cards, loan schemes for people unable to access credit, and community banking models. She notes that people in remote locations often lack access to banking. She ends with an assessment of the postal savings bank as a structural way to address financial exclusion. For its reach into bank "deserts" particularly where the barrier created by the absence of a bank branch or credit union is considerable for many rural and remote communities, she concludes that the reintroduction of the postal savings bank may well be an old idea whose time has come again.

Regulations designed to promote the financial inclusion of Canadians in mainstream banking are complemented by a patchwork of regulations governing payday lending. Katrine Dilay and Byron Williams (Chap. 7) examine the current structure and recent developments in payday lending regulations in Canada. Following a description of the regulation of small loans prior to the advent of payday loans, they summarize the major regulatory changes occurring in 1981 when the earlier legislation was repealed and substituted by an addition to the Criminal Code that criminalized lending at rates above 60% per annum. When the introduction of the considerably higher-cost payday loan in the early 1990s posed a regulatory challenge to the legislated usury limit, the federal response was to exempt these loans in 2008 in jurisdictions (provinces and territories) that implemented sub-federal payday loan regulations. The result was a relatively decentralized regulatory patchwork quilt, akin to the situation in the United States, and different from the more centralized regulatory regimes in the United Kingdom and Australia.

Dilay and Williams argue that payday loan regulations in most of Canada recognize its potentially harmful nature but intend to enable "efficient" producers to provide their product at a price at or below the price cap in a way that minimizes harm to the consumer. The chapter examines the salient elements of the payday loan regulations that vary somewhat across jurisdictions but most often address price caps, borrowing limits, disclosure, enforcement, and financial literacy. In the face of dynamic changes to the industry and increasing pressure from online lenders, regulations are still very fluid. Rather than advocating for any ideal regulation, Dilay and Williams argue for an open consultation process, such as the process of public hearings undertaken in Manitoba wherein all the affected stakeholders can participate in deliberations.

Survey of the Literature

Payday lending is a mature industry and one that faces chronic challenges associated with critics' claims that the product harms its customers through location strategies, high fees, repeat loans, and now new problems associated with internet payday loans. The literature on payday lending is quite preoccupied with the investigation into the question of whether payday loans benefit consumers. More recently it has also explored the impact of different types of regulation on the industry and its consumers (discussed below). The literature considers the size and changing nature—for example, corporatization—of the industry. The literature is concerned with long-standing issues such as repeat borrowing and privacy and newer issues such as online payday loans. Finally the literature increasingly connects payday loan use with issues such as corporate marketing, bounded rationality, and consumer "tunneling."

Recent Studies and Their Sources

Payday lending has its origins in the United States, and while it has expanded into other countries, the United States continues to be something of the epicenter of the industry. This is because some of the large

US payday lenders have gone international and because the US market is so large. A consequence of this is that the literature on payday lending is the densest in the United States. This literature is helpful to our understanding of payday lending in Canada; however, given the different history, polity, and socio-cultural situation in the United States, results from American studies on payday lending are not directly relevant to Canada.

Prior to the 2000s there were some major studies in the field of financial exclusion, most importantly John Caskey's 1994 *Fringe Banking*, Gregory Squires and Sally O'Connor's 2001 *Color and Money*, and Andrew Leyshon and Nigel Thrift's 1997 *Money/Space*. These are important studies and their scope is quite wide, examining a combination of issues that one might argue fall within the general heading of financial exclusion.

But, reflecting the growth and ongoing concern regarding payday lending, we have seen in the past three years the publication of several books examining the general field (Buckland 2012; Soederberg 2014) and focused studies on payday lending including two books: Carl Packman's 2014 *Payday Lending: Global Growth of the High-Cost Credit Market* and Mehrsa Baradaran's (2015) *How the Other Half Banks: Exclusion, Exploitation, and the Threat to Democracy*.

In addition, tied to the aftermath of the sub-prime mortgage crisis's impact in the United States, there has been a deeper examination of its financial service sector including payday lending by the newly minted Consumer Financial Protection Bureau and the major 2013 study by the Pew Charitable Trusts, the four-part *Payday Lending in America* report. The Pew reports involved a number of methods including a nationally representative survey and a series of focus group meetings.[5]

[5] The Pew Charitable Trusts research project consists of four separate reports on different aspects of payday lending: borrower characteristics, how borrowers choose and repay loans, payday lending regulations, and internet payday lending. The research methodology involved several steps: inserting payday loan questions within an omnibus survey (containing questions on several topics); a follow-up survey with respondents that indicated in the omnibus survey that they had used payday loans; and focus group discussions with a subset of the follow-up survey respondents (Pew Charitable Trusts 2012, p. 31). A total of 49,684 people were involved in the omnibus survey, a total of 451 people were surveyed in the follow-up survey, and there were 10 focus groups. The number of respondents in the follow-up survey represents 0.9% of the omnibus respondents, but this level is consistent with other surveys that seek to include low- and modest-income households because they are more difficult to reach, by telephone, than middle- and non-poor people, because they have fewer or no phones. Moreover, a small share of the US population actually uses payday loans.

Focusing on payday lending in the United States, Baradaran sees payday lending as a manifestation, like sub-prime mortgages, of an unequal economic system that hurts poor people and harms democracy. She quotes US President Barak Obama:

> If you lend out money, you have to first make sure that the borrower can afford to pay it back ... We don't mind seeing folks make a profit. But if you're making that profit by trapping hard-working Americans into a vicious cycle of debt, then you got to find a new business model. You need to find a new way of doing business. (Baradaran 2015, pp. 126–127)

Baradaran's book examines the history and current reality of the payday loan phenomenon and advances the position that the postal service should reintroduce the postal savings bank to provide small loans. Packman (2014) provides an international perspective by examining payday lending in several countries. He presents a political economy analysis of the rise and expansion of the payday lending model. He concludes that the payday loan model does more harm than good, "The business model of payday lending ... has not been designed primarily to improve the financial situation or future financial capability of its borrowers, and in a high number of instances it has been shown to do the opposite, therefore the general perception of the industry being predatory appears correct" (Packman 2014, p. 135).

Pew Charitable Trusts engaged in a major research project on payday lending in the United States which covers a number of practical and important issues regarding the economics of payday lending, the impact of payday lending on consumers, and it offers an important series of recommendations to improve the payday lending product (Pew Charitable Trusts 2012, 2013a, b, 2014).

Industry Dynamics

Payday loans were first popularized in the United States in the 1990s and in Canada in the 2000s. The concept is much older than that; payday loans were available in a different form in the United States in the early twentieth century (Caskey 2012; Baradaran 2015) and available from some employers since then and today. The recent wave of growth is linked with the underlying process of financialization—a process linked with contemporary economic growth and globalization—*which is the expansion of financial motives and increase in the number and size of financial products.*

In the 1990s more of the literature focused on the geographic location of these lenders. This literature established in many jurisdictions including Canada, the United States, and the United Kingdom that payday lenders often locate in low-income neighborhoods (Brennan et al. 2011; Prager 2014; Leyshon et al. 2006). Recent geographic location studies include Barth et al. (2015) and Simpson and Buckland (2016). These studies confirm that fringe banks are located largely in low-income neighborhoods.

Corporatization is another descriptor of changes taking place in the fringe bank market in that companies that offer payday loans and other transactions services are dominated by growing chains with a proliferating number of services. Geographically, the corporate fringe bank model continues to spread to the United Kingdom, Europe, Australia, New Zealand, and South Africa. The industry also continues to grow in countries where it has already been established. The industry in the United States is now worth US$100 billion and has grown at 10% annually through the 1990s so that US payday lenders now lend around US$40 billion per year (Baradaran 2015, p. 122), supplying 12 million Americans with payday loans (Pew 2013a, p. 4).

The origin and center of the payday loan industry is the United States. Caskey's 1994 seminal study identifies the growth of *fringe banks* but not payday lenders per se. At that time check cashers were rapidly growing in importance and numbers, and payday loans were just beginning to be offered, often by the check cashers.

Caskey identified the growth of fringe banks at that time including check cashers and pawnshops. For the pawnshops this was a reversal from previous years, when they were declining. Packman notes that by outlet numbers payday lenders shot up in the 1990s and early 2000s in the United States from approximately 10,000 in 1999 to 12,000–14,000 in 2001 to 20,000 by 2005 (2014, p. 27), suggesting a growth in the industry. Packman notes that by 2005 US payday loan volume hit US$40 billion per year.

If the supply of outlets and nonbank loans is growing, it would make sense that so is the demand. Drawing on a national survey in 2009 and 2011, Mills and Monson (2013) found that US families' reliance on nonbank credit increased. Seven million households, or 6% of the total, used nonbank credit in the 12 months ending in June 2011 (Mills and Monson 2013, p. 4). Overall reliance on four types of nonbank credit—payday loans, pawnshop loans, rent-to-own agreements, and refund anticipation loans—increased from 11.8% in 2009 to 14.2% in 2011 (Mills and Monson

2013, pp. 1–2). Pawnshop loans were the most widely used, and the proportional increase in payday loans was the greatest at 42%.

Corporatization

Corporatization is the consolidation of business operations within one large company that takes advantage of economies of scale and scope. This has occurred to pawnbroking in the United States in the past and is well under way with payday lending in Canada.

In terms of contemporary pawnshop dynamics, Caskey notes that pawnbroking in the United States declined from 1930 through 1970 due to the Great Depression, restrictions on consumer spending during World War II, and, from the 1950s, growing access for middle classes to mainstream bank credit (Caskey 1994, pp. 27–28). Caskey notes that from the mid-1970s, "these fringe banking industries grew explosively" (Caskey 1994, p. 36). By the mid-1980s, he notes the "corporatization" of the pawnshop model through the appearance of chain-based pawnshops in lower-middle-class suburban neighborhoods (Caskey 1994, p. 53).

Chains were established by Cash America Investments, which later purchased a pawnshop chain in the United Kingdom to become an international pawnbroker, and made its Initial Public Offering in 1987 with shares valued at $6.67 that were, as of August 2015, trading for $22.55 (Caskey 1994, p. 54). Then, in 2016, Cash America merged with First Cash Inc. to operate under the First Cash label. First Cash is now primarily a retail merchandiser with a large portion of its business in second hand goods, including items from pawn loans that were never repaid, a large pawn operation and a much smaller payday loan business. This corporatization process involves the establishment of a corporate structure, the bundling of a series of similar services into a core offering, and the creation of store chain. This corporatization process has occurred with other fringe banks in the United States, including Advance America, Ace Cash Express, Cashland, and DFC Global Corp.

Corporate fringe banks extend beyond the United States and Canada in part through the operations of American-based multinational fringe banks such as DFC Global Corp, which, besides its unit in Canada, has operations in the United Kingdom and seven European countries.

Online Payday Lending

Online payday loans are a relatively new means of delivery. Given that storefront payday lenders sometimes deposit loans and receive repayment for loans electronically, it is not surprising that some existing payday lenders have established online delivery as an added channel and that new players focusing strictly on online payday loan processing have entered the market.

In terms of the industry's size, Packman (2014), citing Stephens Inc., estimates the online payday lending industry increased from US$2 billion in 2006 to US$4.3 billion in 2012. The size of the online payday loan market in Canada is difficult to estimate, but one study estimated it to represent 10% of the total Ontario payday lending market (Deloitte 2014, cited in Denise Barrett Consulting 2015, p. 20). Another study estimates the internet payday loan market to encompass one-quarter of all payday loans in the United States in 2012 (Pew Charitable Trusts 2012), while the most recent information suggests that share has already increased to one-third of the market (Zibel 2015, cited in Denise Barrett Consulting 2015, p. 21). The Australian online market is estimated to be one-third of its total (Denise Barrett Consulting 2015, p. 21). The UK's Financial Conduct Authority estimates online payday lending represents 80% of the total (Denise Barrett Consulting 2015, p. 20). One indicator of growth comes from DFC Global, parent company to National Money Mart. DFC Global reported a doubling of its revenue from this source in a two-year period, representing 15.4% of its revenue in 2011 and 33.0% in 2013, followed by a dramatic decline in the first nine months of 2014 (DFC Global Corp. 2014). See analysis in Chap. 4 that suggests the internet business may be facing serious headwinds, particularly in Canada. Unfortunately, no one has reliable current data.

There are limited data on the characteristics of online payday lending clients. Regarding Canadian online clients, a National Money Mart respondent noted that their online clients tend to be younger and better off than in-store clients:

> Online trends younger, to people who are more comfortable with e-commerce as a safe platform. It also trends slightly higher in income. But many of our online customers are also in-store customers." He added that online consumers are service sensitive, not price sensitive. "Ease and speed of service trumps price. That's a general rule of all e-commerce." (Denise Barrett Consulting 2015, pp. 21–22)

Research in the United States also finds that online borrowers are more likely than in-store users to be younger and have higher income and a college degree (Pew Charitable Trusts 2012, p. 28). This study also determined that almost three-quarters of payday loan clients rely exclusively on in-store loans, 16% rely on online exclusively, and 4% of clients use both avenues to obtain loans (Pew Charitable Trusts 2012, p. 27).

Unique Issues of Online Loans

Asymmetric Information

Online payday lending is associated with many of the same issues and concerns as in-store payday lending with some additional concerns. Most importantly, given the fact that the online lender can be based anywhere in the world, regulation is challenging. As research in Canada found, this concern is particularly associated with unlicensed payday lenders. So what do prospective consumers know about them? The prospective client would have more difficulty as compared with a local storefront lender, undertaking an analysis of the online lender.

And what do lenders know about prospective borrowers? With access to information about their income and bank account, they can, of course, make assessments of the client's likelihood or repayment. One US study noted that online lenders use sophisticated analyses to assess prospective borrowers (Pew Charitable Trusts 2014, p. 4). A US study found that online payday lenders rely on specialty credit reporting companies such as Teletrack (CFA 2011, p. 3). Pew Charitable Trusts research found that online lenders are more selective than in-person lenders and they face higher loan losses. Some online lenders reject 80% of applicants, while in-store lenders' average rejection stands at 20%.

Costs Differ for Online Versus Storefront Loans

Pew Charitable Trusts estimated that the cost of providing a loan is lower for online lenders, but that loan losses are more than double: 17% for storefront lenders and 44% for online lenders (Pew Charitable Trusts 2014, p. 5). Pew Charitable Trusts also estimates that Annual Percentage Rate (APR) for online loans at 652% is almost double of the APR for storefront loans, at 391%.

"Lead generators" are an important element of the online loan industry. They "serve as intermediaries connecting Canadian borrowers to worldwide lenders" (Denise Barrett Consulting 2015, p. 20). Lead generators are companies with websites that identify potential payday loan clients and then direct them to payday lenders, receiving a fee for doing so. According to another study these lead generators are paid up to US$110–125 for qualified referrals (Consumer Federation of America

2011, pp. 1, 9) and therefore clearly add to the cost of the payday loan. In the United States, lead generators, internet search ads, and TV/radio advertisements are used to promote payday lending (Pew Charitable Trusts 2014, pp. 6–7).

Online Lenders Less Likely to Follow Regulations

Denise Barrett Consulting (2015) examined online payday lending available to Canadians by analyzing websites and talking with key informants. They found that some online lenders are licensed and some are not and that this distinction effectively predicted whether the lender followed provincial regulations or not.

US research came to a similar conclusion, that unlicensed lenders are the most abusive (Pew Charitable Trusts 2014, p. 27). The results pointed to particular concern about online lenders that required the prospective client's bank account number, passwords, and security question responses "that would give lenders direct access to the borrower's bank account," without giving the client information about the lender (Pew Charitable Trusts 2014, p. 6).

The US study found that online payday lenders sometimes do not disclose where they are physically located, sometimes disclose it as another country (e.g., British West Indies), and sometimes disclose it as another state within the United States (CFA 2011, p. 5). These companies may indicate that they are subject to their local—and not the client's local—laws. The report found that there are a growing number of online lenders who claim exemption from state laws due to tribal sovereignty (CFA 2011, p. 1).

Troublesome Consumer Practices

Pew Charitable Trusts found that there are more complaints—at a 10:1 ratio—to the Better Business Bureau about online as compared with storefront loans (Pew Charitable Trusts 2014, p. 18) and that there are more threats from online lenders and associates toward clients unable to repay the loan, as compared with in-store loans (Pew Charitable Trusts 2014, p. 10). "I had the law office call me. …He tells me I have to get my attorney, and he says we will come to your job, and we'll arrest you" (Online borrower quote, Pew Charitable Trusts 2014, p. 11).

The Pew Charitable Trusts research also found that prospective online clients might receive several payday loan offers based on one request. Pew Charitable Trusts notes that this might be because of the high cost of obtaining names from lead generators so that the lead generators and their clients resell names and contact information to other online lenders: "I'm getting texts, and I'm getting phone calls, and I'm getting emails, and I'm getting all of this stuff" (Online borrower quote, Pew Charitable Trusts 2014, p. 13).

Almost one-half of online borrowers reported that their bank accounts were overdrawn due to payday lender's charges, which is double the rate reported for in-store loans (Pew Charitable Trusts 2014, p. 13). Another one-third of online consumers complained of unauthorized withdrawal of funds from their checking account (Pew Charitable Trusts 2014, p. 14). Twenty-two percent of online borrowers either closed or had their bank account closed to prevent the lender from withdrawing more funds (Pew Charitable Trusts 2014, p. 16).

Repeating Online Loans

Studies in the United States have found that online lending is often structured for the loan to be repeated for more than one pay cycle (CFA 2011, p. 9; Pew Charitable Trusts 2014, p. 8). In some cases online payday lenders can make it difficult to pay off the loan by creating the default to not pay off the loan. Sometimes online payday loans are structured to encourage repeat borrowing by only withdrawing interest and not principal charges for several paydays:

> MyPaydayLoan.com permits borrowers to extend loans with no limit as long as the finance charge is paid every due date. Nationwide Cash automatically rolls over the debt four times, withdrawing the finance charge each time without reducing principal. On the fifth and subsequent paydays, Nationwide Cash withdraws $50 of principal plus the finance charge. Using this payment method, the online lender collects $750 in finance charges ($150 over five paydays) on a $500 loan before the debt is reduced to $450. (CFA 2011, p. 9)

Pew Charitable Trusts found that 31% of online borrowers engaged in payday loans that were automatically extended by withdrawing the fee and not the principal on payday (Pew Charitable Trusts 2014, p. 8).

Do Payday Loans Benefit Consumers?

The vast majority of payday loan impact studies have been undertaken in the United States. John Caskey (2005, 2010) engages what he terms "the big question" regarding payday lending, and that is, do payday loans benefit the borrowers? He argues that answering that question is complicated by the mixed empirical evidence and by ideological differences. Ideological tensions relate to assumptions about human nature such as whether people are rational, and about how well markets serve low-income and low-asset people. In his review of around one dozen impact studies, Caskey concludes that the answer to the "big question" is, so far, ambiguous due in part to these ideological tensions:

> These quasi-experimental studies reflect substantial and careful empirical work, but, in my view, they do not provide a reliable answer to the big question: Do payday lenders, on net, exacerbate or relieve customers' financial difficulties? For one, some of the studies find access to payday lending is beneficial and some find it harmful. But more important, the results of each of the studies are simply suggestive; that is, they are based on at least one of two strong assumptions that may well not be true and therefore cast doubt on the reliability of the results. (Caskey 2010, pp. 25–26)

In a study completed since Caskey's review, Bhutta (2013) examines experiences of consumers in states and times in which payday loans are available and in which they are not available. His conclusion is similar to Caskey in that he sees no relationship between the use of payday loans and credit scores, delinquencies, and the likelihood of overdrawing credit lines (Bhutta 2013, p. 1). To address the limitations of these quasi-experimental studies, Caskey calls for fully randomized design trials and ethnographic studies[6] to understand the impact of payday lending.

Put a slightly different way, Melzer (2014) summarizes the literature to date by stating "there is evidence that the expansion of payday credit aggravates financial difficulties, *at least for a subset of borrowers*" (Melzer 2014, p. 3; italics added). Reporting on a survey of a small number of payday loan clients from the payday lender association database, Lawrence and Elliehausen (2008) report that most respondents were satisfied but concur with Melzer regarding concerns about the subgroup

[6] Caskey proposes a "second fruitful approach that might help answer the big question would be ethnographic studies that carefully follow the budgeting decisions and thought processes of payday loan customers and their households over time. Such studies would necessarily have to be small scale and could be criticized for inevitable subjective data filtering by the ethnographers, but they could also offer rich insights to complement the traditional econometric and experimental approach of economists" (Caskey 2010, p. 37).

of clients who are repeatedly borrowing. Other studies have examined indirect consequences of payday loan use. Fitzpatrick and Coleman-Jensen (2014) found that borrowers in states with restrictive payday loan regulations were less food secure than people in states with permissive payday loan regulations (Fitzpatrick and Coleman-Jensen 2014, p. 553). Melzer, on the other hand, found that payday loan clients were more likely to use food assistance and not make child support payments (Melzer 2014, p. 21).

Lohrenz (2013, p. 21, cited in Wolff 2015) argued that payday lending fees drain money from borrowers who would otherwise have used those funds to purchase other goods and services that would have a multiplier effect on the macroeconomy. It was estimated that consumers losing those fees to payday lenders led to a drain of nearly US$1 billion and 14,000 jobs in the US economy in 2012.

What Do Customers Think About Payday Loans?

The Pew Charitable Trusts also undertook a major study since Caskey's review, including surveys and focus groups of payday clients. One key result is that payday loan clients themselves "experience complicated and conflicted feelings." This is because the borrowers have "appreciation for friendly service, dismay with the high cost, and frustration with lengthy indebtedness" (Pew Charitable Trusts 2013b, p. 39). Moreover, 55% of respondents felt that payday loans take advantage of borrowers (Pew Charitable Trusts 2013b, p. 40). So what would borrowers do if payday loans were unavailable? The Pew Charitable Trusts-sponsored survey found:

> If faced with a cash shortfall and payday loans were unavailable, 81 percent of borrowers say they would cut back on expenses. Many also would delay paying some bills, rely on friends and family, or sell personal possessions. (Pew Charitable Trusts 2012, p. 16)

Repeat Borrowing

One of the chronic and most insidious of problems associated with payday lending is repetitive borrowing by some consumers. This is an issue because payday loans, as promoted by the industry, are small-sum and short-term loans intended to deal with a short-term liquidity problem.

They are relatively expensive and are not intended to overcome longer-term problems.

If people are taking out many loans in a short period of time, they are very likely not choosing the most suitable product. In the early days of payday lending, this issue was associated with rollovers, which were loan extensions that involved additional fees so that APRs grew multiplicatively.[7] Rollovers are largely disallowed by regulations, but some consumers, through one outlet or more, are nonetheless able to obtain several loans in a short period of time. Data in the United States confirm that this is an ongoing challenge there. Data limitations in Canada make confirmation in this country difficult.

As discussed above, Caskey (2010) found that the impact evaluation literature comes to few global conclusions about the impact of payday lending on the consumer. This is partly because payday loans have different effects on different groups of people. One can imagine a variety of scenarios where an individual could benefit from a small loan, even if it is expensive. If the loan allows the person to meet an emergency need, avoid paying a hefty fee, or make a strategic investment, then one can imagine a positive impact. However, there is evidence of a subgroup of payday loan clients who rely repeatedly on payday loans. In this case when the borrower is taking out many loans in a short period of time, perhaps six or seven in less than one year, then this combination stops looking like a series of separate loans and rather it looks like the person has tried to piece together a longer-term loan, at much inconvenience and expense.

The Situation in the United States

There seems to be a consensus in the United States that for a subgroup of payday loan clients, repetitive payday loan borrowing is harmful. Lawrence and Elliehausen (2008) find that in their small sample there were a relatively small percentage of respondents who took out many payday loans in a short period of time. They note that:

> This behavior is not necessarily harmful because some consumers may need a longer period of time to improve their situation. However, reliance on

[7] Early critics of payday lending found that rollovers were common among payday loan consumers. By this it was meant that on the repayment date, the loan was extended, and the original fees were doubled, and additional fees were added. Consequently, fees more than doubled for the rollover loans.

payday loans for an extended period of time seems contrary to the short-term financing intention of the product and may exacerbate rather than relieve financial problems some consumers face. (Lawrence and Elliehausen 2008, p. 315)

Caskey notes a California study where 19% of borrowers took out 15 or more loans in a 1.5-year period, and focus group respondents used terms like "addictive," "repetitive," and "vicious cycle" (Caskey 2010, pp. 4–5). The Pew Charitable Trusts research project states that, for the US payday loan consumer, "repeat [payday loan] borrowing is the norm" (Pew Charitable Trusts 2012, p. 15). The Center for Responsible Lending (CRL) uses the term loan "churn" to refer to the situation in which the consumer is really unable to pay off the loan and is therefore either renewing it with the original lender or borrowing from another lender immediately on the date of repayment or soon thereafter (Montezemolo 2013, p. 3). CRL argues that many payday loans are taken out in a short time period so that "the actual impact of repeat transactions is simply repaying fees to float the same debt rather than being extended new credit each time" (Montezemolo 2013, p. 4). The cost to consumers for trying to convert the payday loan into a longer-term loan is substantial in terms of fees:

- The Consumer Financial Protection Bureau found that "the median borrower in the CFPB sample took out ten payday loans from a single lender during the year, paying $458 in fees alone for $350 in non-churn principal" (Montezemolo 2013, p. 4).
- Data from state regulator databases find borrowers take out nine, on average US$346, loans per year involving US$504 in fees.
- The Pew Charitable Trusts research finds borrowers take out eight 18-day, on average US$375, loans in one year and owe US$520 in fees.
- A study from the Center for Financial Services Innovation found that borrowers take out 11 loans in one year, and Advance America, the United States' largest payday lender, reports its clients on average take out eight loans per year (Montezemolo 2013, p. 4).

Why So Many Payday Loans?

Baradaran argues that payday lenders do not underwrite their loans[8] and this is an inherent weakness of the payday loan model. She argues that

[8] Test the consumer's ability to repay the loan through, for example, a credit score.

payday lenders do not check the credit worthiness of borrowers and do not test the difference between insolvent and illiquid people so that it is not a good credit model. This is an issue for payday lenders but particularly for the internet-based payday loan segment, introduced above.

> The current market for lending to the low and middle income does not distinguish between the two [insolvent and illiquid]. And often, the losses from those who are insolvent raise the prices for those who are merely illiquid. If the two types of borrowers could be adequately sorted, those who are illiquid could get lower cost loans that would help them stay solvent. But here's the irony: the only loans available to the merely illiquid are high-cost loans that make it much more likely they will becomes insolvent. (Baradaran 2015, p. 135)

Lack of underwriting is linked with some payday loan clients taking out many loans. The Pew Charitable Trusts research project investigated consumer motivation behind borrowing many loans in a short period of time and point to the following factors (Pew Charitable Trusts 2012, pp. 19–29):

- Consumers needing cash to meet an urgent expense. Thirty-seven percent of borrowers said they would accept a loan on "any terms offered."
- Some borrowers who will be unable to pay off the loan, unrealistically, think they can pay off the loan—principal and interest—in two weeks.
- No *caveat emptor*: consumers relying on payday lenders' information that themselves rely on repeat borrowers for their businesses to prosper. Fifty-four percent of borrowers relied "completely" on payday lenders for information about the payday loan.
- Some borrowers find the ease with which they can access payday loans as part of the problem as it creates a "temptation" they cannot resist.

Consumer Behavior and Literacy

It is often assumed within standard economic theory, a theory that is very influential in policymaking circles, that humans are entirely rational and that this is reflected in self-interested behavior that is deliberately achieved by careful data collection and optimization calculations. But in the past 15 years, a growing collection of scholars and scholarship have critically explored that assumption through various types of research and experiments falling within the area of behavioral economics. For instance, Dijkema and McKendry (2016) note, "[o]f course this does not mean that payday-loan use is always a rational decision and/or the best solution for the borrower's needs" (p. 23).

While the study of economics has always involved questions about human rationality, the contemporary school of behavioral economics has emerged through work by Shefrin and Thaler (1993), Thaler and Sunstein (2008), and Mullainathan and Shafir (2013). This research addresses a variety of economic issues including consumer use of credit and its analysis encompasses use by a variety of socio-economic groups including income- and asset-poor people. The scholarship begins with the assumption that people do not consistently behave rationally and, through research, seeks to identify our irrationality or what the literature calls "bounded" rationality. For instance, Thaler and Sunstein (2008) identify a series of characteristics of bounded rationality including anchoring[9] and overconfidence.

Tunneling

Mullainathan and Shafir (2013) specifically examine low-income people's decision-making. What they argue is that while poor people are just like non-poor people in many ways, including being limited by bounded rationality, they do face particular kinds of scarcities that constrain their thinking. They argue that, by definition, a poor person faces scarce resources, liquidity constraints, for example, income and assets. This scarcity forces them to focus thought and energy on meeting their immediate needs. The opportunity cost is that they are unable to focus on longer-term issues like medium- and long-term financial and social goals. They describe this focus in the short run as *tunneling*, in the sense that scarcity causes them to focus on a narrow space of life, the tunnel, and this precludes them from examining other spaces, because they are in this tunnel. Mullainathan and Shafir conducted experiments with people from a variety of backgrounds (poor and non-poor) in simulation experiments and found that the conse-

[9] This is a heuristic that involves using a known state or condition to assess a current state or condition, even if the known state or condition has no relationship to do with the new one. For instance, we might estimate the population of a city we are visiting by "anchoring" that estimate to our own city, even if they are completely different sizes.

quences of tunneling include reduced executive control, increased distraction, forgetfulness, and impulse control (Mullainathan and Shafir 2013, pp. 47–65).

Payday Loan Marketing

Taking up low-quality credit products may be the result of market scarcity—that is, there are no alternatives in the market—or it may, as Mullainathan and Shafir point out, be the result of bounded rationality. Bertrand et al. (2009) ran an experiment to test these competing explanations. Does the way in which sellers frame their products affect the uptake of loans from a South African bank? The banker sent out flyers about a loan product which contained different types and amounts of information. The researchers examined the credit products that people chose to determine if they behaved rationally by choosing the lowest interest rate loan, but they found that people's decision-making was influenced by other factors, such as simplified loan presentations and photos of attractive people.

In a study focused on payday loan uptake, Bertrand and Morse (2011) experimented with payday loan clients by providing different types of information. One group got the standard amount and date due for taking out the loan, and the other group was given the fee for a payday loan and extension for up to three months along with the equivalent fee for borrowing with a credit card (Bertrand and Morse 2011, pp. 1866–1867). The results found that those who received the comparison fee data were 11% less likely to re-borrow four months after the experiment.

Financial Literacy

Financial literacy measurement and education, like behavioral economics, is of interest among policymakers, and they relate to each other in important ways. Behavioral economics seeks to understand human decision-making, dropping the assumption that people always behave fully rationally. Financial literacy practice seeks to educate people so that they make sound financial decisions.

Financial literacy is generally defined as having the knowledge, skills, and attitude to manage one's finances effectively to achieve one's financial and life goals. This includes knowledge about concepts such as risk-reward trade-off with investments, skills such as budgeting, and attitude that enables a person to think and act, even with the constraints they face, to maximize their financial and life goals.

A common finding in financial literacy studies is that many people's capacity to deal with a rapidly financializing economy is inadequate. For instance, Lusardi and Mitchell (2014) scan the literature and find that a large share of Westerners (United States, Canada, Europe, etc.) have low levels of financial literacy: they lack certain literacies, *and* they are overconfident about their ability, the latter a bigger problem for men compared with women. Using universal standards of measurement, women do worse than men, poor people do worse than rich people, and ethnic minorities do worse than majorities, in assessments of US financial literacy.

Of course these universal standards are less relevant for poor people because, for instance, they are less likely to make investments or have mortgages and so will score poorly on questions that test irrelevant knowledge. Lusardi and Mitchell note that financial illiteracy can make people more vulnerable to scammers and less able to plan for retirement. Gathergood (2012) notes that consumers with high debt levels lacked self-control, heavily discounted future spending, and exhibited low levels of financial literacy.

The Impact of Regulation on Payday Lending

In their current form payday loans have been offered in the United States for over 20 years, in Canada and the United Kingdom for over ten years, and in other parts of Europe and the world (e.g., South Africa) more recently. Payday loan regulation in the United States and Canada has been a state or provincial responsibility, which adds diversity to the regulations in these two countries. Some municipalities in Canada and the United States have also engaged in limited regulation through, for example, zoning rules that require certain distances between outlets.

Under the UK Office of Fair Trading, payday lending was influenced by non-binding guidelines but now, under the Financial Conduct Authority, it faces binding regulations including repeat loan limits and a price cap (Fejos 2015). As a consequence of the substantive time and large number of jurisdictions in which payday lenders have operated—and noting that some jurisdictions have changed their policy regime over time—there is the opportunity to study the impact of different regulations on the payday loan market and consumer.

Some important qualifications are warranted before proceeding:

- First, data are often a limiting factor in assessing the payday loan market, particularly in Canada. Without sufficient quality and quantity of data it is difficult to make assessments of the market and the impact of regulations.
- Second, since jurisdictions are quite small—a US state or a Canadian province—their regulations are not absolute in that residents, especially residents that live near a border, are able to access payday loans under a different regime in an adjoining state of province.
- Third, and related to the jurisdiction size point, the internet is another source for payday loans, and there is some evidence that it is a growing source.
- Finally, payday loans are a product that has attracted strong opinions in one form or another. There are proponents and opponents of payday lending or, more broadly, the use of microloans to advance the interests of asset- and income-poor people. It is sometimes difficult to distinguish between strong results and strong passions.

Some New US Payday Loan Regulations

The creation of the Consumer Financial Protection Bureau is one of the main outcomes of the US government response to the sub-prime mortgage crisis. One of its major initiatives is a broad-based proposal to reform the small-sum credit market including short-term loans such as payday loans and longer-term loans such as title loans. The proposal includes regulations that are intended to "prevent" a debt trap and to "protect" borrowers from a debt trap.

With respect to reforms targeting payday loans, debt trap prevention involves underwriting loans and limiting loans to one or two in a 60-day period. In terms of debt protection, the regulations involve limiting rollovers to two followed by a 60-day cooling off period, and, if needed one option would involve installment repayment.

In 2010 the state of Colorado in the United States implemented a serious reform requiring payday lenders to transform their loans into a longer-term six-month loan that is repaid with installments. The rationale for this reform was that the two-week high-fee balloon payment payday loans were considered too harmful and that, to reduce consumer harm and improve consumer benefit, the state of Colorado advanced a new payday loan model. The maximum loan size is US$500, and the APR is limited to 129% (Pew Charitable Trusts 2013b, p. 9).

According to a report by Pew Charitable Trusts, the new payday loan model in Colorado found that since the law was enacted, there are fewer payday lender outlets but they are still broadly available, there are fewer payday loans, fees are lower and more transparent, the vast majority of loans are repaid within five months, and consumers are more satisfied with the new service as compared with the old one.

Payday Lender Costs

A common goal of payday loan regulation is to protect consumers from unsafe payday loan products. One way this has been achieved is to devise regulation that allows efficient payday lenders to operate but disallows inefficient lenders to do so. Price caps and other regulations—for example, restricting the number and type of repeat loans—are put in place to enable the former but not the latter. An underlying assumption of this approach is that (1) some consumers want and can benefit from payday loans and (2) payday loans are an expensive service to offer. On the latter point, why is delivering payday loans more costly than, for example, a mortgage?

> [T]he cost structure of the consumer finance industry is such that operating costs increase less than proportionately with loan size. This relationship exists because many of the costs occur whenever an application is accepted, a loan is made, or payments are serviced. These activities must be performed regardless of the size of the loan. Companies producing larger loans have lower costs per dollar of credit extended than those producing smaller loans. Thus, for a given interest rate, larger loans are more profitable than smaller loans. (Lawrence and Elliehausen 2008, p. 301)

Other variables that affect payday loan costs include loan volume which relates to economies of scale and number of related services offered, which relates to economies of scope (Table 1.1). Other factors affecting costs include the default rate, the cost of capital, the price or price cap, the firm's profit margin, the number of first-time customers (an expensive clientele for payday lenders), and the number of loans per client per year (more is better for the payday lender; the reverse is the case for the borrower).

Table 1.1 Some important factors affecting payday lenders costs

Cost item	*Type of cost*
Volume of loans per period	Economies of scale
Number of services, in addition to payday loans offered	Economies of scope
Loan default rate	Particular cost
Cost of capital	Particular cost
Price/price cap	Market or set price
Firm's profit margin	Owner expectations
Share of first-time borrowers	Consumer characteristic
Share of borrowers taking out multiple loans per period	Consumer characteristic

The Impact of Price Caps

The most extensive studies of the impact of payday loan regulations come from the United States (Pew Charitable Trusts 2012, 2013b; McKernan et al. 2010; Edmiston 2011; Kaufman 2013).

Price caps are a common component of regulation. What happens when a price cap is implemented? One theory is that remaining firms move their prices—up or down—to the price cap. This in fact has been the case in the United States (Kaufman 2013). Baradaran argues that there is evidence that payday loan firms, at times, either implicitly or explicitly, collude around price caps, "consistent with Thomas Schelling's theory of implicit collusion around pricing focal points" (Baradaran 2015, p. 131). The argument is that the price cap enables firms to not compete and rather, to price their loans at the cap level.

What is a reasonable price cap that enables an efficient payday lender? The Pew Charitable Trusts study noted, according to an industry analysis, "In a state with a $15 per $100 rate, an operator … will need a new customer to take out 4–5 loans before that customer becomes profitable" (Pew Charitable Trusts 2012, p. 15). And Pew Charitable Trusts research demonstrated that in states with "hybrid" regulations—caps around $10 per $100 borrowed, restrictions of the number of loans per year a person can take, and allowing installment repayment—payday lenders continue to operate in large numbers (Pew Charitable Trusts 2012, p. 20). Caskey reports on Zinman's (2010) study that examined payday lending in the state of Oregon before and after introducing restrictive caps, $10 for $100 loaned:

> The new law capped finance charges at roughly $10 per $100 advanced and set a minimum loan term of 31 days for a maximum APR of 150 percent.

> Most payday lenders decided that their business would not be sufficiently profitable under this restriction. At year-end 2006, there were 346 payday loan storefronts in the state. By February 2008 there were 105. (Caskey 2010, p. 7)

While these studies disagree about the viability of operating a payday loan outlet within a $10 per $100 cap, clearly some were able to do so even in the Zinman study. Presumably loan volumes and other factors (e.g., providing complementary services) would lend to the viability of offering payday loans at this rate.

Limiting the Amount of Borrowing

Another common component of regulation is to limit the total amount that a person is able to borrow through payday lending. This is done in various ways such as limiting the number, size, or frequency of the payday loans. But Kaufman (2013) found that efforts to limit total borrowing have been less successful:

> Overall, it appears that customers were able to borrow the desired amount no matter whether the limit was structured as a size cap or a simultaneous borrowing ban. This suggests that unless states enact much more binding limits on the maximum amount borrowed it may not matter whether or not they also have limits on simultaneous borrowing. (Kaufman 2013, p. 16)

The Impact of General Payday Loan Restrictions

One argument is that restrictive regulations push credit-strapped people to alternative lenders, including anything from other fringe banks to illegal and dangerous loan sharks. But several studies in the United States find that this is not the case. Pew Charitable Trusts, McKernan, Kaufman, and Wolff find that in states with more restrictive regulations, there are fewer payday lenders and that there is no evidence that people are relying more on other loan sources.

In some jurisdictions payday loan regulations essentially disallow payday loans. For instance in North Carolina in 2001 a usury limit of 36% took effect for payday loans (Wolff 2015). Payday loan outlets were all closed by 2006. Credit union small loans remained, but the APR for these was 12%. Wolff (2015) concluded:

> Research by the University of North Carolina's Center for Community Capital (2007) documented that the rate cap benefited North Carolinians,

and that most low- and moderate-income residents—even those who had previously used payday loans—welcomed the change. Researchers concluded, "[m]ost surveyed households consider themselves better off or unaffected by the closing of payday loan stores." Households found a variety of ways to manage financial stresses and expressed their happiness that payday loans were no longer in the state." (Wolff 2015, p. 33)

Edmiston (2011) reviewed US data and literature on this point. He noted that indebtedness in Georgia, United States, declined after the mid-2004 move to more restrictive regulations. What he found was that the trend line of growing indebtedness started to drop after the introduction of greater restrictions, while the trend continued on at roughly the same rate for the rest of the United States (Edmiston 2011, p. 73). But Edmiston found that people in low-income counties with payday loan outlets have slightly higher credit scores than the national average (Edmiston 2011, p. 77). He concludes:

The evidence showed that consumers in low-income counties may have limited access to credit in the absence of payday loan options. As a result, they may be forced to seek more costly sources of credit. The evidence also showed that, in counties without access to payday lending, consumers have a lower credit standing than consumers in counties with access. (Edmiston 2011, p. 83)

McKernan et al. (2010) used data from a nationally representative US survey to examine the relationship between state-level regulation and consumer use of fringe banks. They found that prohibition of payday lending caused people in that state to reduce their use of payday lending by 35% as compared to states without prohibition. These residents can still obtain a payday loan in an adjoining state that does not prohibit payday lending or through the internet. Lower rate caps did not affect consumer uptake of payday loans. And they noted that prohibitions and price caps on one type of fringe bank product, for example, payday loans, do not lead consumers to increase their use of other products, for example, pawnshop loans (McKernan et al. 2010, p. 19).

The Pew Charitable Trusts (2012) investigated this question using their nationally representative dataset in which almost 50,000 people were screened through an omnibus survey leading to 451 participants of a full-length survey and eight focus groups specifically on payday lending. They explored the question of how state regulations affected payday loan use.[10] They found that in states with restrictive regulations, people do not increase their use of online payday loans or other fringe bank products (Pew Charitable Trusts 2012, pp. 22–24). States with more restrictive regulations have fewer payday loan outlets and people simply use fewer physical and online fringe bank loans. Pew Charitable Trusts found that where payday loans were not available people cut back on expenses, delay paying some bills, borrow from friends/family, and/or sell or pawn personal possessions (Pew Charitable Trusts 2012, p. 16). Pew Charitable Trusts noted:

> Prior research has found "no evidence that prohibitions and price caps on one AFS (Alternative Financial Services) product lead consumers to use other AFS products." Our research builds on that finding, revealing that the vast majority of would-be borrowers do not even substitute a new method (using the Internet instead of a storefront) to obtain the same AFS product, which in this case is a payday loan. (Pew Charitable Trusts 2012, p. 24)

While there are limited data about online lending, what data are available do point to higher risks for consumers. This should not, however, be used as a rationale to not regulate payday lending from physical storefronts. Repeat borrowing continues to be a major concern, and this problem is well documented in the United States. Repeat borrowing points to the need for substantial reform of the sector as has been done in Colorado, for instance. The Pew Charitable Trusts study revealed that the majority of payday loan customers want more regulation of payday lending (Pew Charitable Trusts 2013b, pp. 47–50).

The state-based and varied regulation of the payday loan industry in the United States has led to a number of interesting studies. While impact assessments cannot definitively determine whether or not payday loans benefit consumers, it is clear that some consumers—relying on repetitive borrowing, accessing their loans online, tunneling as a result of personal and professional pressures—can be harmed by payday loans. Continued

[10] For their study the Pew Charitable Trusts categorized US states into three categories: (1) Twenty-eight "permissive" states, where most Americans live, where the payday loan rate caps are greater or equal to $15/$100; (2) "Hybrid" states where rate caps are approximately $10/$100, there are restrictions on the number of loans each borrower can take, and sometimes borrowers are allowed to repay the loan over several pay periods; and (3) "Restrictive" states where the rate cap is placed at 36% APR, and payday loan storefronts are not found (Pew 2012, p. 20).

regulation is needed as is consumer education that draws on the insights from behavioral economics.

Where We Are Now

Payday lending is a mature industry with chronic challenges. While there is evidence that growth of the payday loan industry has slowed down in some rich countries, companies are expanding their services to include online loans and expanding into new regions such as South Africa and Eastern Europe. Payday loan companies, perhaps better labelled fringe banks since they offer many services, have consolidated and now many have a corporate footprint.

Payday lending continues to face major criticism and to be the subject of discussion for reform. Discussion in Canada has continued in the media (Grant and McFarland 2015; Pollon 2015) but policymaker dialogue is relatively muted. Payday lending regulations in the United Kingdom have "caught up" to regulations in the United States and Canada. But it is in the United States where there continues to be the most lively discussion about payday loans and their reform. In Canada there was a proposal that the postal system be used to deliver banking services to unbanked people (Anderson 2013). More recently there was some interesting discussion that took place within a cross-sectoral panel put together by the Ontario government but their areas of consensus were very weak.

The panel convened by the Ontario government consisted of representatives from consumer, government, and business sectors to strengthen Ontario's payday lending regulations (Deloitte 2014). The panel report reviews Ontario's regulations point by point and notes some areas in which the panel came to a consensus and other areas where a consensus was not reached. They noted that the industry and loan model is always changing so that effective regulations must be broad enough to continue to regulate the sector. They also agreed that more data are needed to make effective regulations, that regulations should also be strengthened for non-compliant payday lenders and products, and there needs to be more financial education available to consumers. The panel was unable to agree on recommendations about other items such as fee caps, repeat loan limits, loan size limits, and so on.

A holistic response to bank exclusion evidenced by the growth of payday lending would include regulation of mainstream Financial Institutions (FIs) (Buckland 2012; Dijkema and McKendry 2016). Restricting, reforming, or allowing fringe banks through state intervention are insufficient to address bank exclusion. A critical component to the solution to payday lending is that mainstream FIs identify the need, learn from the current providers (i.e., the payday lenders), and put in place products that meet this need. This is not happening through the "market mechanism" so it is justifiable that the federal government steps in to engage with mainstream FIs to generate this outcome. For instance, the federal government, through the Financial Consumer Agency of Canada, could broaden and deepen the Access to Basic Banking Regulations so that banks are required to maintain branches in modest-income neighborhoods, develop financial services the income-poor people need, and train staff to understand the financial reality of asset-poor people.

In Canada though, we simply have insufficient data to determine the extent of the problems associated with payday lending and then what legislation would be best. There is a clear need for government to collect these data so that careful analysis can be done. Federal agencies such as the Financial Consumer Agency of Canada and/or the Industry Canada-based Consumer Measures Committee are obvious choices to take on this task.

The contribution of our book is the examination of the ethical issues, the client base, the nature of the industry, the mainstream banking alternatives, and the regulations that govern payday lending in Canada. The book had its origins in the work prepared by many of the authors for a series of regulatory hearings in Manitoba dating from 2007 through 2016. Updated and expanded here, the objective of our book is to present evidence, theory, and argument demonstrating both the complex impact of payday lending on their clients and why there is a pressing need for careful regulation of payday lending to minimize these harmful consequences. Based as it is on a large-scale mixed methodology including socio-economic, financial, econometric, and legal components, the collection of research presented here aims to fill a major gap in the comprehensiveness of the existing research on payday lending.

References

Anderson, John. 2013. *Making the Case for Postal Banking in Canada*. Ottawa: Canadian Centre for Policy Alternatives.

Baradaran, Mehrsa. 2015. *How the Other Half Banks: Exclusion, Exploitation, and the Threat to Democracy*. Cambridge, MA: Harvard University Press.

Barth, James R., Jitka Hilliard, and John S. Jahera, Jr. 2015. Banks and Payday Lenders: Friends Or Foes? *International Advances in Economic Research* 21 (2): 139–153.

Bertrand, Marianne, and Adair Morse. 2011. Information Disclosure, Cognitive Biases, and Payday Borrowing. *Journal of Finance* 66 (6): 1865–1893.

Bertrand, Marianne, Sendhil Mullainathan, Dean Karlan, Eldar Shafir, and Jonathan Zinman. 2009. *What's Advertising Content Worth? Evidence from a Consumer Credit Marketing Field Experiment.* Working Papers, Economic Growth Center, Yale University.

Bhutta, Neil. 2013. *Payday Loans and Consumer Financial Health.* Finance and Economics Discussion Series, No. 2013-81, Board of Governors of the Federal Reserve System (U.S.).

Brennan, Marilyn, Brian McGregor, and Jerry Buckland. 2011. The Changing Structure of Inner-City Retail Banking: Examining Bank Branch and Payday Loan Outlet Locations in Winnipeg, 1980–2009. *Canadian Journal of Urban Research* 20 (1): 1–32.

Buckland, Jerry. 2012. *Hard Choices: Financial Exclusion, Fringe Banks, and Poverty in Urban Canada.* Toronto: University of Toronto Press.

Buckland, Jerry, Tom Carter, Wayne Simpson, Anita Friesen, and John Osborne. 2007. *Serving Or Exploiting People Facing a Short-Term Credit Crunch? A Study of Consumer Aspects of Payday Lending in Manitoba.* Winnipeg, Canada.

Caskey, John P. 1994. *Fringe Banking: Check-Cashing Outlets, Pawnshops, and the Poor.* New York, NY: Russell Sage Foundation.

———. 2005. Fringe Banking and the Rise of Payday Lending. In *Credit Markets for the Poor*, ed. Patrick Bolton and Howard Rosenthal. New York: The Russell Sage Foundation.

———. 2010. *Payday Lending: New Research and the Big Question.* Working Papers, No. 10–32, Federal Reserve Bank of Philadelphia, Philadelphia.

———. 2012. Payday Lending: New Research and the Big Question. In *Oxford Handbook of the Economics of Poverty*, ed. Philip Jefferson. New York: Oxford University Press.

Consumer Federation of America. 2011. *CFA Survey of Online Payday Loan Websites.* Washington, DC.

Consumer Protection BC. 2016. *BC Aggregated Payday Loan Data – Self-Reported for License Years ending on October 31.* Victoria, BC. https://www.consumer-protectionbc.ca/wordpress/wp-content/uploads/2017/10/2016-Payday-Aggregate-Loan-Data-Table-for-Web.pdf

Consumers' Association of Canada (Manitoba) Inc. 2015. *Privacy in Online Lending: An Analysis of Online Payday Lenders' Privacy Policies and Consumer Expectations for Privacy Protection.* Winnipeg, Canada.

Deloitte. 2014. *Strengthening Ontario's Payday Loans Act: Payday Lending Panel Findings and Recommendations Report.* Toronto.

Denise Barrett Consulting. 2015. *Consumer Experiences in Online Payday Loans*. Toronto.

DFC Global Corp. 2014. *Form 10-K for the Year Ended June 30, 2013*. Berwyn, US: DFC Global Corp. https://www.sec.gov/Archives/edgar/data/1271625/000119312513352311/d590562d10k.htm

Dijkema, Brian, and Rhys McKendry. 2016. *Banking on the Margins: Finding Ways to Build and Enabling Small-Dollar Credit Market*. Hamilton: Cardus.

Edmiston, Kelly D. 2011. Could Restrictions on Payday Lending Hurt Consumers? *Federal Reserve Bank of Kansas City Economic Review* 96 (1): 63–93.

Fantauzzi, J. 2016. *Predatory Lending: A Survey of High Interest Alternative Financial Service Users*. Canadian Centre for Policy Alternatives and ACORN Canada.

Fejos, Andrea. 2015. Achieving Safety and Affordability in the UK Payday Loans Market. *Journal of Consumer Policy* 38 (2): 181–202.

Financial Consumer Agency of Canada. 2016. *Payday Loans: Market Trends*. https://www.canada.ca/en/financial-consumer-agency/programs/research/payday-loans-market-trends.html

Fitzpatrick, Katie, and Alisha Coleman-Jensen. 2014. Food on the Fringe: Food Insecurity and the Use of Payday Loans. *Social Service Review* 88 (4): 553–593.

Gathergood, John. 2012. Self-Control, Financial Literacy and Consumer Over-Indebtedness. *Journal of Economic Psychology* 33 (3): 590–602.

Grant, Tavia, and Janet McFarland. 2015. Payday Loans: Predatory Loan Sharks or Crucial Fix in a Pinch? *The Globe and Mail*. http://www.theglobeandmail.com/report-on-business/payday-loans-predatory-loan-sharks-or-crucial-fix-in-a-pinch/article24463029/. Accessed 27 July 2015.

Kaufman, Alex. 2013. *Payday Lending Regulation*. Finance and Economics Discussion Series, No. 2013-62, Board of Governors of the Federal Reserve System (U.S.).

Lawrence, Edward C., and Gregory Elliehausen. 2008. A Comparative Analysis of Payday Loan Customers. *Contemporary Economic Policy* 26 (2): 299–316.

Leyshon, Andrew, and Nigel J. Thrift. 1997. *Money/Space: Geographies of Monetary Transformation*. London: Routledge.

Leyshon, Andrew, Paola Signoretta, David Knights, Catrina Alferoff, and Dawn Burton. 2006. Walking with Moneylenders: The Ecology of the UK Home-Collected Credit Industry. *Urban Studies* 43 (1): 161–186.

Lusardi, Annamaria, and Olivia S. Mitchell. 2014. The Economic Importance of Financial Literacy: Theory and Evidence. *Journal of Economic Literature* 52 (1): 5–44.

McKernan, Signe-Mary, Caroline Ratcliffe, and Daniel Kuehn. 2010. *Prohibitions, Price Caps, and Disclosures: A Look at State Policies and Alternative Financial Product Use*. Washington, DC: Urban Institute.

Melzer, Brian T. 2014. *Spillovers from Costly Credit*. Working Papers, Center for Economic Studies, U.S. Census Bureau.
Mills, Gregory B., and William Monson. 2013. *The Rising Use of Nonbank Credit among U.S. Households: 2009–2011*. Washington, DC: Urban Institute.
Montezemolo, Susanna. 2013. *Payday Lending Abuses and Predatory Practices*. Durham, NC: Center for Responsible Lending.
Mullainathan, Sendhil, and Eldar Shafir. 2013. *Scarcity: Why Having Too Little Means so Much*. New York: Henry Holt, Times Books.
Packman, Carl. 2014. A Short History of Payday Lending. *History Workshop Journal* 81 (1) (Spring).
Pew Charitable Trusts. 2012. *Payday Lending in America: Who Borrows, Where They Borrow, and Why*. Washington, DC: Pew Center on the States.
———. 2013a. *How Borrowers Choose and Repay Payday Loans: Payday Lending in America*. Washington, DC: Pew Center on the States.
———. 2013b. *Payday Lending in America: Policy Solutions*. Washington, DC: Pew Center on the States.
———. 2014. *Fraud and Abuse Online: Harmful Practices in Internet Payday Lending*. Philadelphia: Pew Charitable Trusts.
Pollon, Christopher. 2015. Easy Money. *The Walrus*, June 19.
Prager, Robin A. 2014. Determinants of the Locations of Alternative Financial Service Providers. *Review of Industrial Organization* 45 (1): 21–38.
Service Nova Scotia. 2015. *Opening Statement of Service Nova Scotia (SNS): February 2015 Payday Loan Hearing*. Halifax, Canada: Service Nova Scotia.
Shefrin, Hersh M., and Richard H. Thaler. 1993. The Behavioral Life-Cycle Hypothesis. In *Economics and Psychology*, ed. Shlomo Maital and Sharone L. Maital, 166–200. Cheltenham, UK: Edward Elgar.
Simpson, Wayne, and Dana Bazarkulova. 2013. *Payday Loans Consumer Profile Based on the 2009 Canada Financial Capabilities Survey*. Winnipeg.
Simpson, Wayne, and Jerry Buckland. 2016. The Dynamics of Financial Institution Location in Toronto: Who Is Serving the Inner City? *Economic Development Quarterly* 30 (4): 1–29.
Soederberg, Susanne. 2014. *Debtfare States and the Poverty Industry*. London: Routledge.
Squires, Gregory D., and Sally O'Connor. 2001. *Color and Money: Politics and Prospects for Community Reinvestment in Urban America*. Albany, NY: Suny Press.
Thaler, Richard H., and Cass R. Sunstein. 2008. *Nudge: Improving Decisions About Health, Wealth, and Happiness*. New Haven, CT: Yale University Press.
Wolff, Sarah D. 2015. *The Cumulative Costs of Predatory Practices*. Durham, NC: Center for Responsible Lending.
Zinman, Jonathan. 2010. Restricting Consumer Credit Access: Household Survey Evidence on Effects around the Oregon Rate Cap. *Journal of Banking and Finance* 34 (3): 546–556.

CHAPTER 2

A Statistical Profile of Payday Loan Clients from National Surveys

Wayne Simpson and Khan Islam

Introduction

Concern about the impact of payday lending concentrates on the clients and the harm their borrowing practices are doing to their financial circumstances and prospects. But who are these clients? Are they a narrowly defined segment of the population? Or are they a more diverse population requiring a more complex understanding of their borrowing motivations and practices? And is the population changing through time? Is there greater penetration of payday lending into consumer groups that might be expected to rely on mainstream financial services?

To address these questions, this chapter considers the evidence available from two reputable national surveys conducted by Statistics Canada that ask about payday loan borrowing practices. The **Canadian Financial Capability Survey (CFCS)** was conducted in 2009 and 2014 with the cooperation and support of the Financial Consumer Agency of Canada

W. Simpson (✉)
Department of Economics, University of Manitoba, Winnipeg, MB, Canada

K. Islam
Department of Economics, Philosophy and Political Science,
University of British Columbia, Kelowna, BC, Canada

J. Buckland et al. (eds.), *Payday Lending in Canada in a Global Context*,
https://doi.org/10.1007/978-3-319-71213-0_2

(FCAC) to collect information about Canadians' knowledge of financial matters and instruments and their ability to apply this knowledge in decision-making.[1] The Survey uses a stratified multi-stage survey design administered to a subsample of respondents to the Labor Force Survey,[2] which yielded 14,490 respondents in 2009 and 6528 respondents in 2014 who answered the questions on payday loan borrowing. The payday loan borrower's profile is drawn from survey questions that ask: (1) if the respondent or other household members used the services of payday lending during the previous 12 months, (2) if the respondent or other household members had a payday loan at the time of the survey, and (3) how may payday loans (one, two, or three or more) the respondent or other household members had taken during the previous 12 months. The latter question provides some limited but valuable information on the incidence and extent of repeat borrowing.

The **Survey of Financial Security (SFS)** was conducted in 2005 and 2012 to collect such information as assets, debts, employment, income, and education to understand how family finances change because of economic pressures. Information was collected on the value of all major financial and non-financial assets and on the money owing on mortgages, vehicles, credit cards, student loans, and other debts to provide a comprehensive picture of the net worth of Canadian families. The SFS has a stratified multi-stage dual-frame design,[3] which yielded 5237 families in 2005 and 12,003 families in 2012 who responded to the question on payday

[1] While some of the evidence for CFCS refers to activities undertaken in 2013 or 2008, we refer to the results by their survey date (2014 or 2009) throughout our discussion or, when no date is mentioned, the reference is to the latest CFCS in 2014.

[2] Each province is divided into large geographic strata. The first stage of sampling consists of selecting smaller Primary Sampling Units (PSU) from within each stratum while the second stage consists of selecting dwellings from within selected PSU. The CFCS sample consisted of dwellings from the two rotation groups that completed their last Labor Force Survey interviews in January and February of 2014. The survey covers the civilian, non-institutionalized population that is 18 years of age and over. Response rates were 56.3% in 2009 and 55.6% in 2014, and almost all respondents (93.4% in 2009 and 97.7% in 2014) answered the questions on payday loan borrowing.

[3] The SFS is based on independent samples from two overlapping frames, the Labor Force Survey (LFS) area frame and a frame constructed from the urban portion of the 2009 T1 family file (T1FF). The LFS area frame strata were grouped into urban and rural strata within each province, while the urban T1FF frame was stratified by province and by four levels of predicted household net worth. The response rate was 60% in 2012 and all respondents answered the question on payday loan borrowing.

lending. The only question asked, however, was if anyone in the family had borrowed money through a payday loan in the past three years.

Computer-assisted telephone interviewing (CATI) was used to collect data for both the 2009 and 2014 CFCS. Buckland (2012, pp. 23–24) notes that reliance on telephone interviewing likely underrepresents low-income households without a telephone, and this is corroborated by the finding in Frenette et al. (2007) that survey data inflates incomes at the bottom of the distribution relative to tax and census data, which do not rely on telephone interviewing. The 2009 CFCS used random digit dialing (RDD), but an address-based frame was used in 2014 CFCS. All households with missing telephone numbers were removed from the frame. The CFCS surveys exclude persons living in the territories, on reserve, the Aboriginal settlements, full-time members of the Canadian Armed Forces, and the non-institutionalized population. The Kish sample allocation method was used to select the dwelling from the frame. One member of age 18 years or above was randomly selected from each selected dwellings for the CFCS interview where a proxy interview was not allowed.

Since these are national surveys intended to collect a variety of information on the financial circumstances and behavior of Canadian families, the low incidence of payday loan borrowers leads to small sample sizes. The 2009 CFCS provides a sample of 265 respondents (1.8% of the total sample) who indicated that they used the services of payday lending at least once during the last 12 months and 80 respondents (0.6% of the sample) who reported that at least one household member had a payday loan at the time of the survey. The 2014 CFCS yields 214 respondents (4.2% of the sample) who indicated that their household used payday lending services and 35 respondents (0.8% of the sample) who reported at least one household member with a payday loan at the time of the survey. The survey population of the SFS is the same as the CFCS, covering about 98% of the population in the ten provinces. SFS 2012 is based on a sample of 11,591 dwellings from the Labor Force Survey (LFS) frame that did not participate in the labor force or financial surveys conducted by the Statistics Canada. Then an additional sample of 8409 urban dwellings was selected from the T1 Family File (T1FF) for a total sample size of 20,000. Using a computer-assisted personal interviewing (CAPI) method, the most knowledgeable member of the family's financial situation was interviewed. In SFS 2005, the personal interviews involved a paper questionnaire for a total sample of 9000 dwellings, 7500 dwellings were added from LFS sampling frame, and the remaining 1500 observations were selected from geographic regions where a large proportion of households was defined as "high-income." The SFS provided 137 respondents in 2005 (2.6% of the sample) and 340 respondents in 2012 (2.8% of the sample) who indicated that they had used the services of payday lending during the last three years.

Alternative direct surveys of payday loan users, such as the survey of 1500 users recently conducted by the Financial Consumer Agency of Canada (FCAC 2016), offer larger samples of users, but the sampling method is not random and they do not permit comparison with non-users to identify distinctive characteristics of payday loan clients. An older survey by Environics Research Group (2005) for the Canadian Association of Community Financial Service Providers, now known as the Canadian Consumer Finance Association, combined a survey of 1000 recent payday loan users with a random sample of 1000 Canadians from the general population[4] to facilitate comparison of payday loan clients and non-clients.

Our analysis yields important and sometimes surprising patterns of payday loan borrowing. We consider these patterns in two stages. First, we consider the simple descriptive statistical profiles of the characteristics of payday loan borrowers contrasted with non-borrowers. We start with the economic factors, principally income, wealth, credit availability, and labor market participation, before moving to other demographic factors and to borrowing frequency and aspects of repeat borrowing behavior. We then use multiple regression analysis to help us understand the strength and significance of the relationship between payday lending behavior, in terms of both the incidence and frequency of borrowing, and the specific characteristics of borrowers and non-borrowers we have considered previously. This allows us to assess the robustness of the correlation between payday loan borrowing and individual characteristics, independent of the impact of the other characteristics, to draw final conclusions.

The Economic Factors

An important source of concern for payday loan clients has been their presumed limited financial resources in conjunction with the high cost of payday loans. To assess the economic circumstances of clients, we examine

[4] Absence of detail about the sampling procedures makes it difficult to evaluate them or compare them with those used by Statistics Canada.

their household income, assets and liabilities, use of credit cards, and employment situation. What emerges is a client profile that is concentrated on lower-income households but, it should be emphasized, not the poorest households. This may not be surprising, since payday loan eligibility has generally required the borrower to produce a paycheck and the poorest households in Canada are typically those that are heavily reliant on government transfer payments rather than earnings.

The SFS, for example, indicates that payday loan clients have lower average household income than non-clients, but it also indicates that the gap has been declining. The average household income in 2005 of the client and non-client groups was $40,204 and $66,573, respectively, a gap of $26,369 or 65.6%.[5] By 2012 the corresponding figures were $52,416 and $73,341, a smaller gap of $20,925 or 39.9%. That is, the household incomes of payday loan clients had grown faster (30.4%) than non-clients (10.2%) from 2005 to 2012.

We can look more closely at the incomes of client and non-client households by quintiles in the 2014 CFCS. As Fig. 2.1 illustrates, the proportion of payday loan clients in the poorest quintile of households (18.7%) is only slightly higher than for non-clients (17.0%). The real source of the income gap is the other four quintiles. The second and third quintiles contain 19.1% and 22.3% of the non-client sample, respectively, compared to 25.7% and 25.2% of the client sample; that is, 51% of the client sample belongs to the second and third income quintiles compared to only 41% of the non-client sample. The fourth and highest quintiles contain 19.6% and 10.8% of the client sample compared to 21.9% and 20.0% of the non-client sample; that is, 41.9% of the non-client sample belongs to the top two quintiles compared to only 30.4% of the client sample. What might be most surprising in these figures is that almost one-third of all payday loan clients come from the top two income quintiles of what would appear to be relatively prosperous households. These results are consistent with the FCAC (2016, p. 2) finding that "while payday loans are primarily used by those with low-to-moderate incomes (more than half lived in households with annual incomes under $55,000), many higher-income Canadians also reported accessing these loans. Twenty percent of respondents reported household incomes exceeding $80,000, with 7% over $120,000."[6] It is also consistent with the earlier Environics Research Group (2005,

[5] Currency figures reported in this chapter are in Canadian dollars.

[6] FCAC notes that the median family income was $78,000 in 2014, so that rought one in five payday loan users comes from a family with income above the median.

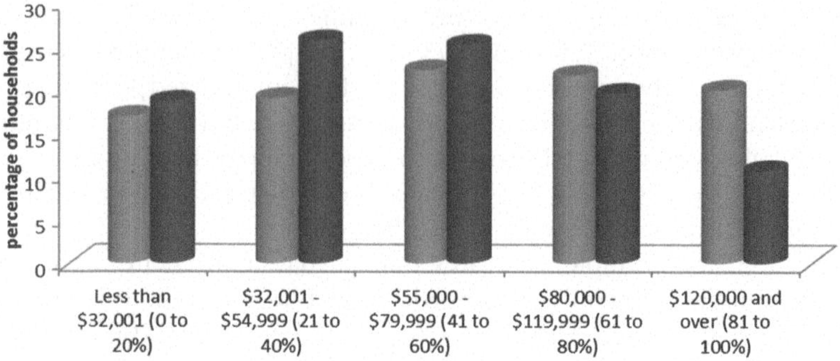

Fig. 2.1 Household income distribution for payday loan clients (*Red/dark*) and non-clients (*Blue/light*) in the 2014 CFCS. Source: Author's calculations using public files of 2014 CFCS

p. 5) result that those in households with incomes above $60,000 were almost as likely to have used a payday loan service as those in households with incomes below $40,000.[7]

An alternative, and potentially more accurate, measure of household prosperity is net worth and its component assets and liabilities. As expected, the SFS for 2005 and 2012 indicate that the average net worth of payday loan clients is much lower than non-clients, although the wealth of payday lending clients is growing more rapidly. The average household wealth of payday loan clients rose from $165,173 to $234,103 (41.7%) between 2005 and 2012 compared to an increase from $740,070 to $867,813 (17.3%) for non-clients.[8] The greater wealth of non-clients reflects greater debt as well as greater asset levels, consistent with the idea of more limited access to mainstream borrowing sources for payday loan clients. Indeed, the average household debt of non-clients has increased more rapidly

[7] Median family income was $63,866 in 2005 according to Statistics Canada: http://www12.statcan.gc.ca/census-recensement/2006/dp-pd/tbt/Rp-eng.cfm?LANG=E&APATH=3&DETAIL=0&DIM=0&FL=A&FREE=0&GC=0&GID=0&GK=0&GRP=1&PID=96428&PRID=0&PTYPE=88971,97154&S=1&SHOWALL=0&SUB=0&Temporal=2006&THEME=68&VID=0&VNAMEE=&VNAMEF=

[8] Since these are cross-sectional surveys, it is important to remember that those in the client and non-client groups are not the same in each survey and that mobility from the client to the non-client group is likely associated with economic fortunes that are at least partly captured in the wealth data.

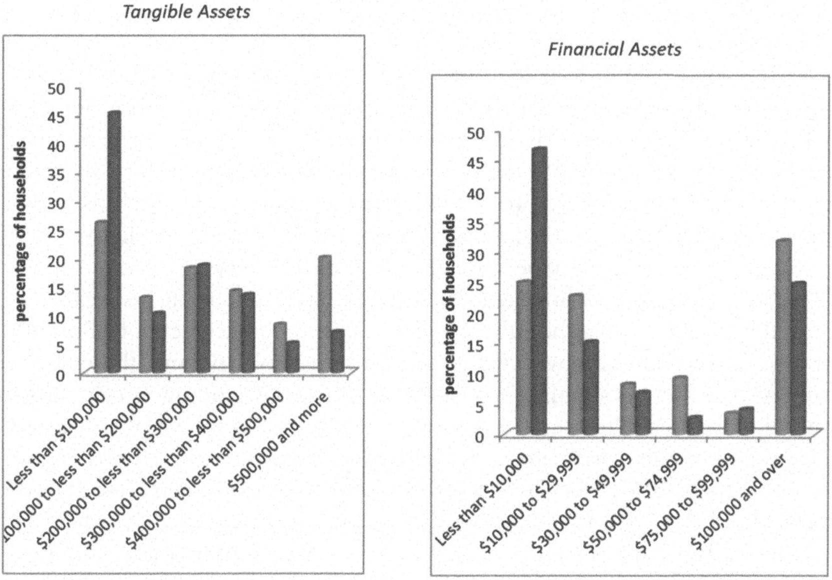

Fig. 2.2 Total assets distribution for payday loan clients (*Red/dark*) and non-clients (*Blue/light*) in the 2014 CFCS. Source: Author's calculations using public files of 2014 CFCS

between 2005 and 2012 from $66,135 to $95,239 (44%) than for clients (from $53,229 to $56,544 or only 6.2%).

If we examine the distribution of assets and liabilities for payday loan clients and non-clients in the CFCS, however, some interesting patterns emerge. Payday loan clients are more clearly concentrated in households with the lowest assets, both in terms of tangible and financial assets,[9] as indicated in Fig. 2.2. The proportion of payday loan clients in households in the lowest financial asset category is 46.2% for tangible assets (under $100,000) and 46.6% for financial assets (under $10,000), compared to

[9] In the CFCS, **tangible assets** include: houses or property (in or out of Canada, including one's principal residence), vehicles (cars, trucks, watercrafts, RVs, trailers, snowmobiles, ATVs, etc.), collections, antiques, jewels, and other valuables. **Financial assets** include cash savings (from savings or chequing accounts), investments (stocks, bonds, term deposits, GICs, non-Regsitered Retirement Savings Plan mutual funds), registered disability savings plans, tax-free savings plans, and private pensions.

only 26.1% and 24.9% for non-clients. The lower tangible asset level of payday loan clients is reflected in lower levels of liabilities, as 66.7% of clients reported total liabilities of less than $50,000 compared to 49.3% of non-clients, figures which have changed little from 2009 CFCS. Lower levels of liabilities for payday loan clients include lower incidence of mortgage debt, 32.5% compared to 40.1% for non-clients, and lower incidence of credit card debt, 73.1% compared to 87.2%, although student loan debt is higher among payday loan clients (12.9% compared to 8.7% for non-clients).

Again, however, it may be surprising to find that very nearly one-quarter (24.7%) of the payday loan clients fall into the highest financial asset category exceeding $100,000, although only 7.1% have tangible assets of $500,000 or more. In conjunction with the results for household income, these figures suggest that there is significant penetration of payday lending into wealthier households where alternative forms of financing should be available. Indeed, the use of credit cards along with payday loans increased considerably between the 2009 CFCS, where 48.3% of payday loan clients used credit cards,[10] and the 2014 CFCS, where 73.1% of clients used credit cards.

The traditional basis for a payday loan has been employment and a pay stub, but this may be changing. The CFCS shows that, while payday loan clients were more likely to be employed or self-employed than non-clients in 2009 (65.3% compared to 58.1%), this difference had virtually disappeared by 2014 (67.0% compared to 66.0%) in 2014 CFCS. Moreover, there were important changes in the distribution of borrowers by income source between 2009 and 2014, as the source of income for payday loan clients shifted from its traditional source of wages and salaries toward social assistance payments, public retirement income (CPP/QPP/OAS/GIS), and other transfer income. Since the most dramatic changes in income sources have occurred for repeat borrowers, we return to this issue in section "Regression Results."

The Demographic Factors

Payday loan clients are younger than non-clients and more likely to be in their prime working years. The SFS reports that the average age of the major income earner in families using payday lending services was 40.8 years in 2012 compared to 53.1 years for non-client families, while the 2014 CFCS finds that 60.3% of payday loan clients came from the 25- to 54-year-

[10] This figure is consistent with a figure of 41% of payday loan users having a credit card in the Environics Research Group (2005, p. 4) poll.

old age group compared to only 45.4% of non-clients. This may be an unsurprising result when we consider the employment requirement still normally associated with payday loan transactions and the higher likelihood of employment for this “prime” age group, but there may also be concerns that this younger and prime working age population seems most susceptible to alternative and more expensive financial arrangements. Between 2005 and 2012, the SFS finds a small increase in the average age of the major income earner in families using payday loans from 37.4 to 40.8 years, suggesting some increased penetration of payday lending into older families.

It is generally presumed that lower education plays some role in household reliance on payday loans because of the strong association of education with earning power and wealth generation, although there is also a common argument in the payday loan literature that links education to financial literacy[11] (Social and Enterprise Development Innovations 2004; Atkinson et al. 2007; Simpson and Buckland 2009). That is, lack of education and financial literacy may limit the capability of borrowers to make rational decisions (Lusardi and Mitchell 2014), an issue we analyze further in our regression analysis in section “Regression Results”. In this section, we simply report that the 2012 SFS finds that the university graduation rate for payday loan clients is only 11.6%, well below the 28.7% rate for non-clients, but it also finds that more than 80% of payday loan clients have at least a high school diploma, a figure that is consistent with the earlier results from Environics Research Group (2005, p. 12). Moreover, results from the CFCS suggest greater penetration of payday loan borrowing into higher education groups, as the proportion of payday loan clients with a post-secondary diploma or university degree increased from 38.1% in 2009 to 56.3% in 2014. These trends raise questions about education and its role in household financial management that would involve further analysis with more sophisticated data.

One implication of the relative youth of payday loan clients is that they are more likely to be supporting children. The 2014 CFCS finds that more than one-third (37.6%) of the client sample responded that they carry financial responsibility for one or more children compared to less than one-quarter (23.9%) of the non-client sample, a gap that is comparable to earlier findings by Environics Research Group (2005). Moreover, 22.4% of the client sample lives in a household with more than one child compared to

[11] Financial literacy refers to consumers’ ability to make effective financial decisions using acquired financial knowledge and education. Financial literacy could also be defined as measuring how well an individual can understand and use personal finance-related information (Huston 2010).

14.1% of the non-client sample. From the SFS we also learn that 15.4% of clients are lone parents in 2012, which is much higher than the 4.7% of non-clients who are lone parents in 2012 and an increase from the 12.4% of clients who were lone parents in 2005. These results suggest that family composition and more specifically marital status and the presence and number of children in the household could be factors in payday loan borrowing, although they also raise additional concerns about how payday loan borrowing may be affecting the financial well-being of Canadian children.

Other demographic factors appear less important. While clients are more likely than non-clients to be aboriginal (15.0% vs. 12.3%) or immigrant (7.2% vs. 4.2%) in the 2014 CFCS, the differences are slight and the proportion of clients who are aboriginal actually declined from 11.7% in 2009. A more interesting result is that the proportion of clients reporting French as their first language has risen sharply from 10.2% in 2009 to 36.5% in 2014, suggesting an increased penetration of payday lending among those who are French speaking. This linguistic pattern has emerged despite Quebec's decision to cap the annual interest rate on loans at 35% and effectively ban the payday lending industry from the province.

Frequency of Borrowing and Repeat Borrowing

The CFCS provides some evidence on the important question of the frequency of payday loan use among clients. What seems clear from the surveys is that only about one-quarter of clients took out a single payday loan during the 12-month period in both 2009 (27.6%) and 2014 (23.4%), a figure that is consistent with the findings in FCAC (2016, p. 9). Hence, most borrowers are repeat users within a year and repeat borrowing practices appear to be growing. It would be useful to have a more detailed breakdown of payday loan borrowing among the most frequent users, but the top survey category is simply three or more loans within a year. FCAC found, for example, that while 29% of payday loan clients took out only one loan over the previous three years, nearly as many (23%) took out six or more loans. Thus, the top category in the CFCS limits our ability to identify those with more serious repeat borrowing practices.

A surprising result may be that repeat payday loan use is not more prevalent among lower-income clients. In the lowest income quintile, 75% of payday loan clients took out more than one loan within 12 months, but repeat use actually rises to 78.2% in the second income quintile of borrowers and 77.8% in the third quintile before dipping slightly to 69.1% in the fourth quintile and then rising again to 87% in the top income quintile.

The absence of a pattern of repeat borrowing by income level may not be surprising, however, in view of our earlier finding that payday loan clients in the lowest income quintile are now more dependent on transfer payments, a source of income that may limit prospects for repeat borrowing.

The changing income sources of repeat borrowers represent an important development. Wages and salaries, the traditional dominant income source of payday loan clients, declined in importance between 2009 and 2014. For the most frequent borrowers who took out three or more loans during the year, wages and salaries as the principal income source fell dramatically from 71.7% in 2009 to 48.8% in 2014. What income sources replaced wages and salaries? Households relying on social assistance constituted 30% of those taking three or more payday loans in 2014 compared to only 18% in 2009, and the proportion of households with three or more loans relying on pension income rose to 15% from 4% during this period. The latter result is consistent with the evidence of rising payday loan borrowing among older Canadians, while both results reflect an increased penetration of payday lending beyond the traditional working population.

Regression Results

In this section we use regression analysis to help us understand the relationship between payday lending behavior and the multiple characteristics of clients and non-clients. First, we report probit models estimated for the CFCS and SFS data to explore further the important determinants of the incidence of payday loan borrowing, that is, whether a family took out a payday loan during the period surveyed. Our econometric framework follows Jappelli (1990), who applies the life cycle consumption model to analyze credit constraint and financial exclusion, and is used by Hogarth et al. (2005) to study the unbanked in the USA and Simpson and Buckland (2009) to analyze financial and credit exclusion in Canada. We then extend the analysis to report ordered probit models estimated on the CFCS data to analyze the effect of different factors on the important question of the frequency of payday loan use, that is, whether a family took out zero, one, two, or three or more payday loans during the survey period (one year).

The probit model estimates are presented in Table 2.1 for both the CFCS and the SFS.[12] The results for the 2005 SFS are taken directly from

[12] The models presented here include the full range of personal characteristics and family circumstances. Other models with more limited regressor lists have been estimated but the important and statistically significant results are unchanged. These results are available from the authors upon request.

Table 2.1 Probit estimates of the determinants of payday loan borrowing from the CFCS and SFS
[Dependent variable is 1 if a member of the household has taken out a payday loan in the last 12 months (CFCS) or the last 3 years (SFS) and 0 otherwise]

	1: 2014 CFCS		*2: 2009 CFCS*		*3: 2012 SFS*		*4: 2005 SFS*	
	Coefficient estimate	*Robust standard error*	*Coefficient estimate*	*Robust standard error*	*Coefficient estimate*	*Robust standard error*	*Coefficient estimate*	*Standard error*
Age					0.019	0.011	−0.018	0.017
Age squared					−0.0003	0.0001	0.000	0.000
18–24 year age group								
25–34	.820[b]	.393	0.0534	0.114				
35–44	.764[c]	.394	−0.0316	0.114				
45–54	.819[b]	.390	−0.139	0.111				
55–59	.761[b]	.414	−0.316[b]	0.141				
60–64	1.038[b]	.411	−0.427[a]	0.165				
65–69	.494	.450	−0.476[b]	0.211				
70 and over	.248	.443	−0.357[b]	0.180				
Sex	−.112	.087	−0.0765	0.0542				
Marital status								
Married			−0.187[a]	0.0614				
Living common-law	.575[a]	.142						
Widowed	.564[a]	.164						
Separated	.521[a]	.168						
Divorced	.182	.158						
Single, never married	.440[a]	.136					0.141	0.158
Family size					0.050	0.109	0.155[b]	0.067
Family size squared					0.005	0.018		
Number of children	0.008	0.068	0.0407	0.0366				

(*continued*)

Table 2.1 (continued)

	1: 2014 CFCS		*2: 2009 CFCS*		*3: 2012 SFS*		*4: 2005 SFS*	
	Coefficient estimate	*Robust standard error*	*Coefficient estimate*	*Robust standard error*	*Coefficient estimate*	*Robust standard error*	*Coefficient estimate*	*Standard error*
Children 0–4							0.054	0.151
Children 5–17							0.080	0.138
Couple with children							−0.114	0.203
Lone parent							0.014	0.236
Financial responsibility for children	−0.488[a]	.145	0.146[c]	0.0843				
Education								
Education not available							1.336[a]	0.410
High school or less							0.371[b]	0.145
High school only					0.091	0.081	0.246[c]	0.128
Some college, university without degree	−0.378[c]	.204					0.267[b]	0.127
College, trade, vocational, or technical school	−0.143	.099			0.029	0.084		
University undergraduate degree	−.367[a]	.132	−0.304[a]	0.0571	−0.282[a]	0.101		
University graduate degree	−.301	.208						
Employment								
Number of earners in household					0.255[b]	0.116	0.099	0.076
Number of earners squared					−0.060	0.035		
Gender of major income earner					−0.009	0.056		

(*continued*)

Table 2.1 (continued)

	1: 2014 CFCS		*2: 2009 CFCS*		*3: 2012 SFS*		*4: 2005 SFS*	
	Coefficient estimate	*Robust standard error*	*Coefficient estimate*	*Robust standard error*	*Coefficient estimate*	*Robust standard error*	*Coefficient estimate*	*Standard error*
Employed			−0.117	0.0714				
Self-employed	−.258	.203						
Not working and looking for work	.019	.206						
Not working and not looking for work	−.061	.173						
Retired	.232	.174	−0.367[b]	0.144				
A student (including work programs)	0		−0.706[a]	0.199				
Doing unpaid household work	−.033	.355						
Household income ($,000)					0.007[a]	0.003	0.325	(0.510)
Household income squared ($,000,000)					−0.00004[b]	0.00001	−0.411	(0.349)
Less than $32,000(2014)/ $25,000(2009)								
$32–$55,000(2014)/ $25–50,000(2009)	.169	.139	0.0819	0.0812				
$55–$80,000(2014)/ $50–75,000(2009)	.141	.148	0.110	0.0873				
$80,000–$120,000(2014)/ $75–100,000(2009)	.078	.157	−0.209[c]	0.112				
$120,000 + (2014)/ $100–125,000(2009)	−.138	.177	−0.395[a]	0.135				
$125–150,000(2009)			−0.401[b]	0.184				

(*continued*)

Table 2.1 (continued)

	1: 2014 CFCS		*2: 2009 CFCS*		*3: 2012 SFS*		*4: 2005 SFS*	
	Coefficient estimate	*Robust standard error*	*Coefficient estimate*	*Robust standard error*	*Coefficient estimate*	*Robust standard error*	*Coefficient estimate*	*Standard error*
$125,000 + (2009)			−0.304[b]	0.131				
Household wealth ($,000,000)					−0.268[a]	0.093	−0.033	0.035
Household wealth squared (×10[12]					0.015[c]	0.009	−0.000	0.002
Household total assets			−1.1e−10[b]	5.47e−11				
Less than $100,000								
$100,000 to less than $200,000	−.594[a]	.185						
$200,000 to less than $300,000	−.135	.130						
$300,000 to less than $500,000	−.494[a]	.138						
$500,000 or more	−.441[a]	.123						
Household debt ($,000,000)					0.025	0.055	0.038	0.046
Household debt squared (×10[12])					−0.163	0.649		
Own home with mortgage					−0.021	0.106	0.106	0.164
Rent; do not own home					0.586[a]	0.095	0.611[a]	0.169
Use of credit card					−0.493[a]	0.068		
cons	−1.510[a]	.481	−1.513[a]	0.195	−2.356[a]	0.289	−2.276[a]	0.465
N	6505		14490		11831		5267	

Results for 2012 SFS include a Manitoba dummy variable which is insignificant and not reported here. Results for 2005 are taken from Simpson and Buckland (2009, Table 7) which include regional cummy variables that are not reported here

[a]Denotes significance at the 1% level

[b]Denotes significance at the 5% level

[c]Denotes significance at the 10% level

Simpson and Buckland (2009).[13] The variable lists for the two CFCS surveys (2014 and 2009) and the two SFS surveys (2012 and 2005) are similar, but the lists across the two surveys differ because of the nature of the questions asked on these omnibus surveys. There are, however, common questions from which we can ascertain the age, gender, marital status, and education of the respondent as well as household income, some indicator of wealth or household assets, and the size of the family. By looking across the surveys on these dimensions, we are able to assess the relative importance of the factors discussed in previous sections.

We begin with the economic factors. While the 2009 CFCS found a strong and significant negative relationship between household income beyond $80,000 and the likelihood of taking a payday loan, the link between household income and payday loan incidence is no longer significant in the 2014 survey. Indeed, although the effects are generally insignificant, the probability of being a payday loan client actually increases for the second, third, and fourth income quintiles relative to the poorest 20% of the survey sample in 2014 before declining for the top 20% of incomes. Both surveys also control for total household assets and that relationship is stronger: Households with greater assets are significantly less likely to use payday loan services.

The results from the 2012 and 2005 SFS also find that the negative correlation between household income and payday loan borrowing is restricted to higher-income households. In both surveys, the quadratic model (including income and income squared) yields a positive coefficient on income and a negative coefficient on income squared, indicating that it is not the poorest households that are payday loan clients but those with somewhat higher, although not the highest, incomes.[14] The negative relationship between household wealth and payday loan borrowing is again strong in the 2012 SFS, which contains the additional related finding that renters are more likely to be payday loan clients than homeowners. Wealthier households are also less likely to be payday loan clients in the 2005 SFS, but this result is not significant.

[13] Pyper (2007) also analyzes the 2005 SFS using logistic regression. She finds that younger families, families with $500 or less in their bank account, families behind in their bill or loan payments, and families without a credit card were more likely to have taken a payday loan.

[14] The coefficients for income and income squared are only significant for the 2012 SFS. These coefficients in column 3 of Table 2.1 imply that households with income up to $175,000 are more likely to take a payday loan and households with income above $175,000 are less likely.

Contrary to the traditional notion of the payday loan requiring a paycheck, employment status does not appear to affect the likelihood of taking a payday loan. The measures of employment status in the CFCS are insignificant, although the 2012 SFS finds that more earners in the household significantly increases the probability of taking a payday loan (other factors considered). A related result of note from the CFCS is that those who are retired are significantly less likely to take a payday loan in 2009, but that result is both weaker and no longer statistically significant in the 2014 survey, consistent with earlier evidence of an increasing penetration of payday lending toward older clients and those whose major income source is pensions.

Some demographic factors also affect payday loan client status, particularly age and marital status. The CFCS reports that respondents in prime working age groups over 25 are significantly more likely to take out payday loans, but that range of age groups has expanded to include the 55–64 year-olds in 2014. Moreover, whereas respondents over 65 were significantly less likely to take out a payday loan in the 2009 survey, the likelihood is no longer statistically significant in 2014, consistent with other evidence of increasing penetration of payday lending into older working and pensionable age groups in the population.

Results from the CFCS for both 2009 and 2014 indicate that respondents who are married report a smaller probability of payday loan use. Beyond that result, a significant negative correlation between payday loan use and financial responsibility for children in the household has emerged since 2009. This is a reassuring result which offsets the impression left from the descriptive analysis that payday loan clients are more likely to have financial responsibility for children; that is, once other factors are considered—such as income, wealth, age, and marital status—financial responsibility for children is negatively, not positively, correlated with payday loan borrowing. The 2012 SFS does find, however, that larger families are more likely to rely on payday lending.

There is consistent evidence across all the surveys that having a university degree or more significantly reduces the likelihood of being a payday loan client. Results from the 2005 SFS also suggest that those without a high school diploma are most likely to take payday loans. Since these results for educational attainments are robust to controls for income and wealth, they suggest that the earning power of higher education is not the sole explanation for this result and that other factors, such as financial literacy, could be involved. This result is consistent with the finding

FCAC (2016, p. 12) that payday loan clients who rated themselves higher on financial literacy used the service less frequently, although their result does not adjust for income differences or draw any direct comparison with the financial literacy self-assessment of those who do not use payday loans.

We estimated ordered probit models on the CFCS data to analyze the effect of the various economic and demographic factors on whether a family took out zero, one, two, or three or more payday loans. The results of these models to explain the frequency of payday loan use are reported in Table 2.2. In general, these results echo those from Table 2.1 for the incidence of payday loan borrowing; that is, the factors that increase the likelihood of being a payday loan client also increase the likelihood of being a more frequent or repeat borrower.

Households with income above $50,000 in 2009 are less likely to be frequent payday loan borrowers but that relationship is no longer significant in 2014, reflecting greater penetration of both the incidence and frequency of payday loan borrowing across the household income spectrum. The stronger relationship remains with accumulated assets, where households with more assets have a lower probability of frequent payday loan borrowing, especially those with assets exceeding $300,000 according to the 2014 data. While asset accumulation obviously reflects both income and time (age), we have controlled for these factors in our analysis. That is, our results suggest that the wealth effect is not simply about richer and older households avoiding payday loans but about financial management and asset accumulation.

Employment status again has no significant effect on payday loan frequency. The significantly lower frequency of payday loan borrowing among those retired in 2009 disappears by 2014, again reflecting increased penetration of payday loan borrowing across the age spectrum. Students are unlikely to be frequent payday loan borrowers, which appears to alleviate any earlier suggestion that student loan debt may be more of a problem for payday loan clients.

Growth of payday lending among older respondents is even more noticeable when the frequency of borrowing is considered. In comparison with the results in columns 1 and 2 of Table 2.1, there is a more pronounced shift toward more frequent payday loan borrowing among all age groups over 25 years of age in 2014 that is also consistent with earlier findings on age and source of income of payday loan clients. Marriage, financial responsibility for children, and more education, especially a

Table 2.2 Ordered probit estimates of the determinants of payday loan borrowing using the CFCS for 2009 and 2014
[Dependent variable is 1 if respondent has taken out a payday loan once in the last 12 months, 2 if respondent has taken out a payday loan twice in the last 12 months, 3 if respondent has taken out a payday loan three times or more in the last 12 months, and 0 otherwise]

	1: 2014 CFCS		*2: 2009 CFCS*	
	Coefficient estimate	*Robust standard error*	*Coefficient estimate*	*Robust standard error*
Age				
18–24 (base)				
25–34	.735[c]	.411	0.0505	0.113
35–44	.703[c]	.410	−0.0239	0.113
45–54	.739[c]	.406	−0.145	0.111
55–59	.654	.427	−0.335[b]	0.141
60–64	.964[b]	.427	−0.429[a]	0.164
65–69	.393	.461	−0.471[b]	0.210
70 and over	.167	.455	−0.363[b]	0.180
Sex	−.116	.086	−0.0645	0.0539
Marital status				
Married			−0.201[a]	0.0611
Living common-law	.573[a]	.140		
Widowed	.551[a]	.159		
Separated	.499[a]	.163		
Divorced	.180	.157		
Single, never married	.451[a]	.131		
Household size				
Number of children	−.001	.070	0.0444	0.0361
Financial responsibility for children	−.500[a]	.145	0.160[c]	0.0836
Education				
High school or less (base)				
Some college, university without degree	−.437[b]	.202		
College, trade, vocational, or technical school	−.173[c]	.098		
University undergraduate degree	−.419[a]	.128	−0.302[a]	0.0568
University graduate degree	−.322	.206		

(*continued*)

Table 2.2 (continued)

	1: 2014 CFCS		*2: 2009 CFCS*	
	Coefficient estimate	*Robust standard error*	*Coefficient estimate*	*Robust standard error*
Employment				
Employed			−0.115	0.0710
Self-employed	−.266	.199		
Not working and looking for work	.015	.201		
Not working and not looking for work	−.022	.170		
Retired	.222	.171	−0.353[b]	0.144
A student (including work programs)	−4.107[a]	.141	−0.723[a]	0.201
Doing unpaid household work	.031	.354		
Household income				
Less than $32,000(2014)/ $25,000(2009)			0.0906	0.0809
$32–$55,000(2014)/ $25–50,000(2009)	.166	.136	0.128	0.0868
$55–$80,000(2014)/ $50–75,000(2009)	.125	.144	−0.197[c]	0.112
$80,000–$120,000(2014)/ $75–100,000(2009)	.082	.154	−0.394[a]	0.135
$120,000 + (2014)/ $100–125,000(2009)	−.126	.175	−0.391[b]	0.184
$125–150,000(2009)			−0.294[b]	0.131
$125,000 + (2009)			0.0906	0.0809
Household total assets			−1.27e−10[b]	5.44e−11
Less than $100,000 (base)				
$100,000 to less than $200,000	−.568[a]	.186		
$200,000 to less than $300,000	−.098	.127		
$300,000 to less than $500,000	−.495[a]	.134		
$500,000 or more	−.440[a]	.119		
N	6505		14490	

[a]Denotes significance at the 1% level
[b]Denotes significance at the 5% level
[c]Denotes significance at the 10% level

university degree, are associated with a lower frequency, as well as a lower incidence, of payday loan borrowing.

Conclusions

This completes our statistical portrait of payday loan clients. Our portrait uses two representative national surveys from Statistics Canada that ask about payday loan borrowing practices as well as other financial practices and circumstances, the 2009 and 2014 Canadian Financial Capability Surveys and the 2005 and 2012 Surveys of Financial Security. While the small sample sizes limit the potential reliability of the profile we draw, these surveys allow us to consider both the characteristics of payday loan clients in comparison with non-clients and how those characteristics have changed over time as payday lending has matured.

The view of payday loan clients as a financially vulnerable population is consistent with our results to a certain extent, but there are also some surprising results that suggest caution in taking this portrayal too far. Payday loan clients are likely to come from households in the lower, although not the lowest, income categories, but our analysis suggests caution in emphasizing income as a dominant factor determining payday loan behavior. The household income gap between clients and non-clients appears to be declining and our regression results from the 2014 CFCS find that the importance of income in identifying payday loan clients and their frequency of borrowing has also declined to statistical insignificance. While the potential under-sampling of low-income households in telephone surveys complicates the analysis, the change over time in the income profile of payday loan clients we observe with the same survey techniques is compelling.

What endures is the role of net worth, since clients remain less wealthy with smaller levels of assets and debt and lower rates of home ownership. The regression results support a strong association between household assets levels or net worth and the incidence and frequency of borrowing, although our analysis also points out that a surprisingly large proportion of payday loan clients come from households with large levels of financial assets.

Nor is the view that payday loan clients are predominantly the working poor without exception. Although clients were more likely to be employed than non-clients in earlier surveys, that no longer appears to be the case. And employment status is not a significant predictor of payday loan incidence or frequency in our regression analyses. Corresponding to this development is an increasing reliance of clients on sources of income other than wages and salaries, particularly social assistance, public retirement income, and other transfer income. This result is particularly noticeable for repeat borrowers, suggesting that the idea of payday loan clients as financially vulnerable working adults needs to be adjusted to include non-workers with limited resources derived from public income support programs.

Payday loan clients are predominantly younger, but not the youngest, adults but the age gap with non-clients is closing. In particular, it is no longer the case that those over 55 years of age are less likely to be payday loan clients or to borrow less frequently, as payday lending expands beyond its traditional clientele to older workers and retirees who may be relying on limited public pension incomes.

While we have no direct tests for financial literacy in our surveys, our analysis does find that payday loan clients have lower levels of education, although that gap with non-clients is closing. Our regression analysis, however, finds that education, especially a university degree, is associated with a reduction in the incidence and frequency of payday loan borrowing even after controlling for income and wealth, which suggests an independent role for education beyond its role in supporting financial security.

There are indications that family structure affects payday loan borrowing practices, but in a complex way. The notion that lone parents and families with large numbers of children are more vulnerable to payday loan borrowing does not stand up to careful empirical scrutiny. For example, the descriptive evidence finds that payday loan clients are more likely to have financial responsibility for children, but this troubling result is actually reversed in the regression analysis. That is, when we control for household income and wealth and other characteristics, those with financial responsibility for children are associated with a lower incidence and frequency of payday loan use. What endures in the regression analysis is that married couples have a significantly lower incidence and frequency of payday loan borrowing, although many factors associated with marriage and marriage stability could be at play.

This, then, is the portrait of payday loan clients that emerges from our statistical analysis: Not the poor, but lacking wealth and assets; somewhat less educated and lacking a university degree; relatively young but getting older; likely working but more often not than in the past; and reliant on public programs as time passes. The concerns remain about households that take out expensive payday loans and especially those that are repeat borrowers over a short period, but they need to be understood in the context of a clientele that is changing. To the extent that a maturing payday loan industry is also penetrating a wider income, wealth, and the age spectrum of the population, these concerns may be both more complex and more imperative than in the past. An important area for future research would appear to be how payday loans are evolving in a mix of household debt instruments, particularly for wealthier households and for households whose chief source of income is derived from public transfers rather than earnings.

References

Atkinson, A., S. McKay, S. Collard, and E. Kempson. 2007. Levels of Financial Capability in the UK. *Public Money and Management* 27 (1): 29–36. https://doi.org/10.1111/j.1467-9302.2007.00552.x.

Buckland, Jerry. 2012. *Hard Choices: Financial Exclusion, Fringe Banks, and Poverty in Urban Canada*. Toronto: University of Toronto Press.

Environics Research Group. 2005. *Understanding Consumers of Canada's Payday Loans Industry*. Report prepared for the Canadian Association of Community Financial Service Providers (now the Canadian Payday Loans Association (CPLA)), June 9. https://studylib.net/doc/10013463/understanding-consumers-of-canada-s-payday-loans-industry

FCAC. 2016. *Payday Loans: Market Trends*. Report of the Financial Consumer Agency of Canada, October 25. https://www.canada.ca/content/dam/fcac-acfc/documents/programs/research-surveys-studies-reports/payday-loans-market-trends.pdf

Frenette, Marc, David A. Green, and Garnett Picot. 2007. Rising Income Inequality in the 1990s: An Exploration of Three Data Sources. In *Dimensions of Inequality in Canada*, ed. David A. Green and Jonathon R. Kesselman. Vancouver: UBC Press.

Hogarth, J.M., C.E. Anguelov, and J. Lee. 2005. Who Has a Bank Account? Exploring Changes Over Time, 1989–2001. *Journal of Family and Economic Issues* 26 (1): 7–30.

Huston, S.J. 2010. Measuring Financial Literacy. *Journal of Consumer Affairs* 44 (2): 296–316.

Jappelli, T. 1990. Who Is Credit Constrained in the US Economy? *The Quarterly Journal of Economics* 105 (1): 219–234.

Lusardi, A., and O.S. Mitchell. 2014. The Economic Importance of Financial Literacy: Theory and Evidence. *Journal of Economic Literature* 52 (1): 5–44.

Pyper, Wendy. 2007. Payday Loans. *Perspectives on Labour and Income*, Statistics Canada Catalogue No. 75-001-XIE, April.

Simpson, Wayne, and Jerry Buckland. 2009. Examining Evidence of Financial & Credit Exclusion in Canada from 1999–2005. *Journal of Socio-Economics* 38: 966–976. https://doi.org/10.1016/j.socec.2009.06.004.

Social and Enterprise Development Innovations (SEDI). 2004. *Financial Capability and Poverty*. Discussion Paper, Policy Research Initiative, Ottawa.

CHAPTER 3

A Socio-economic Examination of Payday Loan Clients: Why and How People Use Payday Loans

Jerry Buckland

Introduction

The rapid rise of payday lending in Canada in the early 2000s fascinated many people such as those in the media and behavioural economists. Part of the fascination was seeking to understand why so many people would use such an expensive credit product. Many field, experimental, and data analysis studies have been completed to understand consumer behaviour. This chapter reports on a series of field methods undertaken in Winnipeg, Canada, in 2015–2016, to understand why and how people use payday loans and what they think about alternatives to payday loans. The 'why and how' questions are informed by a small sample survey, and the exploration into people's views about alternative products—such as slightly larger instalment loans—is done through a focus group conversation with payday loan borrowers.

J. Buckland (✉)
Menno Simons College, Canadian Mennonite University,
Affiliated with the University of Winnipeg, Winnipeg, MB, Canada

J. Buckland et al. (eds.), *Payday Lending in Canada in a Global Context*,
https://doi.org/10.1007/978-3-319-71213-0_3

Mixed Methods Analysis

A small-scale mixed methods research project was undertaken from November 2015 through January 2016 that included a survey, an interview, and focus group meetings.

Participants for the survey, interview, and first focus group were recruited from Winnipeg through a purposive and not random process by local advertising (newspaper and community organizations) and snowball sampling. The goal was to select payday loan consumers who (1) are relatively more vulnerable than the average (meaning relatively lower income and/or reliant on repeat borrowing) and (2) ensure a strong sample among women, newcomer Canadians, and Indigenous people. The survey involved a combination of quantitative and qualitative questions and was completed by 130 individuals; 21 completed the questions online and 109 completed the questions in person. The interviews involved more qualitative and probing questions, and they were undertaken in person with nine people with experience in repeat borrowing and online payday loan usage. Two focus groups discussions involving 16 (7 + 9) people were organized to explore, in a group setting, participants' experiences with payday lending and to get their impressions on some alternatives to payday loans available in other jurisdictions. We report here only on the second focus group meeting.

The participants for the second focus group were selected from Winnipeg with the assistance of a local non-profit organization that recruited from past and present clients and some of their (clients') contacts. The group included nine participants, from diverse socio-economic backgrounds, who currently or in the recent past use/used payday loans. The focus group discussion lasted 2.5 hours. The session began with a brief conversation about the participants' use of payday loans (see appendix for details about the format). A presentation followed that explained how annual percentage rate (APR) is a measurement that allows for comparison of different credit products. Then three models were presented—the Manitoba payday loan and the two other small loan products—and participants were asked to identify the strengths and weaknesses of each product, in addition to their overall preference.

Why and How Do People Use Payday Loans: Results from the Survey

Participant Characteristics and Use of Payday Lender Services

In terms of the demographic makeup of the survey respondents, one-half identified themselves as male and one-half as female. Just less than one-half of the respondents identified themselves as an Aboriginal person. One-half of the survey respondents were employed full-time, and 50% had high school education or less. Just under one-half (48%) of respondents were single and 43% rented an apartment. Participants for the interviews and focus groups represented an older age grouping as compared with the survey respondents. The age ranges for interviewed participants was 25–93 in which 67% ($n = 6$) were between the ages of 40–59.

There was a relatively even distribution of income levels across the methods. Annual income for the survey respondents ranged up to over $80,000, but 72% of respondents' annual income was less than $40,000. For the participants involved in the interviews and focus groups, the annual household income ranged from $1,555 to $62,000, and most, 59% (10 of 17), earned between $15,000 and $35,000. As expected, because it is a requirement for receiving a payday loan, virtually all respondents had an account at a mainstream financial institution (FI). Among the 130 surveyed respondents, 44% had a credit card and 39% had a tax-protected asset such as a Registered Retirement Savings Plan (RRSP) or Tax Free Savings Account (TFSA).

In terms of how the money from a payday loan is used, respondents shared various purposes. One-half of the survey respondents reported using money from the payday loan to pay basic living costs such as food, rent, clothing, and utilities. Forty-four percent of borrowers used the loans only in emergency and 5% used their payday loans to pay off other loans.

Payday loans and lenders' purpose is variable. The term 'payday lender' as applied to these firms is somewhat misleading as it suggests a consistent link to an employment pay cheque. But, in fact, survey respondents used a variety of future income sources to get a payday loan including: 58% for a payroll cheque, 10% for child tax benefit payment, 6% for employment and income assistance payment, and 6% for an employment insurance cheque. Moreover, survey respondents were not limited to payday loans from payday lenders, another reason why payday lender is less than the ideal name. Other services respondents got from payday lenders include: 54% used check cashing, 26% used money transfer, 25% used bill payment services, 15% used a debit card service, and 11% used a pawn loan.

Why Use Payday Loans as Opposed to Another Type of Loan?

There are different dimensions to understanding the purpose of payday loans for the consumer: for example, how is the money from the loan used, and why payday loans, as opposed to a loan from another source like a mainstream FI? Respondents raised several factors and these can be relatively easily categorized as falling on the 'push side' and the 'pull side.' Push factors included deteriorating income and employment status, lack of small loan product available at mainstream FIs, and poor credit record. Pull factors included characteristics of payday loan services and one's community of practice.

Push factors included deteriorating income and employment status, lack of small loan product available at mainstream FIs, and poor credit record. Job loss and declining income were catalysts for using payday loans. In this case, people have insufficient savings to cushion themselves in the short term and use payday loans to overcome the immediate income gap. In one case, a small business operator went bankrupt, and, since then, he has been using payday loans on a regular basis to try to 'make ends meet.' Another respondent was injured and had to cut back at work:

> I did my first [payday loan when] I broke my wrist in the fall. And so I have been doing them every month now because I am working less, I can't fully work in my job because it is a very hands-on physical job. So my hours got cut like in half. I was full time but now I am part time. It is basically so I can get food until my next pay cheque because my pay cheques were totally going for bills. So I didn't have money for food. (Interview Participant)

Another push factor identified from the research was a lack of access to an appropriate mainstream bank product. Several respondents commented that in the face of a drop in their income, they turned to mainstream banks for a loan but either could not get a product aligned with their needs or could not get a product at all. In some cases, the products the bank was offering were too large or too slow to meet their needs. In one case, the respondent was looking for a loan of $50 and was offered an overdraft for $500, but according to the respondent, this was too high an amount and therefore not well aligned with his needs. In another case, the respondent needed cash immediately, but the mainstream bank product required a process that would take too long:

> Like I said the whole scenario with these companies [mainstream banks] is that I need the money now not 2 weeks from now after you have jumped through hoops, you know signed off my right arm.... (Interview Participant)

In several other cases, people were refused any credit products from their mainstream financial institution. In some cases, this was because of bankruptcy and/or a poor credit record. One respondent stated, 'I want to use my own bank. I have a bank account at BMO. I would love to deal with them rather than [a] payday [loan] company but the downfall is the credit rating' (Focus group participant).

Pull factors include characteristics of payday loan services and one's community of practice. Payday loan services were aligned with the particular needs of many respondents, and the service was, generally speaking, delivered in a friendly and professional manner. As was discussed above, the payday loan service is convenient, quick, is a small sum, and involves a simple repayment process. For some respondents, this model worked very well. Convenience was a point that was highlighted by the respondents. Convenience included several factors including convenient location, long operating hours, and quick processing of the loan application. Many outlets are open into the evening, and according to one respondent, some outlets are open 24 hours a day.

Other respondents explained that their attraction to payday lenders was that the staff created a positive relationship with them: 'They all know me, like as soon as I walk in it's a friendly service' (Interview Participant). In some cases, respondents contrasted their experience with staff from a payday loan outlet with staff from a mainstream bank:

> You walk into a bank, first you got to make your appointment 3 days in advance. You go to the Cash Store, get in and out half an hour, you got your money. …I don't feel belittled when I walk in there [payday loan outlet]. You know, I'm actually treated with respect because I'm a frequent customer. They don't make you feel like you're anything less than an appreciated customer. You go in and get your money, it's all good. You walk into a larger [mainstream bank] branch, you know and they say we will see you in 20 minutes and you sit in the lobby and someone shows up and they look down their nose and ask, 'What can you do for us?' … Like I said I think they are offering a more humane service than the banks do. The banks only cater to people who have money, not to people who don't. (Interview Participant)

Interestingly, some respondents noted that they dealt with payday lenders with cash in order that payday loan information would not appear on their bank statements. These respondents worried that if their mainstream banker saw information about payday lending, because of its stigma, they would be judged.

Respondents' friends and families influenced them in turning to the practice of borrowing from payday lenders. A 'community of practice' is the notion that people learn about and regularly engage in activities through a social process. Two-thirds of the interviewed respondents explained that they learned about payday lenders through a friend or family member, and that these referring people described payday loans in positive terms such as convenient, easy, or quick.

It must be noted that there were some aspects of the payday loan experience that some respondents were not satisfied with. For instance, some respondents noted that their account had been mistakenly debited. Another respondent noted that trying to correct a mistaken automatic debit was very frustrating:

> I talked to someone on the phone.... They were just like I was on hold forever first off which I called the actual branch but I wasn't calling the 1–800 number, whatever. And then yeah like I explained my situation and [the staff person was] just not very helpful at all. (Interview Participant)

Payday Loan Fees

It is sometimes claimed that given the high cost of payday loans, as compared with mainstream FI products, using them is not entirely rational. Interestingly some respondents agreed with this criticism of payday loans and said that they need to be used with caution because of the high fees that can make repaying the loan on payday difficult. These respondents also stated that caution needed to be exercised in the face of payday loan staff who will offer to increase one's credit limit:

> We use it as a bridging gap ... But we've got to be careful on when you want to take it out, because you've got to think about it very carefully. Like yesterday, they were going to give me $380, and I said 'you guys are crazy, I just want $150'. And so I ended up taking $200. You know I was surprised. (Interview Respondent)

Other respondents' views, regarding the caution one needed to observe regarding payday lending, noted that caution is needed for other fringe bank products such as secured credit cards (this is like a credit card but available credit is limited to the amount of cash the person has deposited on the card). Many respondents who discussed this point commented that they did not want a credit card because it is 'faster money [that is] easy to spend. That's not easy to pay back' (Interview Respondent). In another case, the respondent had other credit cards and did not want to get another one.

Another interesting issue related to the customer's understanding about payday loan fees and how they compare with the fees associated with other financial products. This has been identified as an important issue because of the relatively high cost (compared with mainstream FI products) of payday loans. One of the complications associated with this question is that payday loan fees are generally not presented in a way that allows simple comparison to other credit products. Payday loan fees are presented in various ways but, in the province of Manitoba, all fees when combined together cannot exceed \$17 for each \$100 loaned. Virtually, all payday lenders in the province charge \$17 per \$100 loaned. However, when asked about the 'dollar-per-hundred' fee, only one-half of respondents correctly stated it as \$17 per \$100 loaned. Another issue that relates to understanding fees is to be able to compare the fees associated with a number of credit products, using a common indicator such as an annual interest rate. One common indicator of annual interest rate is the annual percentage rate (APR) (For a payday loan in Manitoba the fees are capped at 17 per 100 which yields an APR of $517\% = 17/100 \times 365/12$). At 517%, compared with mainstream credit products, typically ranging between 10% and 20%, payday loan interest charges are very high. Two-thirds of respondents did not know the annual interest rate (via the APR) associated with their payday loan fees.

Repeat Borrowing

One of the topics this research was particularly interested to explore was about repeat borrowing. The distribution of repeat borrowing among survey respondents followed a declining trend in terms of the number of loans per year: 45% of respondents borrowed between 1 and 3 loans per year, 24% borrowed between 4 and 6 loans per year, 6% took out 7 to 9 loans per year, 20% took out 10 to 12 loans per year, and 5% took out 13 or more loans per year. Respondents who took out seven or more loans per year were asked what the reason was for repeated borrowing, and the top three reasons were to meet an unexpected expense (47%), to pay off an existing loan (38%), and to pay for an emergency expense (36%).

In the interviews and focus group discussions we were able to probe the reasons for repeat borrowing in more depth. Interestingly, respondents with repeat borrowing experiences discussed their desire to stick to their budget and to not engage in too much borrowing as it would lead to a sense of 'being out of control.' But these participants noted that it was relatively easy to fall into a debt cycle with payday loans and then to feel trapped in the debt.

> And I think that's the whole ball game with payday loans … they know they have you. I know for most people who are using the service they don't have credit. [A payday loan is] the only thing available to people that can't normally get credit. So they just let you dig and dig and that's got to stop. There has to be a way out. [Focus group participant]

Focus group participants found the loans easy to get but difficult to pay off, particularly as a result of the high interest rate charged on the loans. A number of participants reported using multiple payday loans at once and becoming stuck in a cyclical trap of taking out new loans in order to pay off their previous loans. The participant with the longest history of payday loan use in the group expressed that, 'This pull [payday loans] have, they make it so-called "easy," which is a blind spot because of the interest you're paying back' [Focus group participant]. In some cases, participants borrowed from a second payday lender to pay off the first: 'I take from Cash Mart to pay for Money Mart. Money Mart's the one that will not extend it. It's due, it's due and that's it' [Interview Participant]. In other cases, respondents waited the appropriate time before borrowing again.

Repeat borrowers identified various reasons for doing so. Some participants noted that their pay cheque regularly ran out before the pay period ended. Some participants relying on social assistance faced a chronic budget deficit and found that their income was inadequate for their needs and so regularly took out a payday loan. But with chronic borrowing, the person regularly pays large fees on top of the principal, so that respondents found that this situation is not sustainable: 'So if they're getting a 200 dollar loan, on 200 dollars that would be almost 250 bucks. So if they're only getting 200 dollars they're still in the hole for 250 bucks. So they're always in the hole' [Interview Participant]. In some cases, the chronic borrower was just trying to cover basic necessities, and in other cases a respondent shared that she was trying to finance more superfluous costs: 'not only in terms of living expenses, but also because I do sometimes like to spoil myself with luxuries. You know, I do like clothing especially' [Interview Participant].

In other cases of repetitive borrowing, the deficit was seasonal and not year-round. In this case, there are certain seasons or times of the year when the person is in a deficit position. One respondent noted the deficit she faced during Christmas time because of the extra costs that she faced. This same respondent noted that she also faced a deficit in the early fall because she was regularly laid off from work at that time.

Other repeat borrowers explained that while they were not chronically in deficit, at least not at the beginning, unexpected bills came up before they were able to repay an existing payday loan so that they had insufficient money to repay the loan. Here an additional loan is needed because of bad planning or unexpected bills that could not be planned for. But the consequence is a debt cycle and, in some cases, a person moving into a chronic deficit:

> If you are borrowing money, say you borrow $700.... Well now 2 weeks later you have to pay $700 back. But it might fall to your rent payment coming up, if you pay the $700 back, you just got no money to pay the rent, or money for gas or anything else. So you might have to re-borrow maybe $400 back just to tie you over. So you know the amount might be little overwhelming to pay them back in one pay cheque as opposed to dragging over two. [Interview Participant]

In some cases, the one-time or seasonal repeat borrower became a chronic borrower. In some cases, this led to a debt cycle where an increasing portion of the person's income is directed towards financing their debt. As this amount grows, it becomes increasingly unsustainable, particularly when the credit has not been used to build the person's capacity to repay the loan.

> That's why the next pay cheque after the one where I get the payday loans, its devastation. That basically takes out 75% of everything that I have, and hence the need for re-loans ... on one pay cheque where I get the two payday loans, suddenly I'm bursting with money, like literally it just seems like there is a parade, and so it's a good short-term feeling. The next pay cheque of course when I have to pay back, I mean basically I'm paying back some $450, sometimes even as much as $500. And given my average pay cheques that will cut me down to maybe $300. [Interview Participant]

Online Borrowing

Very few of the surveyed respondents (6% or 7 of 130) used online payday loans. Even when we deliberately sought to recruit online payday loan clients for the interview, we faced challenges so that only three of nine (33%) interviewed respondents had used online payday loans.

Online borrowers tended to borrow from both online and physical branches, and most online borrowers used their smart phones to obtain the loan. The main reasons why participants chose online over physical payday loans were because of the convenience and the quickness of the service. A smaller number of respondents noted that they preferred online loans as it allowed them to save their documents electronically. One respondent noted her rationale for using online loans was to avoid a feeling of shame that she associated with it:

> I would prefer the on-line [over the physical] payday loan. I would try to think of the right way to say it, but um, [the physical payday loan involves] a little embarrassment I guess, or judgement. [Interview Participant]

What Do People Think About Alternatives to Payday Loans: Results from the Focus Group Meeting

One of the focus group conversations probed participants' views about payday loans as compared with a set of financial products designed to substitute for them. The focus group participants included nine people, and the purpose was to hear their thoughts regarding the strengths and weaknesses of the payday loan product available currently in Manitoba from a number of payday lenders as compared with two other small loan products found elsewhere: Vancity credit union's Fair and Fast loan and the state of Colorado's (United States) regulated payday loan. The Vancity loan which ranges from $100 to $2,500 has a term of 12–24 months and a 19% interest rate. The state of Colorado regulates payday lenders so that they offer a six-month payday loan, with an APR of 129%, and it involves instalment repayments. In addition to asking participants for their views about these products, they were asked about their use of payday loans, and if they had any other suggestions for improving payday loans.

Frequency and Period of Use

Frequency of payday loan use varied considerably. Four of the participants reported using payday loans 12 times a year (i.e., once a month), while two participants used them 4–6 times a year. After getting caught up in using multiple payday lenders at one time in order to pay off previous loans, one participant did not trust them for a long time and now only accesses payday loans in emergency situations, though he did not specify how often.

One participant who has been using payday loans for roughly 25 years reported a personal record high of engaging with ten payday lenders at one time until he was eventually forced to declare bankruptcy. Because of his family's difficult financial situation, and because he could no longer obtain payday loans, his spouse began to take them out. They continue to use payday lenders, and, as a couple, they currently use two pawnshops and one payday lender about once a month.

Purpose for the Payday Loan

Respondents identified a wide variety of purposes for a payday lender, including:

- To pay for things which they might not otherwise be able to buy
- To carry them over between paydays, child tax benefit cheques, tax returns, etc.
- In emergency situations or when faced with unexpected expenses
- To pay off previous loans
- To meet basic needs (food, transportation, pay off bills, etc.)
- To support addictions (i.e., gambling, alcoholism, drug-use)

Why Payday Loans?

When asked why payday loans as opposed to borrowing from a bank or credit union, the most common reasons indicated by the participants were bad credit and/or convenience. For those with a history of bad credit, their use of payday loans was less a choice and more of a necessity, as they were unable to access the services of mainstream financial institutions (FIs) during a time of need.

The majority of the participants expressed that they turned to payday loans because of the convenience. Additionally, some participants liked the short duration of the loan, the quick acquisition process, and the simplicity of repayment. Two of the participants shared that payday loans are such an easy way of getting 'extra cash' that they simply use them for shopping and avoid high interest rates by repaying the loan early.

Other participants, however, found the loans easy to get but difficult to pay off, particularly as a result of the high interest fees. A number of participants reported using multiple payday loans at once and becoming stuck in a cyclical trap of taking out new loans in order to pay off their previous loans. The participant with the longest history of payday loan use in the group expressed that:

> This pull they have, they make it so-called 'easy', which is a blind spot because of the interest you're paying back. [Focus group participant quote]

Among focus group participants, those who are less financially stable and access payday loans because of poor credit appear to be particularly vulnerable to this risk, as compared to those who simply use the loan for extra cash and do not struggle with repayment.

Participant Assessment of Payday and Other Loans

The next step in the focus group discussion was to ask participants to compare payday loans that are available in Manitoba with two other loan products. In order to have respondents make this comparison, two points were discussed by the facilitator: the concept of annual interest rate and the characteristics of the two products. The first explanation was about the rationale for using an annual percentage rate (APR) as the standard price for payday loan fees. The main justification for using APR is that it enables a simple comparison between different credit products, even if those credit products' duration varies (Box 3.1).

The next step in the focus group was for the facilitator to describe salient characteristics about the payday loan available in Manitoba with

Box 3.1 Presentation explaining credit and the rationale behind using of annual percentage rate (APR) as the standard price for payday loans

Loans (or mortgages, small loans, credit cards, credit lines) are a commercial product and involve a seller and buyer, or creditor and borrower. Like all commercial products, creditors charge a price for their product, which, in this case is called an interest rate. Fringe bank products like payday loans are sometimes priced in unique ways, for instance, in a dollar fee, for example, \$17/\$100 borrowed. But presenting the 'price' of credit in a unique way like this makes it more difficult to compare the payday loan fee with the fee for other loans. So, for instance, in Manitoba, payday lenders often advertise their loans as costing \$17/\$100. Some consumers believe that this is equivalent to a 17% APR. In fact \$17/\$100 loaned is the fee for a 12-day loan, or a 17% interest for 12 days. To convert it into an annual interest rate, for example, APR, we must do the following: APR = Fee/Loan × 1/Share of term in the year = 17/100 × 365/12 = 5.17 × 100% = 517%.

two other credit products, Vancity Fair and Fast Loan and the payday loan available in the state of Colorado in the United States (Table 3.1). The payday loan available in Manitoba is quite similar to the product in most other Canadian provinces and many states in the United States: short term, small sum, single repayment, and quite expensive. The Vancity loan is unique in Canada in that it is of longer term, up to two years in duration, involves instalment repayment, and is lower priced. The payday loan found in the US state of Colorado is of medium-term duration, six months, involves instalment repayment, and its price is between the payday loan in Manitoba and the Vancity loan.

After the presentation on annual interest rate and the different loan products, participants were asked to describe the strengths and weaknesses of the three credit products. From the responses, we identified four key points related to, interest rate, repayment structure and duration, loan size, and credit reporting.

Table 3.1 Comparison of payday loans in Manitoba with two other products

Character	*Payday loan in commonly found in Manitoba*	*Vancity fair and fast loan*	*Colorado state (US) model*
Loan size	<$1500	$100–$2500	<USD 500
Duration	2 weeks	12–24 months	6 months
Repayment	One-time; 'balloon'	Instalment	Instalment; early repayment possible without penalty
Approval process	60 minutes first time; less time for 2nd loan and beyond	Rapid	Rapid
Credit report	Not applicable	Use alternative report to assess; loan use is reported	Not applicable
Character	Payday loan in commonly found in Manitoba	Vancity fair and fast loan	Colorado state (US) model
Fees in 2 weeks on a $300 loan	$51	$2	$15
Annual percentage rate	517%	19%	129%
Fees in 1 year	$1,224 [If you were able to take 2 × 12 = 24 consecutive payday loans]	$57	$387

Interest Rates

When presented with the three different small-loan models, focus group participants were largely in favour of the Vancity Fair and Fast Loan model because of its lower interest fees. Most of the participants agreed that the 517% APR on Manitoba payday loans is too high, instead favouring the Vancity model that has an APR of 19%.

Two participants said they are satisfied with Manitoba payday loan fees, particularly because the interest is reduced if the two-week loan is paid off early. These individuals use payday loans about 3–6 times a year as an easy way to get extra money to be able to buy things in between paydays and other cheques.

Repayment Structure and Duration

A portion of the group identified the instalment repayments and possibility of early repayment without penalty as the main strengths of the Colorado state model product. As for the Fair & Fast Loan offered by Vancity, the group was split between those who felt the long-term and instalment repayments were a strength and those who felt it was a weakness. Those who saw it as a strength did not like the one-time repayment structure of the Manitoba payday loan. They would prefer to pay the loan back slowly.

Those who saw it as a weakness were adamant that they preferred to pay off their loan within the two-week period that is standard in Manitoba. These participants were committed to not getting caught in a longer-term repayment obligation. They strongly endorsed the Manitoba payday loan model:

> You don't have to worry about it for a long time. [Focus group participant quote]

Loan Size

The larger loan, which is available through the Vancity product was appealing to some of the participants because it allows users to get a larger sum of money as compared to the Manitoba payday loan. One participant acknowledged that a larger loan could potentially help those who are stuck in a cycle of repeat borrowing because you would be able to pay off more money at a reduced rate. However, others saw it as a temptation to borrow too much and be unable to repay. One participant who shared this concern noted,

> Having a large amount is difficult because you maybe can't trust yourself with it. [Focus group participant quote]

Some of the participants were not interested in the large loans offered by Vancity because their credit needs were more modest. Most participants agreed that the US$500 maximum offered by the Colorado state model was an inadequate amount.

Credit Reporting
Some participants stated that they felt that a strength of the payday loan system in Manitoba is that there are no background credit cheques and no credit reporting. Some participants expressed concerns that they would not be approved for a loan through the Vancity model which assesses users' credit scores prior to providing the loan. The opportunity to build their credit rating did, however, appeal to a few participants who expressed support for this feature of the Vancity model and said they would rather have the loan repayments appear on their credit record. Although they were conscious of the fact that failure to make payments on time could actually hurt their credit scores, the opportunity for improvement remained an attractive feature.

Discussion

In the process of investigating different small-loan models, we found that some payday loan clients prefer the current Manitoba payday loan, while others prefer other options, most notably the Vancity Fair and Fast Loan. In some cases, people used payday loans infrequently, and in other cases participants used them frequently. We heard stories of participants being harmed by payday loan dependence and stories of participants who were helped by using the loans in a strategic fashion. But even the strategic approach may be inconsistent with the 'perfect rational agent' that economic theory posits. This strategy seems consistent with bounded rational behaviour—a view promoted by behavioural economists (Thaler and Sunstein 2008; Mullainathan and Shafir 2013)—that real people follow slightly irrational behaviour when they are subject to time and institutional constraints.

Several focus group participants explained that for them there were few alternative loan products. Some of them were unable to get credit from mainstream banks due to bankruptcy or a poor (or no) credit rating. For some of these underbanked participants, loans from friends/family and pawn loans were the few options they had. However, relationship-based loans and pawn loans are small as compared to payday loans. Also, pawn loans require depositing a household item with the pawnbroker.

Some respondents noted that due to the high cost of repaying the loan, they fell into a dependence on payday loans. Two participants who took out at least 12 payday loans per year struggled with addiction issues. They noted that the consequences of their personal and financial struggles were bankruptcy or accumulating unrepayable debt. For these participants, payday loans were not helping them, but were delaying their need to address personal and financial issues. Moreover, the accumulation of unrepayable debt added an additional challenge.

Other borrowers did not take out as many loans, perhaps 3–6 per year, and referred to other reasons for using the loans, such as convenience and ease of accessing them. Some of these focus group respondents talked about using payday loans in a more strategic way in that they limited the number of loans they would take and these funds would be devoted to certain items, for example, paying particular bills or for emergency purposes. One respondent explained that she had adequate savings to pay for bills, but preferred to use payday loans for some bills in order to keep her savings intact. This approach to using payday loans is consistent with 'mental accounting,' a term used in behavioural economics (Shefrin and Thaler 1993), associated with a bounded rational strategy undertaken by individuals facing constraints. Rather than seeing money as perfectly fungible, it is understood to fit in different categories, for example, employment income, benefit income, emergency expense, and gift expense.

The principal purpose of the focus group was to explore participants' views about alternative financial products. Several respondents were quite interested in the Vancity loan because of its longer-term and lower annualized interest rate. They felt that this loan would be easier to pay off because of the instalment plan and the lower fees.

Some participants preferred the short term one-time repayment for reasons described as 'less worry' and 'pay it off and be ok for a little bit.' Other participants talked about 'not trusting' oneself with a larger or longer-term loan. For them, the small-sum and short-term loan offered them the discipline to limit their borrowing. Once again these strategies seem consistent with a bounded rational strategy in which people are making decisions with limited information, time, and self-control. For them there is a benefit to short-term, one-time repayment so that this product is worth the cost.

Two types of payday users became apparent through the focus group conversation:

- Those who are able to use small loans from time-to-time, in a strategic fashion, and are able to repay them in a timely fashion and
- The more vulnerable repeat borrowers who eventually become dependent on the loans.

In this way, the ease of accessibility and the convenience of Manitoba's current payday loan system can help some borrowers and harm others. The credit-challenged payday loan users appeared to be the most vulnerable to potential risks and would benefit most from an alternative product.

References

Mullainathan, Sendhil, and Eldar Shafir. 2013. *Scarcity: Why Having Too Little Means So Much*. New York: Henry Holt, Times Books.

Shefrin, Hersh M., and Richard H. Thaler. 1993. The Behavioral Life-Cycle Hypothesis. In *Economics and Psychology*, ed. Shlomo Maital and Sharone L. Maital. Cheltenham, UK: Edward Elgar.

Thaler, Richard H., and Cass R. Sunstein. 2008. *Nudge: Improving Decisions about Health, Wealth, and Happiness*. New Haven and London: Yale University Press.

CHAPTER 4

A Business Analysis of the Payday Loan Industry

Chris Robinson

The Business of Payday Lending

The public face of payday lending for most Canadians is the ubiquitous storefronts of the chains: Money Mart, Cash Money, Cash4You, Speedy Cash, and Fast Cash are the biggest groups. Money Mart is the largest and one of the first entrants into the business, following on from its roots as a check casher in Edmonton. For many Canadians, its yellow and red storefronts and its name are almost synonymous with payday lending. In addition, Canadians can get payday loans from a few smaller regional chains, independent community stores, and internet lenders.

The five largest chains hold the lion's share of the volume, but the chains and the independents have much the same business model. The chains engage in more branding activities and have more administrative costs, but also seem to enjoy higher volumes. Although they advertise a brand, each store in a chain is really a small business, similar in some ways to a convenience store. Each store has only a few employees with no more than two on duty at any time, and the chains require quite a bit of low-cost part-time labor. The dollar volume of loans is quite low, a critical issue we will expand on in this chapter.

C. Robinson (✉)
Faculty of Liberal Arts and Professional Studies, School of Administrative Studies, York University, Toronto, ON, Canada

J. Buckland et al. (eds.), *Payday Lending in Canada in a Global Context*,
https://doi.org/10.1007/978-3-319-71213-0_4

The internet payday loan business is very different, and we have very little data. The larger chains will also lend online, but they follow the same practices as their storefront operations except that a direct debit to a bank account is used instead of a physical check to repay the loan. The internet-only lenders are a different kettle of fish. Nobody knows how much of the payday loan volume they generate—estimates range from 5% to one-third, but they are little more than guesses. We will discuss the internet payday loan business in more detail in a later section in this chapter. Now we turn to the public face, the storefront payday lenders.

Payday lending stores and companies have the following characteristics:

1. They are small businesses.
2. They charge very high fees compared with other lending institutions.
3. They have high operating leverage, which means profits change a great deal with changes in volume.
4. Most of the costs are the operating costs—70–80% of all costs—and these are largely fixed for the scale of most stores.
5. Bad debts affect profits significantly but are much less important than the operating costs.
6. They require little capital.
7. They have limited economies of scope compared with most financial institutions. Only two business lines make a significant contribution: payday loans and check cashing. The check cashing business is declining steadily and some of the smaller operators no longer do it at all.
8. The payday lending business depends upon repeat customers rather than one-time users. The majority of loans are to repeat customers.
9. The business shows significant concentration in a few chains.

I will show the evidence supporting this characterization in the rest of this chapter.

The Players in Canada

Although payday lenders are now required to register in each province, that registration requirement did not start until the provinces passed enabling legislation, and thus there are no definitive estimates of the number of outlets until after 2010, with some provinces taking quite a bit longer. Payday lenders are not required to belong to an industry association, but one has existed for over 15 years. The first incarnation was called the Canadian Association of Community Financial Services Providers (CACFSP). About 2006 it changed its name to the Canadian Payday Loan Association (CPLA), with headquarters in Ottawa. In 2016 it changed its name again to the Canadian Consumer Finance Association (CCFA), and it is now located in Hamilton, Ontario. Dollar Financial's wholly owned subsidiary Money Mart has been the largest member and the leader in the industry association since its inception. The current CEO of the CCFA is a former Dollar Financial Corporation employee and three of the eight directors are employees of Money Mart and Dollar Financial. The CCFA says its members operate a total of 961 stores and online payday businesses, and it lists 16 companies, including the five largest listed in Table 4.2. Some of the member companies offer online payday loans only and have no storefronts. Very few members operate only a single storefront.[1]

The payday loan business grew very rapidly for two decades, but that growth has ended, and there are fewer stores now than at the peak. Ernst & Young (2004) reports a 2003 estimate by the CACFSP of 1000 outlets. By 2006, the CPLA Executive Director Robert Whitelaw told me in a private conversation that the CPLA estimated there were 1350 outlets. The CPLA scoured the Yellow Pages in hard copy for all of Canada to find lenders who were not members. The number of outlets may have exceeded 1800 in the period around 2010–2012, when Cash Store Financial had expanded quite rapidly and not yet been forced to start closing outlets. It reported 509 outlets at the time of its bankruptcy (Carlstrom 2014, p. 66). Dijkema and McKendry (2016) say there are 1500 outlets, relying on a bankruptcy filing (Carlstrom 2014, p. 66). Using the regulators' counts, and a search of the Yellow Pages for New Brunswick, which has still not proclaimed its payday loan legislation, I created Table 4.1, showing a total of 1431 registered payday loan outlets in 2016, including a few internet-only lenders who have also registered with the provincial regulators.

The regulators do not all use the same dates for their counts, and so this table would never be perfectly accurate as of any chosen date. The table also shows the rate caps when each province first regulated, and the rate

[1] http://canadiancfa.com/ccfa-members/, accessed July 29, 2017.

Table 4.1 Registered payday lenders in each province

	# of stores per province	*Rate cap/$100*		*2015 provincial population 000s*	*Stores per 100,000 population*
		Original	*2018*		
Nova Scotia (NS) (2015)	45	$25	$22	943	4.8
New Brunswick (NB) (2016)	35	21	21	754	4.6
Newfoundland and Labrador (NF)	0	60% interest per annum		528	0
Prince Edward Island (PEI)	1	25	25	146	0.7
Quebec (PQ)	0	35% interest per annum		8264	0
Ontario (ON) (2015)	813	21	15	13,792	5.9
Manitoba (MB) (2016)	40	17	17	1293	3.1
Saskatchewan (SK) (2015)	53	23	23	1134	4.7
Alberta (AB) (2016)	235	23	15	4197	5.6
British Columbia (BC) (2016)	209	23	17	4683	4.5
CANADA (exclude PQ, NF)	1431			26,942	5.3

caps, which have been lowered in four provinces. The rate cap in Ontario dropped to $15 per $100 on January 1, 2018.

Payday loan stores need a large enough population close enough to generate sufficient volumes, and hence they locate in urban centers. Most of them are in the largest Canadian cities. The low concentration in PEI is because there is only one center large enough—Charlottetown—and it is really only economic for one lender. Manitoba has a lower concentration because it was the only province that regulated an appropriate rate cap in the first round of legislation. All the other provinces that allowed payday lending put rate caps in place that were much too high, as I show in a later section of this chapter.

The industry has always been quite concentrated in Canada, more so than in the USA. The first major chain was Money Mart, which started as a check casher in 1982 in Edmonton and expanded later into payday lending. By 1990 it had over 100 branches and by 2000 over 200, mirroring the growth in the industry as a whole. I believe that Money Mart now has more than 50% of the total volume of payday loans in Canada. Since the companies are all privately held, no current financial data is in the public domain. Table 4.2 displays the largest companies in Canada, ranked by number of stores.

None of the provincial regulators requires them to file complete financial statements, and the information the regulators disclose is aggregate across the industry. Cash Store Financial, which was the second largest operator, and may at its peak have had more stores than Money Mart, was a public company. It went bankrupt in 2014. Money Mart bought a number of its outlets and merged them into its own network, usually closing the Cash Store outlet in the process. When the two were competing head to head, their stores were often within sight of each other in the lower-income neighborhoods of most cities. All payday lenders will have captured some of Cash Store's customers, but Money Mart was in the best position because of the purchase and its existing iconic status as the face of payday lending in Canada; hence my estimate is that it now has over 50% of the volume of payday lending, even though it has only 40% of the storefronts.

Dollar Financial Group (subsequent name change to DFC Global), a US alternative finance company, bought Money Mart many years ago, but it continued to disclose substantial segmented data showing separate results for Canada, the USA, and Europe. Lone Star Financial of Texas

Table 4.2 Largest payday lenders in Canada

	No. of stores	*% of total*
Money Mart[a]	574	40
Cash Money[b]	186	13
Cash4You[b]	91	6
Cash Canada[a]	56	4
Speedy Cash[a]	24	2
Top five (above)	931	65
The rest	500	35
	1431	100

[a]Dijkema and McKendry (2016, p. 28)

[b]I counted the stores listed on the companies' websites: www.cashmoney.ca/find-a-store/, accessed Feb. 28, 2016; www.cash4you.ca/company/find-a-store/, accessed Feb. 28, 2016; https://www.speedycash.ca/locations/

bought DFC Global on April 1, 2014. Lone Star is a private company and the last financial results we have for DFC Global and its segments are the nine-month statement dated March 31, 2014. We will look at them in a subsequent section of this chapter, because they provide substantial insight into operation of the payday lending business in Canada.

The payday loan companies operated on two slightly different business models. Money Mart and almost all other payday lenders in Canada and the USA lend the money directly to the customer. Cash Store Financial and some other operators in Canada claimed that they were loan brokers, and this business model was called the "broker model." Companies using a broker model process loan applications and collect the repayments, but the money loaned to the customer comes from a never-identified third party. One effect of this split in roles was the appearance of compliance with Section 347 of the Criminal Code and its restriction to a 60% interest rate. Cash Store claimed it did not violate Section 347, nor subsequent provincial payday loan rate caps, because its fees were broker fees, not interest (Robinson and Schwartz 2017).[2] The provincial laws make it very clear that all the charges are to be considered equivalent to interest, or to something defined in the provincial law by various terms such as total cost of credit. Ontario banned the broker model, as a direct attack on Cash Store Financial, which was charging rates far higher than other lenders.[3] We are not aware of any Canadian payday lender that still uses the broker model. In any case, the turnover of payday loans is so fast that the capital required to support the loan portfolio is quite small relative to the annual volume of loans. The separation of the processing and financing parts of the business was an inefficient business model.

Follow the Money: Where Does It Come From and Where Does It Go?

Appendix 1 shows the most recent results available for DFC Global Corp., which are the three- and nine-month income statements for March 31, 2014, by segment. Appendix 1 is a small excerpt from the DFC Global

[2] Another method that one payday lender tried for a while in Ontario was to charge 59% interest plus a large insurance fee to cover the risk of non-payment. These are examples of opportunistic compliance—creating the appearance of compliance while violating the intent of a law—as noted in Chap. 6.

[3] Private conversation between an Ontario government employee involved with the issue and Chris Robinson.

Corp. 10Q Report, which is a mandatory quarterly report by all registrants with the US Securities and Exchange Commission (SEC) that is disclosed to the public on the SEC website. Recall that the Canada segment of DFC is Money Mart,[4] the largest Canadian payday lender. We usually see Canadian subsidiaries as a small part of an American company, but in this case Money Mart is far larger than the American segment. The European segment is larger measured by sales, but that includes the UK and several countries on the continent.

The Canadian segment accounts for 30% of the DFC revenues, but 70% of the operating margin. Annualized Return on Assets (ROA) is 14.7%, compared with 5.6% for the US segment and negative returns of 10.6% and 27.1% for the European and E-Commerce segments. The losses on those two segments are not due simply to a new start-up. DFC has been growing both those segments for a number of years, and the revenues are substantial. The loan loss rate in the E-Commerce segment is nothing short of disastrous. Money Mart appears to be providing all the cash flow to prop up the losing segments, while the smaller US division is modestly profitable. The balance sheet of DFC and market value of equity yields a multiplier of approximately 3.7× to convert Return on Assets to a Return on Equity (ROE), which yields a phenomenal ROE of about 54% per annum for Money Mart.[5] This result is not confined to 2014. Similar results are seen in previous years in the 10K disclosures[6] of Dollar Financial dating back at least to 2006, except that the earlier results do not show the E-Commerce segment separately.

The contribution to revenue of the different lines of business is also revealing. Check cashing is a significant business only in Money Mart. European countries have been abandoning checks and there is little demand for check cashing there. Money Mart began as a check casher and that business continues to be important, but it has been declining for many years, while the payday loan business through stores and the internet has been increasing. The E-Commerce segment now includes the internet

[4] We call it Money Mart throughout because that is the name the public sees. The legal name is National Money Mart Company.

[5] ROA = (Net income + Interest expense after tax)/total assets. An approximate calculation to convert ROA to ROE is to deduct current liabilities from total assets and divide that total by shareholders' equity at market value. An estimate of market value at March 31, 2014, is the agreed valuation for the merger of $9.50 per share.

[6] 10K is the required annual financial report that all SEC registrants must file and which then is posted on https://www.sec.gov/edgar.shtml.

payday loan business in Canada that Money Mart manages, which gives the somewhat erroneous impression that payday lending is also declining in Canada. Shortly after this March 31, 2014 statement, Cash Store Financial failed and Money Mart picked up a lot of the pieces. If we had subsequent statements, we would observe considerable increases in Money Mart's payday lending. For the nine months ended March 31, 2014, payday lending through the stores contributed 61% of total store revenue in Money Mart, and check cashing contributed 21%. The large pawn loan segment in Europe is primarily due to several purchases of chains of pawnshops in the UK and Spain.

The 2014 10Q does not provide expenses by segment, only for the entire company. The revenue and expense results for the entire company are shown in Appendix 2. Table 4.3 presents an analysis of the expenses to illustrate some of the characteristics of the business. The largest expense is salaries and benefits in operations, but this is only part of the labor cost, because most of the "Corporate expenses" are also labor. Loan losses are the second largest item.

The two right-hand columns express expense lines as percentages of total expenses with certain items removed from that total. I adjust the expenses to focus on operations expenses. Earlier I stated that the great bulk of expenses are fixed in the short term and will not vary much with volume. I remove purchased gold expense because Money Mart and other payday lenders do virtually none of that; it is part of the European pawnshop business. I remove interest expense and foreign exchange loss for three reasons. Dollar Financial has arranged its financing so that most of the debt is in the profitable Canadian operation, but in fact that debt is used to support the entire company, especially its expansion in Europe. Most of the foreign exchange loss is related to the Canadian debt because the DFC statements are denominated in US dollars. Third, in a later section I will estimate the appropriate rate cap for Canada, and the method used in that analysis treats interest expense as part of the cost of capital, not as an expense. With these items removed, the adjusted total expense before taxes is US$789 million. The loan loss provision is 19% of the adjusted total expense, as shown in the middle column of figures in Table 4.3. Everything else relates to running the operations, both at the store level and at the corporate level, except for the Goodwill and Intangible Impairment cost. This adjusted expense amount will not vary

Table 4.3 Analysis of Dollar Financial expenses

Nine months ended March 31, 2014 values in US$ millions			
Revenues			
Consumer lending	$498.8		
Check cashing	89.6		
Pawn service fees and sales	70.8		
Money transfer fees	26.1		
Gold sales	31.3		
Other	55.6		
Total revenues	772.2		
Operating expenses		*% of adjusted expenses*	
Salaries and benefits	187.4	23.8%	28.3%
Provision for loan losses	148.4	18.8	22.4
Occupancy	55.8	7.1	8.4
Purchased gold costs*	28.3		
Advertising	45.3	5.7	6.8
Depreciation	19.6	2.5	3.0
Maintenance and repairs	15.7	2.0	2.4
Bank charges and armored carrier service	16.2	2.1	2.4
Returned checks, net and cash shortages	7.4	0.9	1.1
Other	72.8	9.2	11.0
Total operating expenses	596.9		
Operating margin	175.3		
Corporate and other expenses			
Corporate expenses	77.1	9.8	11.7
Other depreciation and amortization	12.7	1.6	1.9
Interest expense, net*	85		
Goodwill and other intangible impairment &	127.3	16.1	
Unrealized foreign exchange loss*	8.3		
Provision for litigation settlements	0.1	<0.1%	<0.1%
Loss on store closings	0.3	<0.1%	<0.1%
Other expense, net	2.7	0.3	0.4
(Loss) income before income taxes	(138.2)		
Expenses adjusted to focus on operations			
Total expense less items marked*	788.8		
Total expense less items marked* or &	661.5		

To give a better idea of the relative size of expenses related directly to operating the business, we recalculate total expenses with two different sets of expenses removed, then express the remaining expense lines as a percentage of those adjusted expenses

First column of % of adjusted expenses is expense item divided by "Total expense less items marked*"

Second column of % of adjusted expenses is expense item divided by "Total expense less items marked* or &"

much with volume in the short run unless there is a large drop or large increase in volume. If a store loses 20% of its customers, it may be able to reduce part-time staffing, but we see no evidence of such volatility in volume, at least in Canada. A review of past 10K reports of DFC shows a steady increase in number of stores, payday loan volume, and payday loan revenues.

The right-hand column of percentages is based on adjusted total expenses with the Goodwill and Intangible Impairment charge also removed. This charge is very large, US$127 million, and its removal reduces total expenses to US$662 million. It is a non-cash charge. Why do we not want to consider it as part of the expenses of running the business? It arises from past purchases of intangible assets, including the premium paid for takeovers of other alternative finance companies. The management and the auditors have determined in 2014 that the amount paid for those purchases is no longer reflected in the value of the intangible assets, and they have to reduce those asset values on the balance sheet to the current value. The result is this very large expense, which has nothing to do the expense of running a payday loan and check cashing store. Furthermore, the charges must relate primarily to the businesses outside Canada, since as we have already seen, the Canadian operation is producing most of the profits, and hence the value of any intangibles related to it will not have declined.

However you analyze the numbers, it is evident that 70–80% of the expenses are for operations and most of that amount is fixed in the short term. The percentage of expenses for labor costs is surprisingly low for a service business. The corporate expense includes labor at the head office and perhaps also regional offices, if the company has any, but that is not enough to account for such low expenses for labor. In casual conversations with payday lenders and officers of the CPLA, I have learned that a lot of the employees at the store level are part-time, and many of them are students. The wage rates for them will be at or close to minimum wage, and it is unlikely that Money Mart or any other payday loan stores offer much in the way of employee benefits to the store clerks.

Loan Volume, Average Size of Loan, and Loan Losses

So far we have discussed loan revenues and expenses, but critical elements for understanding a payday loan company are the size of an average loan, the dollar volume of loans, the number of loans per store, and the loan loss percentage. Breaking it down to this level shows that this is a classic small business operation that has as much in common with a convenience store as it does with a bank. The reader should understand important measurement practices that relate to all loan volume, revenue, and loan loss figures. Loan volume is the total value of all loans given to customers, whether or not the customers repaid anything. Revenue is the value of all the loan fees that the lender collected. Loan losses are the *estimated* value of the principal value of all loans made during the year that will not be collected, either immediately on the due date or after collection efforts have failed. It is always uncertain at the end of a period how many of the loans still outstanding will be collected. Each payday lender has to estimate how much will be lost and record that value as the provision for loan losses. In the next year, the provision may have to be adjusted either up or down, and so the loan loss provision in any financial reporting period doesn't precisely show how much was lost, although on average over many periods the total loan loss provisions will equal the actual cash lost. These issues are not unique to payday lenders; they occur in any business that offers any form of credit.

Unfortunately, most Canadian provincial regulators do not require payday lenders to disclose any data on volume, number of loans made, and number of borrowers, unlike the US states. BC is the only province that provides detailed statistical evidence on all lending by registered payday lenders, and its five-year results for 2012–2016 are shown in Appendix 3.[7] Let's start with the big picture—loan volume for Canada. Dijkema and McKendry (2016) assert that the annual volume of payday loans in Canada is about CD$2.5 billion, but they provide no hard evidence to support that claim. The volume in BC for 2016 was CD$369.7 million, and that includes internet lenders who registered in BC, including the large storefront chains who also offer internet payday loans, and 310 Loan, which lends only over the internet. BC has 17% of the Canadian population living in provinces that allow payday lending and 14.6% of the payday stores in Canada. Simple extrapolation yields a Canadian loan volume of CD$2.2 to 2.5 billion. Another rough approximation works with Money Mart Data. The Money Mart storefront loan volume for Canada was US$922.9 million for the year ended June 30, 2013 (Money Mart 2013 10K, p. 11;

[7] The BC reporting date is October 31, but the date for the individual companies reporting will vary depending on their financial reporting systems. Small companies that prepare only annual financial statements could be reporting values almost a year old each Oct. 31.

the 10K is annual report required of every SEC registrant), which is most recent volume data available. I estimate that the Money Mart internet annual payday loan volume around that time was US$37 million, for an approximate total Money loan volume of US$960 million, which translates to about CD$1.03 billion. Cash Store Financial was still operating for most of that time, and so Money Mart would have had 35–40% of the total Canadian loan volume. If we use 40%, we can extrapolate total Canadian payday loan volume to be CD$2.6 billion. This figure is in 2013 or 2014 dollars, and we might expect it to have risen because of inflation, but Appendix 3 shows that loan volumes in BC peaked in 2014 at CD$385 million, declined to CD$340 million in 2015, then rose again in 2016, but not all the way back to the 2014 level. We can be sure that there is some internet lending occurring that is not captured by any of these estimates, both in Québec and other provinces. A reasonable range of values is about CD$2.3–$2.7 billion annual volume.

Payday loans turn over much faster than more conventional loans and hence require much less capital to support them. A striking contrast between the size of the payday loan industry and mainstream banks shows how small the payday loan industry is. An average branch of TD Canada Trust has CD$89 million in mortgage loans and CD$59 million in personal loans outstanding at any time. The entire payday loan industry in Canada has somewhere in the range of CD$80–$100 million in loans outstanding.

Now let us turn to the loan size, all figures in CD$. The upper limit on payday loans is $1500 in S. 347 of the Criminal Code, but few loans reach that limit. Appendix 3 records an average loan size of $460 in BC in 2016. Of the 804,257 loans made: 67% were $500 or less, 28% $501–$1000, and only 5% greater than $1000.

At the store level the annual loan volume is $1.8 million, and the fee revenue on those loans is $384,000. Most payday stores operate about 360 days a year, for 8–12 hours per day. Using these figures we calculate that the daily loan volume of a single store is $5000 and the daily revenue is just over $1000. Or to put it another way, the average store makes 11 loans per day, or one per hour.[8] When we consider the high loan loss rates and the resources needed to make those loans—store rent, staff wages, owner or manager pay, telephone, internet, heat and electricity—we see that this is an incredibly inefficient way to deliver small loans. Given the fixed nature of most costs in the short run, the critical success factor for a

[8] $1.8 million ÷ 360 = $5000 volume per day. $384,000 ÷ 360 = $1067 revenue per day. $5000 ÷ $460 average loan size = 10.9 loans per day.

payday loan store is getting enough volume of loans quickly to cover fixed costs. Most small retail stores face this as their number one challenge, especially in large cities with high rental costs.

The low loan volume obscures an even more important effect: the frequency that a customer borrows. Chapter 2 shows that 25% of borrowers reported only a single loan across Canada, which means 75% are repeat borrowers. The Canada-wide data does not provide a lot of detail about how many loans the repeat borrowers took out, because the highest frequency is three or more loans per year, and since it is survey data, it is possible that respondents under-reported the frequency. The BC data in Appendix 3 provides much more detail. BC has the same frequency of one-time borrowers at 25%, but 36% of the borrowers took out six or more loans per year and over 4,000 borrowers took out more than 15, which means they were almost continuously indebted to a payday lender. Even worse, this data will not capture the full frequency of borrowing for anyone who goes to more than one lender. The average borrower took out five loans per year and on average paid $500 in fees. Some of the very frequent borrowers would have paid more than $1000 a year in payday loan fees.

The business model of the payday loan industry requires repeat borrowers, not one-time customers. Ernst & Young (2004) provides this evidence both from the numerical survey data and from interviews with payday lenders. The cost of providing a first-time loan is far higher than the cost of servicing a repeat borrower. The operators who responded to the survey had to estimate the different costs of first-time and repeat borrowers, and so the actual numbers show wide variation, but first-time borrowers are far more costly. Ernst & Young (2004, p. 33) used a value of operating costs for serving a first-time borrower of 2.68 times the cost of a repeat borrower. The report also observed that for every loan to a new customer, 15 loans were made to repeat customers. The report concluded: "Clearly, the long-run survival of a payday loan operator will depend on achieving a steady repeat customer business" (p. 37).

Let's take a closer look at the financial information from Dollar Financial for more detailed evidence on loan volume and loan losses. Table 4.4 shows its loan volumes, loan losses, and loan loss percentages for 2011–2013 for all four segments, and the nine months ended March 31, 2014, using data extracted from its June 30, 2013 10K and March 31, 2014 10K reports. In 2013, Dollar Financial changed its segment reporting to show all internet lending (which it calls E-commerce in the

Table 4.4 DFC Global US$ loan volumes and loan losses

	2011	*2012*	*2013*	*Nine months 2013/2014*	*2013/2014 9 months annualized*[b]
Loan volume $MM[a]				Estimated[c]	
Internet	$340.3	$985.2	$1021.6	$595.9	$794.5
Canada storefront	876.4	893.0	922.9	671.5	895.3
Europe storefront	511.1	603.9	648.7	499.6	666.1
US storefront	480.8	507.6	533.6	417.3	556.4
Total company	2208.6	2990.2	3126.8	2184.3	2912.3
Loan loss $MM[a]				Actual	
Internet	31.2	78.8	108.3	70.3	93.7
Canada storefront	19.6	16.6	20.1	17.9[d]	23.9
Europe storefront	15.5	27.5	41.9	65.7	87.6
US storefront	7.3	8.6	10.8	9.6	12.8
Total company	73.6	131.5	181.1	163.5	218.0
Loan loss as % of volume					
Internet	9.17%	7.99%	10.60%	11.80%	11.80%
Canada storefront	2.24	1.86	2.18	2.67	2.67
Europe storefront	3.03	4.55	6.46	13.15	13.15
US storefront	1.52	1.69	2.02	2.30	2.30
Total company	3.33	4.40	5.79	7.49	7.49

[a]Taken from the DFC (2013, 10K) report

[b]Nine months × 4/3

[c]The DFC 10Q does not disclose loan volumes, only revenues. I estimated loan volume by multiplying the nine months loan revenue by the ratio of volume to revenue for the 2013 annual results

[d]The financial statements show $2.8 million, which is the result of an accounting anomaly that reduced the provision for loan losses by $15.1 million to record the effect of settlement of a lawsuit the company lost

reports) in a separate segment. The values for Canada, Europe, and the USA in Table 4.2 exclude internet lending in those regions. The far right column of Table 4.4 shows the nine-month results annualized by multiplying by 4/3. The company grew rapidly in the full years, but reversed that growth trend in the final nine-month period, with most of the growth coming in 2011–2012 from internet lending and takeovers and new store openings in the UK and Europe. The loan loss percentages have continued to grow in each segment, though the rates remain much lower in Canada and the USA. The evidence is clear that the rapid growth occurred at the expense of sound underwriting practices in the internet lending segment and at least some parts of the European storefront business. Changes occurring in the UK regulation of payday lending also increased the provision for losses, and will restrict future growth in the UK, according to the 10Q.

Compare the loan loss percentages in Table 4.2 with the BC loss rates in Appendix 3. The BC loan loss rates are much higher than those Money Mart experiences in its storefronts. Since Money Mart probably has half the loan volume in BC, the loan loss rate of the other stores must be much higher, about 6% on average. The concentration in the market creates a challenge for rate regulation. Competition ought to force payday fees down, but if one or a few players have significantly lower cost structures, they can continue to charge fees that generate excess profits, because the other players cannot afford to offer lower prices. Rate regulation that allows all the smaller, more inefficient players to continue in business will produce excess profits for the most efficient players. We will return to this issue in the section on determining a payday loan rate cap for Canada.

Table 4.5 presents a simple calculation in $US: DFC revenue per segment divided by volume of all "good" loans. The value of good loans is the total loan volume divided by (1 – loan loss rate). The numbers in Table 4.5 are striking. The American states have either banned payday lending or regulated it fairly tightly with rate caps of $15 per $100 or lower in most states. The average US loan rate for Dollar Financial is very stable, at $13 per $100 in each year. The average rate on Canadian loans

Table 4.5 Dollar Financial average loan rates by segment

	2011	*2012*	*2013*
Internet	28.1%	28.7%	32.7%
Canada storefront	19.8	20.2	21.3
Europe storefront	22.4	26.0	28.2
US storefront	13.0	13.0	13.0

The numbers are revenue of the segment ÷ [(consumer loan volume of the segment) × (1 – loan loss rate)]. The revenue and volume values come from the Dollar Financial 2013 10K, and the loan loss rates are my calculations using the loan loss dollar values from the 2013 10K was rising slightly every year, to $21.3 per $100 in 2013. The Canadian provinces failed to regulate properly, and the average rate is 64% higher than the US rate in 2013. Table 4.1 shows the provincial rate caps were $17–25 per $100 until recently, and only Manitoba had a rate cap under $20. Ontario has over half the population of the total residing in provinces which allow payday lending, and so we would expect the Canadian average to be not far from the Ontario rate of $21 in 2013. The averages in Table 4.5 will always be somewhat lower than the rate caps in the segment. When a borrower is unable to repay a loan immediately and instead pays it off piecemeal over subsequent periods, the additional fee charged is much less than what is allowed on the original loan.

The European storefront rates are much higher than even the very high Canadian rates, because there was little regulation prior to 2014. In 2014 the UK started to regulate payday lending, and the current rate cap in place since 2016 is 0.8% interest per day. For the average US or Canadian loan that lasts less than 14 days, this would be a rate of less than $11 per $100, and it would reach $24 per $100 only on a full-month loan. The UK is the largest part of the European segment, and so this change has lowered the average rates in that segment, but we have no disclosures since 2014 to tell us how much it has declined. Regulation is changing in other countries as well, but it is beyond the scope of this book to record all those changes and incorporate them into this analysis of Dollar Financial.

The internet lending rate is astonishingly high and rising, to $32.7 per $100 in 2013. It hardly seems credible that charging a borrower one-third of the principal of a loan is sustainable in the long run. A one-time borrower might be able to cope with repaying a third more than he borrowed only two weeks before, but the repeat borrowers that provide the great majority of the payday lending business will be unable to meet such costs repeatedly. With this reflection, let me turn to a short discussion of the internet lending business.

The Internet Lending Business

We have very little hard data on the internet business. We can see there are many websites offering payday loans, including websites for the established companies like Money Mart, Cash Money, and 310-Loan. 310-Loan was established by several private investors to engage in projects in finance through the internet in the early days of the net, and payday lending became a major product. 310-Loan registered in each province when the various provincial acts were passed, but it has no storefront business. QC Holdings Inc., an American payday lender, bought 310-Loan in 2011, and continues to operate it in Canada as an internet payday lender. We do not know the size of the internet payday business in Canada or elsewhere, though we reported some very rough estimates in Chap. 1, but we can glean some clues from the DFC reports up to the time it ceased reporting as a public company.

Table 4.4 chronicles both the strength and the weakness of the internet payday lending business. DFC grew that segment's volume from $340 million in 2011 to over $1 billion in 2013. But then the business contracted dramatically in the nine months ended March 31, 2014, and the 10Q report does not provide an explanation. The loan loss percentage rose to 11.8%, which seems so high that it calls into question the viability of the business. I believe Money Mart and other storefront chains that also offer internet lending are generating their own leads, but the companies that operate only on the web also have to pay for prospects, and they will reject a high percentage of those who try to borrow from them. On a net operating business basis, the DFC internet segment earned nothing and therefore contributed nothing toward the corporate general expense, while the Canadian storefronts were highly profitable. The internet segment also recorded a charge for impairment of intangibles of over $50 million, leaving its net income contribution as a large loss. When a company has to write off such a large value of intangibles relative to its income and asset base, this is a clear signal that the business is in serious trouble.

Despite the inclusion of the Canadian internet sales of Money Mart in the global internet segment, the revenue from Money Mart's internet payday lending can be extracted. DFC has to report results on a corporate basis for National Money Mart Company because it has borrowed money in Canada, and the lenders need to see the National Money Mart results including internet lending. Appendix 1 shows the storefront consumer lending revenue of Money Mart was US$139.9 million for the nine months ended March 31, 2014. The total consumer lending revenue for Money Mart was US$149.8 million for the same period (DFC Global 2014a 10Q, p. 52), and hence the internet lending revenue was US$9.9 million, which is only 6.6% of Money Mart's total payday lending business. Furthermore, we can also extract the loan loss rate of the internet business. From the same sources, the provision for loan losses for Money Mart was

US$5.7 million, while the provision for the storefront business was US$2.8 million; so the internet loan losses were US$2.9 million. Converting revenue to volume using the same method as Table 4.4 yields an estimated internet loan volume in Canada of $27.5 million for nine months, which multiplied by 4/3 gives an annual volume of $36.7 million, or about CD$39 million. The loan loss rate is 10.55%, compared with the storefront loan loss rate of 2.67%. Clearly, the internet business is not working any better in Canada than in the rest of the company, and it is a very small part of the Canadian segment of Dollar Financial. Money Mart is the iconic brand of payday lending in Canada. Most Canadians use the name Money Mart synonymously with payday loan. The financial results of Money Mart show that it is very successful, including keeping a tight lid on loan losses. If it cannot attract a larger internet business and make it profitable, I question the viability of internet payday lending in Canada in the long run. The rate cap reductions in Ontario, Alberta, and BC will make it even less likely that the internet payday lending will occupy a significant niche. Accordingly, I can assess what the proper rate cap should be by looking at the storefront business without worrying about the internet segment. First we take a brief detour to look at other products of the alternative finance sector that are closely related to payday loans.

Other Borrowing Options in the Alternative Financial Services Sector

Payday lenders and other players in the alternative financial services sector offer some other debt choices that are not exactly payday loans but may serve the same purpose for some customers in some situations.

Check Cashing

The second most important source of revenue for payday lenders is check cashing. Check cashing is more important in the USA because of the much greater proportion of the population which is unbanked. In Canada or the USA, a payday loan customer provides government-issued identification and endorses a check which the check casher accepts for cash minus a fee. The specific nature of the required identification and the type of check accepted varies a bit between lenders.

In Canada there would seem to be no need for this service, because virtually all Canadians have bank accounts in which to deposit checks. However, the banks have the right to place a "hold" on any check, which is a delay in payment of funds to the payee until the bank is satisfied that it will receive the funds from the payor. Regulations in Canada require that the bank advance to a consumer (but not necessarily to a business payee) immediately up to $100 on any check drawn on a Canadian bank. The permitted hold on the remaining funds for a Canadian check of $1500 or less is four business days after deposit if the check is deposited in person at a bank branch and five business days if deposited in an ATM. There are longer holds possible for larger checks, foreign checks, and some other situations.[9] In economic terms, the check casher is lending the customer the money now as a loan whose term is the length of the hold period, which is an extremely short time, and hence the check cashing fee is a very short-term loan with some risk involved, if the payor does not honor the check when it is presented through the payment system.

Pawnbroking

Pawnbrokers have a very long history as alternative financial services providers. They take small, valuable items as security for loans whose term is usually no longer than one year. Because of the security taken, their rates are much lower than payday loan fees. In Canada, they are restricted by Section 347 of the Criminal Code to no more than 60% per annum, which is usually interpreted as 5% per month or part thereof for a pawn loan, though I have observed a large pawnshop in Toronto charging only 2% per month, simple interest, which is lower than some credit cards charge on overdue balances. The pawnbroker's skill is not as lender, but as a valuator of the varied items offered as security for the loans. As long as the loan does not exceed the value of the security, the risk of loss is very small. Pawn shops also buy the same items that they accept as security for loans and place them for sale at once. Their relationship with payday lending is becoming very strong, because payday lenders like Dollar Financial are buying individual pawnshops and chains of them and adding payday lending as another business line. Pawnshops often offer payday loans. This combination is particularly noticeable in the UK, where Money Shop, a

[9] See https://www.canada.ca/en/financial-consumer-agency/services/rights-responsibilities/rights-banking/cheque-hold-access-funds.html#toc0

subsidiary of DFC, offers both services in most locations. Money Shop appears to be the largest storefront payday lender in the UK now. In addition, pawnshops are becoming almost indistinguishable from used goods stores, although they carry a more limited range of products.[10] Cash Converters of Australia offers to buy used goods, advance pawn loans on the security of used goods, and provide payday loans. At the time of writing, Cash Converters has 11 stores in Canada.

Installment Loans

In recent years, some payday lenders have started to offer installment loans with much longer terms in various jurisdictions and various types. For readers not familiar with the mechanics of installment loans, let me explain. In finance circles we usually speak of blended principal and interest, which is another term for installment loan. A standard consumer loan, car loan, and mortgage loan are repaid in equal periodic amounts that combine interest and repayment of principal. This contrasts with most corporate loans, which are interest only until maturity, and payday loans, which are a single repayment of principal + fee/interest. With the use of powerful computers and readily available software, we can create any form of repayment schedule we want, and the payments need not be the same size each time, nor do the periods have to be the same length. However, both the lenders and the borrowers like to keep these schedules simple so that everyone understands what the obligations are, and so most consumer loans are repaid in equal periodic installments. The commonest period is monthly, but weekly and bi-weekly payments also exist.

Installment loans have entered the payday world in two different forms. One is a longer-term, very high interest rate loan offered as a product by a lender. The other form is an option to convert a payday loan to an installment loan if the borrower is unable to repay it on the due date.

Money Mart is now advertising installment loans for $1000–15,000, 12–60 months to repay, in its stores and on its website. Money Mart does do a credit check for installment loans, but it claims that its approval process also involves a steady source of income, which brings it closer to the payday loan

[10] The main product categories they will accept as security, buy for resale, or take on consignment are jewelry, high-quality watches, gold and silverware, electronics, bicycles, and chinaware.

process.[11] Take the example of a loan of $1000 for 12 months. This is a bit larger than the average payday loan, but in the same order of magnitude. If the annual percentage rate (APR) is 59.5% compounded monthly, the monthly repayment is $112.78. A Manitoba payday loan for one month (assuming the person is paid monthly) of the same amount would require a repayment of $1170 in one month. A family that cannot make ends meet one month will be hard-pressed to find an extra $1170 next month. The total amount paid on the installment loan is $1353.36. Let me ignore the time value of the money that the lender gives up by getting repayments over 12 months instead of one month for now. The borrower pays a fee of $170 for the money for one month, or $353.36 to have use of a declining portion of it for 12 months. For the onetime borrower, this is a much more manageable repayment schedule. The interest rate implicit in the one-month payday loan is an APR of 204% versus 59.5% for the installment loan. I believe that the biggest problem with payday loans is not the very high fee, but the requirement for repayment of the entire balance on the next payday. Installment loans overcome this problem to some extent.

One interesting issue with this new installment loan is what it does to the normal payday lending pattern and the lender's revenue stream. If many payday borrowers who have been getting into a debt trap and borrowing repeatedly to pay off the first loan switch to this loan and are able to cope with the repayment schedule, the total revenue of the payday lender will decline considerably. Twelve ordinary payday loans a year in Manitoba for $1000 would generate $1700 in fees versus the $353.36 from the one-year installment loan. Since the average borrower borrows more than four times a year at the least, the lender could lose a lot of revenue if the reason they are borrowing so often is the inability to repay the initial loan. For example, someone who borrows $500 six times in one year in Manitoba and repays each loan on time will pay $510 in fees. On the other hand, one- and two-time borrowers who switch to installment loans will be more profitable for the payday lender if they choose long enough repayment periods.

Colorado has banned traditional payday loans in favor of installment loans of a minimum of six months, and high fees relative to mainstream

[11] https://www.moneymart.ca/loans/installment-loans/installment-loans-faq, accessed July 22, 2017. Less than a year earlier, Money Mart was advertising a more limited version of installment loans, $1500–3000 with a term of 12–24 months and an APR of 59.9%. These loans were offered at that time in Manitoba, Ontario, and Newfoundland and Labrador.

financial institutions. The fee schedule is complicated—a fixed origination fee that the lender earns over six months + maintenance fee per month + 45% interest per annum, APR. Pew Charitable Trusts (2013, p. 13) shows that this change reduced the annual percentage interest rate charged on the average loan from 329% to 129%, and the average of fees paid per borrower per year from $476 to $277. Previously, Colorado had a rate cap of $15 per $100 fixed fee per payday loan. The new scheme is quite a bit cheaper, but still high cost. It avoids the unmanageable balloon repayment on the next payday that is such a problem with traditional payday loans. The volume of payday loans in 2009, the year before the change from the traditional scheme, was $576 million. The volume in 2014 was $193 million.[12]

The other way to introduce installment loans is to allow a borrower to take out a traditional payday loan with the customary fixed fee and repayment due on the next payday, but also give the customer the option to convert the loan to an installment loan on or before the due date. The state of Washington has such a program. The regular payday fee is 15% on the first $500 and 10% on any additional amount, with a maximum of the lower of $700 and 30% of income. A borrower may not take out more than eight loans in a 12-month period. The borrower also has this right to an installment:

> BORROWERS' RIGHTS TO INSTALLMENT PLANS Borrowers are entitled to an installment loan at any time prior to default. Borrowers do not have to pay a fee for the installment plan and have from 90 to 180 days (depending on the original loan amount) to repay the loan in a series of installments. (Washington 2014, p. 7)

There is still an active payday loan industry in Washington, even though it has several regulations that reduce fees substantially from the previous levels.

Once a province starts creating conditions for smaller installment loans that require less stringent credit checks than the banks enforce, competition from lenders who are not payday lenders is sure to arise, and it has. Older readers may recall names like Household Finance and Avco that flourished during the household formation and consumer boom after World War

[12] http://coag.gov/uccc/info, Comparison Table of Deferred/Payday Lenders, 2005–2014, accessed March 6, 2016.

II. The banks and trust companies wouldn't provide loans for things like furniture and appliances, and the finance companies filled that space. Banks, credit unions, and trust companies moved into much more consumer lending by the 1970s, and the finance companies were driven out of business. The new breed of installment lenders operates primarily over the internet, but is regulated and visible, unlike many of the internet payday lenders. Progressa, Mogo and easyfinancial are three Canadian examples. They do check credit ratings, but lend much more freely than the mainstream institutions, and they charge rates in the range of 40–60% per annum. These rates do not violate Section 347, and they are much lower than payday loan fees, but they are a great deal higher than the mainstream loan rates and higher than credit card interest rates.

Rent to Own

Rent to own also has a long history, but seemed to disappear for some decades in Canada because of the easy credit available from the mainstream. It has reappeared, and it is hard to distinguish clearly from the easy credit terms the furniture and appliance stores offer. We will not delve into this sector too deeply because it seems to be quite small. The basic operation charges a high but not outrageous interest rate with varying terms, sometimes longer than a year. The rates I have seen are around 30% as an APR, or 2.5% per month. There is a hidden catch, however. The loan is calculated on the Manufacturer's Suggested Retail Price (MSRP). This is a standard benchmark in many industries, but it is frequently much higher than the price that the retailers actually charge, and that applies particularly to the sort of goods that rent-to-own stores carry, particularly electronics, small appliances, and furniture. The largest chain in Canada appears to be easyhome (the name is not capitalized), with 180 stores.

What Rate Cap Should Canadian Regulators Set?

A Brief Look at the USA and UK Rate Caps

I preface this analysis with some information on US and UK regulation. Appendix 4 contains data on US payday lending by state.[13] Nineteen US

[13]This data is a bit older than the Canadian figures we provide by province in Table 4.1, but regulation has not changed much in the US in recent years and so the table is still valid. Much of the data is for 2014. I do not specify the currency, because rate caps are always in the same currency as the loan; that is, they are a percentage of the loan. The dollar value of

Table 4.6 US rate caps and stores per 100,000 population

Rate cap	*No. of states*	*Average no. of stores/100,000*
15% or lower	12	6.9
Over 15% but less than 18%	7	10.6
18% or higher	4	15.7
Low rate, complicated, not a single value	5	*
No rate cap, but payday lending allowed	6	9.2
Payday lending banned	17	n/a

*No store counts available for three of the five states, and the number of stores has almost certainly diminished in all of them since the date of the table because of tighter regulations in those states. Washington and Virginia counts in 2014 yield 2.2 stores per 100,000

states (including District of Columbia) have enacted rate caps that are too low for payday lenders to operate, and they have exited those states. A common limit seen in those states is an annual interest rate of 36%. The rate caps for those states that allow payday lending are summarized in Table 4.6. The largest number caps the loan fee at $15 per $100, or lower. Seven states allow more than $15 but less than $18, four have a cap greater than $18, and six states have no rate cap. Some of these states have sliding caps: for example, 15% of the first $500 loaned, 13% of any amount above $500. Five states have rate caps combined with other regulations that are too complicated to capture in a single percentage, but they are effectively lower than $15. Missouri has a rate cap of 75% of the initial principal; that is, $75 per $100 borrowed, but it also applies to the total of all charges when a borrower is unable to repay on the due date. In 2008 there was no rate cap, and at that time Missouri had more payday loan outlets than all of Canada. The average rate charged appeared to be $19 per $100.[14] Some of the caps apparently a bit higher than $15 are actually $15 per $100 plus a flat $5 fee for registration on a statewide database, which involves extra work and expense for the lender.

Most states have more payday loan stores per capita than any Canadian province, despite the fact that the rate caps are generally lower than Canadian rate caps. For example, Florida has a rate cap of $10 per

the rate cap conventionally is always applied to a loan of $100, and hence the dollar values are equal to a flat percentage of the fee. The convention of "x dollars per hundred" is commonly used to distinguish the fee charged on the loan from an interest rate of x% per annum.

[14] In 2008 I looked at the rates on the internet for a number of Missouri lenders, both chains and independent stores. I did not keep the links, only the general observation on the average rate.

\$100 + \$5 per loan, a population somewhat less than the total of all Canadian provinces that allow payday lending, and yet it has four times the number of payday loan stores that Canada has. This evidence is important in determining an appropriate rate cap for Canada.

The UK recently has instituted a rate cap of 0.8% of principal per day, or 80p per £100 loan per day. This cap yields a different fee pattern from the US and Canadian experience. The typical North American loan matures on the next payday, which for almost all borrowers is on a bi-weekly or twice monthly schedule, resulting in loans with less than 14 days maturity. Under the UK cap, a typical ten-day Canadian loan would cost only \$8 per \$100, a rate which would be too low for most Canadian stores. If the loan lasts a full 30 days, the fee would be £24 per £100, which is just a bit higher than the highest Canadian fee. Given a 30-day time to maturity, we would not see such frequent borrowing and so the UK limit would also produce lower fees for all the repeat borrowers.

Analyzing Rate Caps for Canada

I present a detailed analysis in this section that supports \$15 per \$100 as the appropriate and fair rate cap for Canada. In the past, every Canadian province except Québec and Newfoundland and Labrador has set the rate cap higher than required to sustain an efficient firm, and if their rates were lower than the regulated caps, the lenders raised their rates when the rate caps were set in regulations. Alberta has lowered its rate cap to \$15, and the Ontario rate cap is now \$18, but going to \$15 on January 1, 2018. The other provinces maintain rates that I argue are too high. Before I set out the detailed financial analysis, let me present three pieces of simple evidence that the past and current Canadian rate caps are too high, and should be set around \$15 per \$100.

Prior to the legalization of payday lending through the amendment to the Criminal Code Section 347, there were over 1000 payday lending outlets operating in Canada. While doing unpublished research for Industry Canada in 2005–2006 and for the Association of Community Organizations for Reform Now (ACORN) in 2006 and for the Manitoba Public Interest Law Centre in 2007–2008, I observed the rates that many different payday lenders charged. Money Mart charged a complex fee with three factors: an effective annual interest rate of 59%, a fixed dollar amount, and a percentage of the principal plus interest. This complicated schedule yielded a fee of about 19% of the principal for an average size loan for two weeks. Cash Money charged a flat $20 per $100, as did a number of other firms. A few smaller firms charged flat rates ranging from $15 to $20. Cash Store Financial (then operating under the name Rent Cash) claimed it was charging $20, but it was in truth deceiving its customers, because it discounted all loans, which means it deducted the fee from the amount loaned, at the start of the loan. Thus a loan of $100 on paper would only net the customer $80. In addition, it charged other fees on the first loan and a fee to load a debit card. Thus the actual rate was over 25%. A few other small operators charged rates of $22–25. Instaloans, a large chain that Cash Store subsequently purchased, charged $22.50. The fact that these operators continued in business and were expanding is incontrovertible evidence that the rates they were charging were sufficient or more than sufficient. Money Mart in particular was expanding rapidly both before and after the change to the Criminal Code.

When the provinces set their regulations, every province except Manitoba set rate caps that were higher than Money Mart, Cash Money, and many others were charging (see Table 4.1). The response from the chains was unanimous: they all changed their rates to the maximum permitted in each province. For eight provinces, this was a substantial increase from the rates that they had already been charging. Only Manitoba's $17 per $100 rate was determined by a thorough and effective regulatory process that involved independent expert evidence and public hearings in which the industry and the public interest were represented. The companies' response to this lower rate in Manitoba was to remain in business. After the bankruptcy of Cash Store Financial, the number of stores in Manitoba declined, but in 2016 there were still 40 payday loan stores, almost all of which had been in operation since well before Manitoba passed the law and regulations that allowed them to operate within the law. The events in Manitoba provide clear evidence that the regulated rates are too high, and should be no higher than $17, but I will demonstrate with more detailed analysis the rate cap in Canada should be no higher than $15, as we see in many American states.

The USA and Canada are quite similar in culture and economic conditions. Table 4.6 and Appendix 4 make it evident that payday lenders can flourish in the USA at a rate of $15 or even lower. I have already pointed out the situation of Florida, with more payday lenders than all of Canada. Very few of the US states that allow payday lending have set rate caps higher than $18, yet only three Canadian provinces will be under $18 as of January 1, 2018. This evidence suggests that the rate cap most likely to avoid excess profits while permitting payday lending to continue is $15 per $100 or even lower.

Finally, I have already shown in a previous section that the Canadian segment of Dollar Financial was vastly more profitable than the other segments. The contribution margin[15] each year up to last disclosure available in 2014 was double the other segments. Yet Dollar Financial continues to operate in many US states, and in 2014 was expanding greatly in the UK and several European countries. Once again this shows that the Canadian rate caps were too high and remain too high outside of Ontario and Alberta.

Let me turn to a rigorous economic analysis of the revenues and costs of a payday lender in Canada now, to demonstrate more conclusively that a fee cap of $15 per $100 should be the limit the provinces set. For the rest of this analysis, all dollar values are $CD. The financial model I developed estimates a cost structure for an efficient payday lending store, including cost of capital, for a single store that can be either a sole proprietorship or one outlet in a chain of stores.[16] This model is an adaptation of the widely accepted method for regulation of utilities. I determine an efficient cost structure, allowable capital investment and required rate of return on the capital, and volume of production, where production in this case is payday loans. I then apply different prices to the loans and see what profit the model generates for each case. Since the model allows for a fair return on capital invested, the profit this model generates is excess profit. In other words, the model builds into the expenses the amount that the owner can reasonably expect to earn for the money invested and the risk taken. If the profit is positive, the owner is charging fees that are too high.

Chapter 5 presents a careful ethical analysis in more depth to justify the imposition of regulation in the payday lending industry.

The model inputs that have the most significant impact on the results are: loan volume, the fee charged on the loans (which is the value that is the subject of the regulation), operating cost, and bad debts expense. Cost of capital and capital expenditures are much less important. The reader should look at Table 4.7 while reading. I will explain how the table works and the

[15] Contribution margin for a line of business, a segment of a business, or a specific product line is revenue directly attributable to the line or segment minus costs directly attributable to it.

[16] I developed this model in successive research engagements for Industry Canada (2004–2005), Association of Community Organizations for Reform Now (2006) and the Public Interest Law Centre and Public Utilities Board of Manitoba (2007–2016).

Table 4.7 Regulatory model of payday loan rate caps

Model for a single store (in CD$)

Base case $10 operating		*Base case $11 operating*	
$ Volume of loans	$2,340,000	$ Volume of loans	$2,340,000
Revenue model		Revenue model	
Average loan term	18	Average loan term	18
Loan fee	15%	Loan fee	15%
Cost model		*Cost model*	
Operating cost/$100 loan	10	Operating cost/$100 loan	11
Cost of capital real	8.00%	Cost of capital real	8.00%
Cash on hand	32,055	Cash on hand	32,055
Loans receivable	115,397	Loans receivable	115,397
Capital investment per store	50,000	Capital investment per store	50,000
Initial store loss	100,000	Initial store loss	100,000
Regulatory deposit	25,000	Regulatory deposit	25,000
Payables and accruals per	48,430	Payables and accruals	48,430
Net investment per store	274,022	Net investment per store	274,022
Bad debt rate/loans	2.20%	Bad debt rate/loans	2.67%
Economic income statement		*Economic income statement*	
Fee revenue	343,278	Fee revenue	341,628
Total revenue	$343,278	Total revenue	$341,628
Operating cost	234,000	Operating cost	257,400
Capital cost	21,922	Capital cost	21,922
Bad debt cost	51,480	Bad debt cost	62,478
Total economic cost	$307,402	Total Economic Cost	$341,800
Excess profit	**$35,876**	**Excess profit**	**–$171**

source of all the estimates in a minute, but first an overview. The table represents a single store. If it is part of a chain, then the operating cost line and the capital investment include costs that are not directly part of the store, but instead are the administrative or head office costs. I have not modeled any fees other than the flat fee charged on every loan, but most provincial regulations allow an additional fee on past due loans that is effectively higher than the cost of capital for the additional time the loan remains unpaid, and so this model is somewhat biased to show lower revenue and therefore slightly biased to support higher rate caps than are needed in practice.

This model is a perpetuity. The column of revenues and expenses is a single year, but that year is repeated every year in the future. That distinction is essential to understanding what the dollars represent. They are "real" dollars. That is, they are expressed in today's purchasing power. If we want to express them in "nominal" dollars, which means the dollar values we will observe in the future, we cannot use a perpetuity; we need a huge spreadsheet in which we estimate inflation factors for every future year and then inflate the values in the model every year. We will also have to discount all the values. And since we cannot have an infinite spreadsheet, we will have to choose a future year in which we convert everything to a perpetuity in any case. If the payday loan industry were just starting now, we could not use a perpetuity because we would have to allow for future growth in number of outlets. However, the evidence is clear that the industry is not growing rapidly any more. Outlets will open and close, particularly as population shifts, but the net effect will be a fairly stable number of outlets.

Table 4.7 is similar to a common valuation model, Free Cash Flow to the Firm (FCFF). Pinto et al. (2015) have done a standard work for Chartered Financial Analysts and provide a detailed explanation of FCFF valuation, but the same model appears in every valuation textbook, since professional valuators, investors, and money managers all use it as a fundamental analytical tool. I use the same principles in the payday lending model, but the objective function is the price of the loan, not the value of the company. In very simple terms, my model sets up an equation in which the single unknown variable is the price of the loan, and the cash flows and the value of the firm are given. What we want to know is what price on the loan will produce a zero "Excess Profit." An important piece to understand before you look at any details is the meaning of "Excess Profit." This model treats the cost of capital, the return to investors, as if it is an explicit expense in dollars, even though it will not appear that way in a financial statement. Excess profit means the excess beyond what is needed to fairly compensate the investors, or in the theoretical language of an economist, the economic rent. In Table 4.7 and what follows, an Excess Profit of zero is not the same as zero net income. An Excess Profit of zero means that with the revenues and costs included in that particular case, the investors are compensated for their investment and the fee that is charged is fair. The consumers are not paying more than they should. If Excess Profit is negative, the company might still show a positive profit on its financial statement, but the investors are not receiving enough compensation. If the Excess Profit is positive, the investors are capturing economic rent and the company is overcharging the customers. In addition, this model is for a single store, including appropriate costs for management, and so if it is a single store in a chain, the Excess Profit would be multiplied by the number of stores in the chain.

With that said, all of the inputs to such a model are imperfect estimates, and so we should not interpret a small negative or positive value of Excess Profit as being materially different from zero, the case of no economic rent. In my judgment, a value of Excess Profit in the range of negative \$5000 to positive \$5000 should be interpreted as no different from a value of 0. A value of negative \$5000 to negative \$10,000 is a reasonable indication that the store is not returning enough to the investors, and a negative value greater than \$10,000 is clearly not a good economic result. The reverse holds true for positive values greater than \$5000.

Table 4.7 summarizes two representative cases from the model and constitutes my base model.[17] In each case, the fee is \$15 and the volume of loans is \$2.34 million. The difference between the two is size of the two cost factors that are most important. The left-hand column assumes operating costs of \$10 per \$100 of loan volume and a bad debt rate of 2.2% of loan volume. These assumptions produce a very large Excess Profit. The right-hand column assumes operating costs of \$11 per \$100 of loan volume and a bad debt rate of 2.2% of loan volume. These assumptions produce a very small negative Excess Loss that is indistinguishable from 0. In my opinion, these two cases are the best representation of the range of results of an efficient payday loan store, and they support a fee cap of \$15, or perhaps even a bit lower.

Where do these numbers come from? Unfortunately, no payday lender in Canada is a public company now, with financial statements that we can reference. The provincial regulators do not require any financial disclosure at all, except for the limited evidence from BC in Appendix 3. The data that I use come primarily from the already cited 2013 and 2014 results of the Canadian segment of DFC, which is Money Mart. While this is not ideal, there are excellent reasons for using Money Mart to represent payday lenders in Canada in general for determining what the rate cap should be.

First, Money Mart has captured something like 50% of the entire payday lending market, and perhaps more than that. Regulation based on its results already regulates a large part of the payday lending in Canada with the appropriate data.

[17] The base model in a financial modeling is the best single estimate of the relevant parameters. We know that there is variation in what will happen, but the base model is my best estimate of current and future results.

Second, a principle of rate-based regulation is a restriction on costs allowed in the rate base. The costs must be necessary for the provision of the regulated good or service, and they must be the costs under efficient management. Money Mart is an efficient provider of payday loans, to the extent that it is possible for such an operation to be efficient. Its loan loss rate is consistently much lower than the average in the market. It has the largest scale of operations, and the largest volume of loans per store, and given the fixed nature of most of the operating costs, that means its costs per $100 of loan will be the lowest or close to the lowest, in the industry.

In addition, the rate cap reductions in Ontario, Alberta, and BC will inevitably force less efficient operators out of business. Money Mart and the other large chains will capture most of that business in their existing stores, and that increase in volume will reduce their operating costs per $100 loan.

The details of how to estimate the numbers for every line in this model are too lengthy to include in this book. Robinson (2016) provides a complete explanation. The common industry practice is to express values as $ per $100 of loan volume. Ernst & Young (2004) follows this convention also. This practice has a significant drawback because it is not sensitive to material changes in activity. If store X that has been making 15 loans a day gets additional volume of 10 loans per day when a competitor on the next block closes, store X will increase its revenue by two-thirds, but its costs will not rise by anything close to the same amount. Measuring its costs historically as $ per $100 of loan will overstate its expenses and understate profit going forward. Nonetheless, I use this method in the model as a starting point, and then explain how to allow for that effect. In order to properly evaluate the performance of payday lenders today, the values from 2013 to 2014 must be adjusted to take account of the Cash Store Financial (CSF) exit early in 2014.

The loan volume per store estimate starts with the 2013 full year result for Money Mart, which had $1.973 million in loan volume per store. All monetary values are converted to Canadian dollars, but the effect is minimal in any case because the two currencies were almost at par in 2013. Most of the values for Money Mart come from the full year 2013 rather than the slightly more recent nine months ended March 31, 2014, because the quarterly report (10Q) does not contain all the segmented expense detail that the full annual report (10K) does. Appendix 3 shows indirectly the effect of the CSF failure. BC loan volume declined in 2015 by $45 million, but increased by $29 million in 2016 to reach a level above the

2013 volume. CSF was the second largest payday lender in Canada at the time of its failure, and Money Mart would have picked up a significant part of the value, especially because it bought some of the CSF stores and rolled their operations into its existing stores. Robinson (2016) brings a variety of different data and approaches to arrive at an estimate of $2.34 million per store. Remember, all this is in real dollars, although adding inflation would not change the numbers a great deal.

The operating cost includes most of the costs: labor cost, rent, telecommunications, office supplies and equipment, utilities, and so on. There is an elephant in the room that only becomes visible upon close reading of the DFC 10K, and it is in the room every year. DFC recorded extremely large corporate expenses whose nature is undefined. Recall that Money Mart had been a successful stand-alone operation before DFC bought it, and it was far more profitable than the other segments. Essentially, Money Mart provided all the surplus money to pay for the unprofitable expansion into internet lending and the European storefronts. Or perhaps it also provided excessive perquisites for the head office executives. In Robinson (2016), I compared DFC with Cash America, another US payday lender of about the same size that operates only in the USA. The unidentifiable expenses of Cash America were 6.1% of revenue, whereas the unidentifiable expenses of Dollar Financial were 29.5% of revenue. In my opinion, this level of mysterious costs is quite unreasonable, and a great deal of it would not be allowed in a rate regulation setting in which the companies must provide full disclosure. I cannot determine what percentage would be allowed. If all of these corporate costs were allowed, the operating cost per $100 loan volume was $12.01. With all of them excluded, it was $9.53.

The issue of operating costs is further complicated by two factors. While we are analyzing payday lending in this book, the companies also get significant revenue from check cashing and small amounts from some other consumer financial services. All the costs are joint, and there is no "correct" way to divide them between the different lines of business, except for the bad debt losses which apply almost entirely to the payday loan business. I allocated them based on the percentage of revenue for payday lending as a percentage of all business, which is the commonest method of allocating indivisible joint costs.

The other complication I have already introduced: the substantial increase in volumes that occurred with the failure of CSF. If my estimate of $2.34 million loan volume per store in real dollars is correct, the operating cost per $100 loan will decline from the 2013 numbers, because the operating costs will not rise proportionately with the volume increase.

Taking all these factors together, I estimate that the most likely range of operating costs now in real dollars for an efficient lender like Money Mart is $10–11 per $100 of loan volume.

The model also estimates the capital investment of an efficient payday lender, again using Money Mart data as a basis. Virtually all stores are leased, but investment in leasehold improvements was required. The store would lose money during the first year of operation, and the owner must be fairly compensated in the future by earning a return on that loss. Receivables are not large because the loans turn over so fast, and the cash and the payable offset to it are not significant. Add up all the investment and the value is very small. I estimate the real cost of capital (which includes both debt and equity) to be a quite high value of 8%. One change from the estimates in Robinson (2016) is the average maturity date of the loan, at 18 days. A borrower who repays on time will likely have less than 12 days outstanding, since most borrowers will be paid every two weeks. Some borrowers will not repay at once, but will eventually pay off, and that is why the longer average maturity of 18 days is used. But none of the estimates on the capital side have a significant effect on the Excess Profit, within any reasonable variation.

Finally, the bad debt cost for Money Mart in 2006 was 1.3% of loan volume. It has risen since, to 2.2% in the full year ended June 30, 2013, and to 2.67% in the nine months ended March 31, 2014.

Thus we have the numbers in Table 4.7. Even if we assume the high end of the operating cost and bad debt estimates, a fee of 15% leads to essentially zero Excess Profit.

Table 4.8 introduces many different variations on the combinations of fees, loan volume, operating cost, and bad debt expense. Almost all of them result in positive or zero Excess Profit for a fee of $15. The results suggest that possibly a fee of $14 or even $13 is sustainable. Only if cost control is bad does the Excess Loss become significant. Note two of the cases in Panel 7. If the payday lender exercises somewhat better underwriting, which reduces volume and increases operating cost, a reduction in loan loss experience to 1.5% will still lead to zero Excess Profit at a fee of $15. If the lender reduces operating cost to $9.53 per hundred dollars of loans and keeps a lid on bad debts at 2.2%, it can reach an economic breakeven with a fee of only $13.

The reduction of the fee cap in Ontario, Alberta, and BC will force the industry to consolidate more. The largest chains will get more business

Table 4.8 Variations on the base case

Panel 1: Vary Fee, Bad debt. Operating Cost $10				
Loan volume	$2.34MM	$2.34MM	$2.34MM	$2.34MM
Fee	14	15	14	15
Operating cost per $100	$10.00	$10.00	$10.00	$10.00
Bad debt rate	2.20%	2.20%	2.67%	2.67%
Excess profit	**$12,991**	**$35,876**	**$453**	**$23,229**
Panel 2: Vary Fee and Operating Cost				
Loan volume	$2.34MM	$2.34MM	$2.34MM	$2.34MM
Fee	14	15	14	15
Operating cost per $100	$9.50	$10.00	$10.50	$11.00
Bad debt rate	2.50%	2.50%	2.50%	2.50%
Excess profit	**$16,688**	**$27,803**	**–$6712**	**$4403**
Panel 3: Vary Volume, 15% fee, Op Cost $10, Bad debts 2.5%				
Loan volume	$1.9MM	$2.2MM	$2.5MM	$2.6MM
Fee	15	15	15	15
Operating cost per $100	10	10	10	10
Bad debt rate	2.50%	2.50%	2.50%	2.50%
Excess profit	**$20,671**	**$25,534**	**$30,397**	**$32,018**
Panel 4: Vary Volume, 15% fee, Op Cost $11, Bad debts 2.67%				
Loan volume	$1.9MM	$2.2MM	$2.5MM	$2.6MM
Fee	15	15	15	15
Operating cost per $100	11	11	11	11
Bad debt rate	2.67%	2.67%	2.67%	2.67%
Excess profit	**–$2043**	**–$767**	**$509**	**$935**
Panel 5: Vary Operating Cost, 15% fee, 2 million loan volume				
Loan volume	$2MM	$2MM	$2MM	$2MM
Fee	15	15	15	15
Operating cost per $100	9.53	10	11	12
Bad debt rate	2.50%	2.50%	2.50%	2.50%
Excess profit	**$31,692**	**$22,292**	**$2292**	**–$17,708**
Panel 6: Vary Bad debt expense, 15% fee, 2.34 million loan volume				
Loan volume	$2.34MM	$2.34MM	$2.34MM	$2.34MM
Fee	15	15	15	15
Operating cost per $100	11	11	11	11
Bad debt rate	1.80%	2.50%	3.00%	3.50%
Excess profit	**$23,240**	**$4403**	**–$9052**	**–$22,507**

Panel 7: Some Special Cases:

Stronger underwriting: $1.8MM volume, loan losses 1.5%, 15% fee, op cost $12.15: Excess profit = **$1050**

Lower fee and lower cost: $2.34MM volume, fee 13%, cost 9.53, bad debts 2.2%: Excess profit = **$1104**

Higher fee: Fee 16%, volume 2 MM, Cost 11/100, Bad debt 2.67%: Excess profit = **$17,848** without opening new stores as the smallest players exit. This consolidation in turn will reduce the operating cost per $100 loan. The three provinces account for 84% of the population of Canada that lives in provinces that allow payday loans. Other provinces may follow suit. In two or three years, the changed landscape might justify a fee cap of $13 or $14.

The Financial Effect of Loan Size Limits and Other Regulations

Section 347.1 of the Criminal Code limits payday loans to no more than $1500 principal and no longer than 62 days. As we have already seen, most loans are under $1000 and repayment is required on the next date the borrower receives regular income, which will be less than 30 days, and most often quite a bit sooner. BC and Saskatchewan also restrict the size of a loan to 50% of the borrower's net income on the next payment date. Manitoba restricts the size to 30% of the next income. The other provinces have no restriction, but payday lenders almost always restrict their lending to 50% or less of the next pay. The USA has no nationwide limit on payday loans, leaving most regulation to the individual states. The state loan limits range from $500 to $1500 and from 20% to 50% of pay.

The provinces limit the amount charged on overdue loans (see Appendix 1 of Chap. 4). Although loan losses are in the range of 2–4.5%, many borrowers are unable to repay the loan on the due date, and payday lenders are accustomed to accepting partial repayment and repayment over a longer period. The provincial regulations place limits on charges on overdue loans from 2.5% to 5% per month, which are high interest rates, but much lower than the initial payday loan fee.

Some provinces place limits on the frequency of borrowing. For example, BC requires that a payday lender, who lends for the third time within 62 days to a borrower, must spread the repayment over at least two pay periods if paid monthly and over at least three pay periods if paid more frequently. No repayment can exceed 35% for the three-period case nor exceed 50% for the two-period case.[18] This regulation is a small move toward installment lending. Ontario is implementing a similar regulation, effective July 1, 2018.

The purpose of a limit on the size of the loan relative to income is to prevent borrowers from digging themselves into too deep a debt hole and

[18] Business Practices and Consumer Protection Act: Payday Loans Regulation Section 23, at http://www.bclaws.ca/EPLibraries/bclaws_new/document/ID/freeside/16_57_2009, accessed July 22, 2017.

Table 4.9 Effect of payday loan limits and fees

Panel A: Fee is 15% of loan, loan limit is 20% of income, and thus the maximum loan is $300								
# of loans/yr	1	2	3	4	5	6	7	8
Loan fees	$45	$90	$135	$180	$225	$270	$315	$360
Fees as % of take-home pay	0.12%	0.23%	0.35%	0.46%	0.58%	0.69%	0.81%	0.92%
Panel B: Fee is 21% of loan, loan limit is 30% of income, and thus the maximum loan is $450								
# of loans/yr	1	2	3	4	5	6	7	8
Loan fees	$94.50	$189	$283.50	$378	$472.50	$567	$661.50	$756
Fees as % of take-home pay	0.24%	0.48%	0.73%	0.97%	1.21%	1.45%	1.70%	1.94%
Panel C: Fee is 21% of loan, loan limit is 20% of income, and thus the maximum loan is $300								
# of loans/yr	1	2	3	4	5	6	7	8
Loan fees	$63	$126	$189	$252	$315	$378	$441	$504
Fees as % of take-home pay	0.16%	0.32%	0.48%	0.65%	0.81%	0.97%	1.13%	1.29%

A client has take-home pay (after taxes, CPP, EI premiums, etc.) of $1500 every two weeks ($39,000 per year). What are the total fees per year and fees as a percentage of take-home pay if the client borrows the maximum amount one to eight times in a single year?

spending too much of their income on loan fees. The loan fees, the size of the loan, the short time to the next payday, and the economic situation that the borrower was in that obliged him to take a payday loan all interact. Table 4.9 shows the effects of three different sets of limits and fee caps on a single client as an illustration, but the same understanding would arise from any reasonable client situation. The client has take-home pay of $1500 every two weeks or $39,000 per year. This client earns well above minimum wage, but still a bit below the average industrial wage in Canada.[19] This client is somewhere in the middle of the income levels of payday loan clients, according to the statistics in Chap. 3. The great majority of payday loans are made to repeat borrowers as shown in section "A Brief Look at the USA and UK" of this chapter. Therefore, most loans will be to customers on the right side of the table, with several loans per year.

We can see that the effect of taking out several payday loans in a year is material to someone with this level of income, though not crushing. For

[19] Without going into a lot of detail about deductions from gross pay like income tax, employment insurance premiums, and Canada Pension Plan, we cannot compare net income very precisely with any benchmark.

example, if this client took out the maximum number of loans under a regime of 30% of income as a limit and a fee of $21, the annual cost would be 1.94% of take-home pay. A single loan could be reasonably regarded as having an immaterial effect. The effect on the dollar cost of a higher permitted limit is more significant than the higher fee schedule. The current range of fees in Canada is $15–23, and the current permitted maximum percentage of income for a single loan is 30% in Manitoba. Therefore, this table does represent a reasonable picture of the effects of a change in permitted loan limits. Of course, a consumer who ignored the limit and borrowed only the absolute minimum that he or she needed would not be affected by a limit unless it were too low to permit borrowing the required amount.

A more significant effect is seen by considering what happens at repayment date. For example, consider a person who borrows $300 at $15, which is the situation in Panel A, the low-cost and low-fee panel, and must repay $345 in two weeks. Take-home pay before repaying the loan is $1500. That means for the two weeks after repayment, until next payday, the person will have ($1500–$345) $1155 or 77% of disposable income. The person had not been able to meet the unexpected expense out of surplus cash flow because there isn't any and does not have a liquid emergency fund to use. Why is there no emergency fund? The person has been living paycheck to paycheck because current consumption and repayment of existing debts consumes the entire income. How is this person to live on $1155 when $1500 has been required every two weeks? If we move to Panel B, the person borrowed $450 and must repay $544.50, leaving $955.50 for consumption during the next pay period, or only 64% of the regular consumption. We see that the lower fee cap and lower loan limits of Panel A mitigate this problem, but it is still significant. The combination of a $15 fee and 20% limit on borrowing is close to the lowest limits in any US state, and still in this example a person would have to manage for two weeks on 77% of disposable income. The result is often that the client is forced to borrow again, after all possible spending economies, and gets trapped in a cycle of high-cost debt. This is the reason for concern over the percentage of pay borrowed. The cost of the fee makes it even worse, but the principal payment alone will be a serious challenge for many borrowers.

A reduction to a permitted borrowing level of 5–10% of take-home pay would reduce the challenge of repayment to a more manageable level. At that rate, however, the loan size would be so small that most customers would find payday loans would not meet their needs. In our example in the table, the maximum loan allowed at 10% would be only $150. We have already seen that the average loan is much larger than this. Borrowers would be forced to go to different payday lenders to get the money they need. During the 2016 hearings in front of the Public Utilities Board of Manitoba, the public had the opportunity to speak in an open session with the Board. No written notes were provided nor were these speakers under oath or required to be experts. One speaker, a senior manager with a payday lender, said that they could see their customers crossing the street to another payday lender when the loan limits prevented them receiving the loan they wanted. A man who borrowed frequently from payday lenders came to the hearing to speak, having seen a notice inviting the public on the bulletin board of his community center. He told the Board that he routinely borrowed from two or three different lenders at the same time. Unless there is a registry of all payday loans that every lender can access with real-time data, it is not possible to prevent multiple borrowing in cities where there are several payday lenders. Such a registry is expensive to maintain for such a small industry, and will contribute considerably to the costs, which ultimately will be recovered through higher fees. Florida has such a registry, and by law a fixed fee of $5 is charged on every loan to cover the cost of the registry.

Furthermore, given the high operating costs, dividing the loans into many smaller loans would render the business model unsustainable. Accordingly, I do not believe that changing the maximum permitted loan will improve the experience of borrowers significantly. Reducing the maximum fee will of course reduce the total share of the budget going to loan fees, but it will not help with the difficult challenge of the large balloon repayment due on the next payday.

The Installment Option

Allowing the borrower to convert the loan to an installment schedule on the due date is a reasonable alternative that might work for both lender and borrower. Although we do not seem to have any written evidence, we know this happens informally at the individual outlet level. We provide the story of Judy in Chap. 1. Judy had such an arrangement, to repay the loan in installments as quickly as she could every payday after the missed due date. If the alternative is no repayment, the lender will accept some sort of installment. Rollover fees have been banned in Canada and the USA for some time, and there are also rules against borrowing again too soon in some US states, sometimes enforced by use of a statewide registry of borrowers and their loans (e.g., Florida).

Take the example in Panel A of a loan for $300 with $345 due in two weeks. Let us suppose that the borrower could convert to a 12-week, six-payment installment schedule on the due date, with the first payment due immediately. Let us further suppose the interest rate is 60% per annum APR for two-week repayment periods. The installment payment every two weeks will be $60.82, which is much more manageable than $345 at once. Furthermore, even with the high interest rate of 60% per annum, the borrower is a lot better off with the conversion instead of the common practice of going to another lender. If the borrower goes to another lender to pay off the first loan, the fee will be 15% of $345, or $51.75. The interest paid on the installment loan is $19.97. The lender has already charged the high flat fee that is meant to recover the fixed operating costs of maintaining the business and extension of the loan into an installment would be much less time-consuming. Now suppose we create an example in which the mathematics is a little simpler, with an additional fee of 1% of the original principal for every two weeks the borrower is late in repaying.

To make this example concrete, imagine a loan of $400 to someone who is paid $1500 every two weeks, under the recommended new rate cap of 15%, which means that in two weeks the person will owe the lender $460. The person cannot pay on the due date. What will be the payments if the person chooses various longer dates for the installments?

- Two weeks late: $400 + $60 + $4 = **$464**
- Four weeks: $400 + $60 + $8 = $468. Each payday 468/2 = **$234**
- Six weeks: $400 + $60 + $12 = $472. Each payday 472/3 = **$157.33**
- Eight weeks: 476/4 = **$119**
- 10 weeks: 480/8 = **$60**
- 12 weeks: 480/12 = **$40** and so on.

While the addition of two or four additional weeks to repay seem to leave the person with a very difficult budgeting situation, it appears more manageable at six weeks or longer.

Conclusion

The payday loan industry in Canada is quite concentrated already in a few chains and will consolidate even more with the recent reductions in the rate caps. The average payday loan store handles only 11 loans per day with an average volume of CD$5000 and revenue of CD$1000, which is a remarkably inefficient way to deliver small loans. Most of the costs are fixed in the short run and, combined with the low volume and limited revenue from other products and services, force payday lenders to charge very high fees. Loan losses are significant, but the operating costs are 70–80% of the total costs, and the challenge for a payday lender is to generate enough volume to cover the operating costs. The entire industry has less outstanding in loans to consumers than an average Canadian bank branch.

A significant proportion of payday borrowers take out many loans a year. These borrowers are caught in a debt trap. They are borrowing just to repay the previous loan, the total fees are a significant cost relative to their limited income, and the repayment of principal alone on the next payday is likely to be a significant hardship. Allowing borrowers caught in a debt trap to convert a payday loan to an installment loan at the first repayment date may mitigate the repayment problem, but it will do nothing to deal with underlying conditions that led to the financial shortfall in the first place. The payday loan industry depends on repeat borrowers to remain in business, because there are not enough one-time users of the service.

The payday loan industry in Canada has been reaping excessive profits because the provinces did not set the rate caps at the proper level. Recently, Alberta and Ontario have lowered the limit to $15 per $100, but in the past the rate caps ranged from $17 to $25. A careful financial analysis using a properly calibrated financial model of a payday loan store shows that $15 per $100 is the rate cap most likely to eliminate excess profit while still allowing a fair return to the investors.

The internet payday loan business seems highly unprofitable, with unsustainable levels of loan losses.

Finally, reducing the maximum loan size permitted will not provide substantial relief to payday borrowers. The problem for those caught in a debt trap is the requirement to repay the loan in a single lump sum on the next payday, more so than the size of loan permitted. An installment plan, as already suggested, is one way to respond to this problem.

Appendix 1: Segment Results of DFC Global Corp

(In US$ millions)						
	Europe retail	*Canada retail*	*US retail*	*eCommerce*	*Other*	*Total*
For the nine months ended March 31, 2014						
Sales to unaffiliated customers						
Consumer lending	$131.9	$139.9	$53.0	$174.0	$—	$498.8
Check cashing	15.2	48.6	25.8	—	—	89.6
Pawn service fees and sales	70.3	0.4	0.1	—	—	70.8
Money transfer fees	8.2	14.7	3.2	—	—	26.1
Gold sales	26.0	4.1	1.2	—	—	31.3
Other	20.9	20.8	9.3	0.3	4.3	55.6
Total sales to unaffiliated customers	272.5	228.5	92.6	174.3	4.3	772.2
Operating margin	22.2	122.2	21.7	10.1	(0.9)	175.3
Provision for loan losses	65.7	2.8	9.6	70.3	—	148.4
Depreciation and amortization	12.7	6.4	1.4	8.8	3.0	32.3
Interest expense, net	36.8	43.0	—	(4.0)	9.2	85.0
Goodwill and other intangible assets impairment charge	52.7	—	—	52.5	22.1	127.3
Unrealized foreign exchange (gain) loss	(12.9)	21.5	—	—	(0.3)	8.3
Provision for (proceeds from) litigation settlements	—	0.1	0.1	—	(0.1)	0.1
Loss (gain) on store closings	0.2	(0.1)	0.1	—	0.1	0.3
Other expense (income), net	0.4	(1.4)	—	—	3.7	2.7
(Loss) income before income taxes	(88.8)	32.8	19.0	(51.4)	(49.8)	(138.2)
Income tax (benefit) provision	(5.8)	14.0	8.1	3.0	—	19.3
Total assets	$581.3	$394.8	$257.4	$288.6	$89.5	$1611.6

This table is extracted from the DFC Global Corp. 10Q report, March 31, 2014, pg. 43 (Total assets line) and pg. 44

Appendix 2: DFC Global Corp

Interim Unaudited Consolidated Statements of Operations
Three months and nine months ended March 31, 2014
(In US$ millions, except share and per share amounts)

	Three Months Ended March 31		*Nine Months Ended March 31*	
	2013	*2014*	*2013*	*2014*
Revenues				
Consumer lending	$181.7	$159.2	$549.8	$498.8
Check cashing	31.9	28.9	97.4	89.6
Pawn service fees and sales	21.4	24.0	62.8	70.8
Money transfer fees	8.4	8.2	27.9	26.1
Gold sales	17.8	8.6	51.0	31.3
Other	22.4	19.4	64.3	55.6
Total revenues	283.6	248.3	853.2	772.2
Operating expenses				
Salaries and benefits	61.3	63.6	181.0	187.4
Provision for loan losses	49.7	44.2	128.2	148.4
Occupancy	17.6	19.0	51.4	55.8
Purchased gold costs	15.3	7.8	40.4	28.3
Advertising	18.5	15.1	50.4	45.3
Depreciation	6.5	6.7	19.9	19.6
Maintenance and repairs	4.6	5.4	13.3	15.7
Bank charges and armored carrier service	5.9	5.7	17.5	16.2
Returned checks, net and cash shortages	2.6	2.7	7.5	7.4
Other	28.7	25.8	76.9	72.8
Total operating expenses	210.7	196.0	586.5	596.9
Operating margin	72.9	52.3	266.7	175.3
Corporate and other expenses				
Corporate expenses	27.9	25.9	91.4	77.1
Other depreciation and amortization	6.1	4.4	18.8	12.7
Interest expense, net	28.4	27.1	91.3	85.0
Goodwill and other intangible assets impairment charge	31.1	127.3	36.6	127.3
Unrealized foreign exchange loss	2.1	18.6	0.4	8.3
Provision for litigation settlements	—	0.1	2.7	0.1
Loss on store closings	0.3	0.3	0.9	0.3
Other expense, net	12.7	1.5	12.3	2.7
(Loss) income before income taxes	(35.7)	(152.9)	12.3	(138.2)
Income tax provision	0.7	6.2	20.6	19.3
Net loss	(36.4)	(159.1)	(8.3)	(157.5)

This table is extracted from the DFC Global Corp. 10Q report, March 31, 2014, pg. 4

Appendix 3: BC Aggregate Payday Loan Data

Indicator (CD$)	*2016*	*2015*	*2014*	*2013*	*2012*
Total loan volume ($ millions)	396.7	340.9	385.3	351.4	318.2
Total cost of borrowing ($ millions)	80.3	73.9	84.3	76.4	68.4
Total number of payday loans	804,257	736,585	857,830	796,580	738,688
Total number of individual borrowers	161,447	158,962	198,003	146,701	125,172
Average loan amount ($)	460	463	449	441	431
Average cost of borrowing ($)	100	100	98	96	93
Average number of loans per borrower	5.0	4.6	4.3	5.4	5.9
Total loans initially defaulted (%)	15.1	13.8	24.2	25.0	22.7
Total loans ultimately written off (%)	4.4	4.5	5.1	4.0	4.4
Number of licensed locations	209	226	274	275	274
Number of individuals with this range of loans during the year					
1 loan only	41,691	40,099	49,628	33,074	16,857
2–5 loans	62,207	67,724	77,416	55,104	26,948
6–10 loans	35,937	31,315	40,509	34,077	18,809
11–15 loans	17,510	14,934	21,585	17,723	11,049
More than 15 loans	4102	4890	8865	6608	1260

Source: Consumer Protection BC. 2016. *BC Aggregated Payday Loan Data – Self-Reported for License Years Ending on October 31.* https://www.consumerprotectionbc.ca/images/content/licensing/payday_lenders/2016%20Payday%20Aggregate%20Loan%20Data%20Table%20for%20Web.pdf

Appendix 4: US Payday Loan Data by State

	No. of stores	*Population size per state **	*Stores per 100,000 population*	*Maximum (US$) charge allowed on a $300 loan per 2-week pay period*	*Rate cap*
States with limited regulation					
Alabama	1070	4,858,979	22.02	53	17.7%
Alaska	34	738,432	4.60	50	16.7%
California	2119	39,144,818	5.41	45	15.0%
Florida	1275	20,271,272	6.29	35	11.7%
Hawaii	15	1,431,603	1.05	53	17.7%
Idaho	213	1,654,930	12.87	no limit	
Illinois	522	12,859,995	4.06	47	15.7%
Indiana	376	6,619,680	5.68	44	14.7%
Iowa	218	3,123,899	6.98	39	13.0%

(*continued*)

(continued)

	No. of stores	*Population size per state **	*Stores per 100,000 population*	*Maximum (US$) charge allowed on a $300 loan per 2-week pay period*	*Rate cap*
Kansas	352	2,978,204	11.82	45	15.0%
Kentucky	578	4,425,092	13.06	54	18.0%
Louisiana	931	4,670,724	19.93	55	18.3%
Michigan	646	9,922,576	6.51	42	14.0%
Minnesota	74	5,489,594	1.35	29	9.7%
Mississippi	1036	2,992,333	34.62	33	11.0%
Missouri	934	6,083,672	15.35	225	75.0%
Nebraska	180	1,896,190	9.49	53	17.7%
Nevada	339	2,890,845	11.73	no limit	
New Mexico	121	2,085,109	5.80	47	15.7%
North Dakota	56	756,927	7.40	61	20.3%
Oklahoma	358	3,911,338	9.15	45	15.0%
Rhode Island	29	1,056,298	2.75	30	10.0%
South Carolina	367	4,896,146	7.50	45	15.0%
South Dakota	126	858,469	14.68	no limit	
Tennessee	1208	6,600,299	18.30	53	17.7%
Texas	2617	27,469,114	9.53	no limit	
Utah	116	2,995,919	3.87	no limit	
Wisconsin	423	5,771,337	7.33	no limit	
Wyoming	87	586,107	14.84	30	10.0%
Total	16,420				
Colorado 6		5,456,574	n/a	16	
Maine 7		1,329,328	n/a	25	
Oregon 8		4,028,977	n/a	18	
Washington 9	160	7,170,351	2.23	45	
Virginia 10	189	8,382,993	2.25	69	

References

Carlstrom, Steven (Affidavit sworn April 14, 2014). *Application Record for Ontario Superior Court of Justice (Commercial List)*. Court File No. CV-14-10518-00CL [online]. http://cfcanada.fticonsulting.com/cashstorefinancial/docs/Application%20Record.pdf

DFC Global Corp. 2013. *Form 10-K for the Year Ended June 30, 2013*. Berwyn, US: DFC Global Corp. https://www.sec.gov/Archives/edgar/data/1271625/000119312513352311/d590562d10k.htm

———. 2014. *Form 10-Q, for the Nine Months Ended March 31, 2014*. Berwyn, US: DFC Global Corp. https://www.sec.gov/Archives/edgar/data/1271625/000119312514195203/d724100d10q.htm

Dijkema, Brian, and Rhys McKendry. 2016. *Banking on the Margins: Finding Ways to Build and Enabling Small-Dollar Credit Market*. Hamilton: Cardus.

Ernst & Young. 2004. *The Cost of Providing Payday Loans in Canada*. Ernst & Young, Tax Policy Services Group.

Pew Charitable Trusts. 2013. *Payday Lending in America: Policy Solutions*. Pew Charitable Trusts.

Pinto, Jerald, Elaine Henry, Thomas Robinson, and John Stowe. 2015. *Equity Asset Valuation*. 3rd ed. CFA Institute and John Wiley and Sons.

Robinson, Chris. 2016. *An Economic Analysis of the Payday Loan Industry and Recommendations for Regulation in Manitoba*. http://www.pubmanitoba.ca/v1/payday_loan_review2016/cac_5_tab_3_economic_analysis_c_robinson.pdf

Robinson, C., and M. Schwartz. 2017. A Corporate Social Responsibility Analysis of Payday Lending. http://ssrn.com/abstract=3044087; forthcoming in *Business and Society Review*, 2018.

The Washington State Department of Financial Institutions. 2014. *2014 Payday Lending Report*. http://dfi.wa.gov/sites/default/files/reports/2014-payday-lending-report.pdf

Check for updates

CHAPTER 5

Ethical Issues Related to Payday Lending

Chris Robinson and Denys Robinson

INTRODUCTION

Countless articles in newspapers and magazines and books like Baradaran (2015) condemn payday lending as a social evil and payday lenders as unethical businesses exploiting the poor and downtrodden. Reputable organizations concerned with social welfare such as the ACORN and Cardus in Canada and Pew Charitable Trust and the Center for Responsible Lending in the USA have done extensive research into the problems caused by payday loans, like the debt traps for repeat borrowers and the excessive fees in the absence of effective regulation. These organizations and many more have called for government regulation or outright bans. Governments in the USA, Canada, the UK, Australia, and other countries have responded for the most part with restrictive rate caps and other forms of regulation, and in some US states and Canadian provinces, with outright bans on payday lending.

Historically, two central reasons for regulating businesses are: addressing market failures and concern for human welfare. Payday lending is an

C. Robinson (✉)
Faculty of Liberal Arts and Professional Studies, School of Administrative Studies, York University, Toronto, ON, Canada

D. Robinson
Masters student, Public Policy and Administration, Ryerson University, Toronto, ON, Canada

J. Buckland et al. (eds.), *Payday Lending in Canada in a Global Context*,
https://doi.org/10.1007/978-3-319-71213-0_5

oligopoly in Canada leading to non-competitive pricing behavior and abuse of market power. Moreover, the evidence in earlier chapters shows harm to customers and thus there is a prima facie case for regulating payday lending.

We pose and answer four questions to guide our examination of whether governments should regulate payday lending.

1. Do payday lenders harm payday borrowers?
   (a) Do they knowingly exploit payday borrowers?
   (b) Is there a wrong other than exploitation occurring in payday lending relationships?
2. Do payday lenders have an obligation to not exploit payday borrowers, even if it is legal to do so?
3. If the answer is yes to any of these previous questions, should the government do something about it?

Ethical reasoning is not black and white; it does not provide tidy yes or no answers to difficult questions. Different models of ethical reasoning might yield conflicting answers. We try to strengthen our argument by appealing to more than one strand of philosophic thinking. Accordingly, we provide three viewpoints on the ethical issues. First, we summarize the payday lending industry's argument for little or no regulation. Second, we present a normative analysis of payday lending that relies largely on a consequentialist argument in favor of regulation appealing to the work of other authors in this volume who present the extensive descriptive evidence of how payday lending functions and affects its clients and why it is harmful. Third, we summarize an analysis of payday lending using a corporate social responsibility model that incorporates economic, legal, and three different ethical perspectives. We conclude that the ethical analysis and the evidence of harm and obligation not only justify government regulation but also provide significant guidance as to what that regulation should be.

The Industry Argument Against Regulation

The industry describes the one-time borrower who has an unexpected cash crunch and no one but a payday lender will give her the money right away or at all. Either she has a terrible credit rating, or the bank will not grant loans that small. For example, she needs her car repaired. The story explains how she needs the car to get to work or she will lose her job. If a utility bill is the issue, it will cost her far more to reconnect her utilities after they are cut off than the payday loan will cost. If she writes a check to cover expenses and doesn't have enough in the bank to cover it, she will have to pay NSF fees and have her credit rating downgraded. Dollar Financial calls her ALICE, which is an acronym for the payday lender's alleged target customer: Asset Limited Income Constrained Employed. The payday lender provides a valuable social service by allowing Alice to keep her job or avoid extra expenses for her utilities. Yes, she pays a substantial fee to the loan, but the alternatives are worse. She knows the amount of money she will repay on the due date and has an agreement in writing.

In ethical terms, the industry argument is:

- The borrowers enter into the agreement freely (no coercion);
- They know the terms of the agreement (no fraud) and they are competent to understand the terms;
- The loan is not inherently harmful and the person needs it;
- There is no alternative means for the person to get a small, short-term loan.

The industry organizations and their member firms no longer claim that there should be no regulation. The argument now is to avoid banning payday lending altogether, and to make the regulation as "permissive" as possible. "Permissive" can refer to many different aspects of regulation of the loans, but the most important one by far is the limitation on the maximum fee that a payday lender can charge. To explain the permissiveness argument we need to divide the industry into two segments: storefront lenders and internet lenders. Storefront lenders are the public face of payday lending: Money Mart, Cash Money, and other chains and single stores in Canada and Advance America, ACE Cash Express, and others in the USA. While these storefront lenders also lend over the internet, they follow the law and their storefront practices in their online business. A separate group encompasses those payday lenders who operate exclusively on the internet. The limited evidence on the business practices of this second group suggests that some of them are violating the laws of every country in which they lend money, and that they engage in unethical practices in accessing the bank accounts and information of their customers. Consumer Council of Canada (2015) provides some evidence of this behavior in Canada.

These internet-only lenders are virtually invisible and they do not appear at regulatory hearings. The industry's associations of storefront payday lenders have been sponsoring research on internet payday lending, and they claim that the internet lenders represent a serious threat to society, because of their higher rates, worse business practices, and the difficulty of holding them to account. From this it follows, so proponents of payday lending argue, that the storefront payday lenders should not be regulated tightly because they are needed to prevent the greater evil of internet payday lenders.[1]

We will return to unpack the industry position after we have laid out more nuanced ethical analyses.

Exploitation, Fraud, and Coercion in Payday Lending

Alan Wertheimer provides the following definition of exploitation:

> An exploitative transition is one in which A takes unfair advantage of B. A engages in *harmful exploitation* when A gains by an action or transaction that is harmful to B where we define harm in relation to some appropriate baseline. A engages in *mutually advantageous exploitation* when, in relation to the same baseline, A gains unfairly or excessively by an action or transaction that is beneficial to B. (Wertheimer 1996, p. 209)

Unfair advantage then is taking a disproportionate part of the benefits from cooperation when compared to an appropriate baseline. What base-

[1]This argument was presented orally at the hearings in front of the Manitoba Public Utilities Board in 2016, but we do not have a formal written source to cite. The CPLA paid a person to speak in the public hearings and make this argument with a claim that research exists to support this viewpoint, but not to present under oath. This person was billed as if she were a member of the public speaking out of personal interest, and by getting her into the hearing under this guise, the CPLA was able to evade a submission of a written research paper and exempt its paid speaker from cross-examination. The industry associations also claim that payday lending is necessary to prevent organized crime from entering the business. We have never seen a scrap of evidence that organized crime currently lends any significant amount of what could be called payday loans.

line? Wertheimer settles on the hypothetical market price as an appropriate baseline to determine what counts as exploitative (Wertheimer 1996, p. 232). The logic is that, in a competitive market comprised of willing participants, a non-exploitative price is reached because neither party to any transaction has any special advantage in the transaction. In other words, the price that would be arrived at in the case where no one has the capacity to take advantage of anyone is the non-exploitive price. The non-exploitive price might not be the just price, since there might be external moral factors to consider—for example, the competitive market price for food might not be a just price when selling to someone who is poor and starving.

The evidence in Chap. 4 shows that payday lenders charge more than the competitive rate unless the regulations force them to charge no more than the fee that allows a fair rate of return and hence continued operation of the business. Payday lenders have shown that they will charge exploitative rates if left unregulated. Whether for reasons of financial exclusion, failures of understanding, poor financial decision-making skills, or some other factors, people will take loans at these rates. Thus failure to regulate the payday lending industry will lead to their clients being exploited.

Other accounts of exploitation are relevant for those concerned about the ethics of payday lending.[2] Ruth Sample's account of exploitation as found in her book *Exploitation: What It Is and Why It's Wrong* raises an important further question for those concerned about exploitation. One of the ways that we can exploit people is by taking advantage of a previous injustice done to them (Sample 2003, p. 57).

On Sample's account, one of the ways the payday lending industry exploits its borrowers is by taking advantage of the fact that they do not or cannot access cheaper credit through the traditional banking system. Insofar as this financial exclusion is the result of or constitutes an injustice—the payday lending industry is exploiting their customers by leveraging this against them.

While showing that financial exclusion is the result of or constitutive of an injustice is well beyond the scope of this chapter, there are prima facie reasons for thinking this is so. Financial exclusion is disproportionately experienced by otherwise disadvantaged groups and can be seen as part of

[2] For those interested in philosophical discussions of exploitation an excellent starting place is Zwolinski and Wertheimer's article in the Stanford Encyclopedia of Philosophy: https://plato.stanford.edu/entries/exploitation/

a pattern of unequal access to social institutions. Payday lending clients report feeling more comfortable in payday lending outfits, which could be a consequence of conscious or unconscious bias on the part of front-line bank employees.

In addition to exploiting their clients, payday lenders have also coerced and defrauded their clients. We can distinguish between consensual exploitation involving an unfair offer and nonconsensual exploitation involving coercion or fraud (Wertheimer 1996, p. 14). There is evidence that some payday lenders engage in coercive and/or fraudulent behavior, as related in Chap. 5. For example, some of the lawsuits and court cases filed in Canada included allegations that the lenders harassed defaulting borrowers in ways not permitted under the law. Rent Cash Financial (subsequently renamed Cash Store Financial) deliberately misled consumers with its posted rates and then subsequently tried to evade the Manitoba and Ontario payday loan laws altogether by renaming its payday loans as lines of credit, as documented in Chap. 7. Bruser (2016) reports on a lender who used the small claims courts to extract excessive payments from clients, relying on the judges' lack of education about how interest rates and loan contracts operate.

While there is a distinction between fraudulent and coercive lending and collection practices and charging exploitatively high fees, the reality is that these practices do not occur in isolation. Payday lenders frequently encourage their clients to take out loans larger than they need. Employee behavior is influenced by their employment environment. Payday loan stores must achieve enough volume to cover their fixed costs, as we explain in Chap. 4, and this leads them to encourage overborrowing. Even the industry-sponsored study by Ernst & Young (2004) states the industry is totally dependent on very frequent repeat borrowing for survival. It has been understood for sometime in the criminology literature that a factor in criminal behavior is subcultures that normalize the behavior (Heath 2014, chap. 11). This is often discussed in the contexts of street gang crimes, but companies have their own (often very consciously organized) cultures which can easily become criminogenic as in the case of Enron or, more recently, Wells Fargo. The package of criminal and unethical behavior in the payday lending industry should give regulators serious concerns for public well-being.

There is good reason to think that payday lenders are exploiting their customers and that this is wrong. While some of their exploitative behavior, specifically the coercive and fraudulent behavior documented elsewhere, is already illegal, charging exploitative fees is still permissible in most Canadian jurisdictions. While we should be concerned that exploitation is occurring, we should also be concerned about the ethical environment produced in the industry. Employees do not make decisions in a vacuum and a culture of ethical disrespect for their clients should be an area of major concern.

Cross-Subsidization and Repeat Borrowing

Baradaran (2015) and Mayer (2013) come from slightly different perspectives to identify an ethical issue inherent in the nature of the business. Payday lenders do not check creditworthiness other than to see if the person has a source of income. They do not charge differential rates for customers of different risk levels in the way that other lenders do. A significant portion of the operating expense of payday lenders is the cost of staff and debt collection agencies attempting to get repayment from the borrowers who default and the losses when they cannot collect. In order to compensate for this cost, the lower risk responsible borrowers pay excessive fees to subsidize the high risk borrowers who have much higher default rates. Mayer calls it cross-subsidization and argues that it is unethical. Banks either refuse loans to the risky customer or charge higher rates. Baradaran calls this the "sorting function" of banks.

The more common term in banking practice is underwriting—the process of determining the creditworthiness of the borrower. In economic theory, this is an example of adverse selection. Because there is so little control on quality of payday borrowers, there is an incentive for bad risks to gravitate to that market. Note that "bad risk" does not mean that everyone who has limited financial resources is a bad lending risk. If none of them ever repaid the loan, there would be no payday loan industry. Whatever descriptive term we use, the consequence is that the higher risk default group is subsidized by the lower risk group, and the fees are higher than they should be for the better borrowers. There is no ethical case for extending loans to borrowers who will not repay, and so fewer people should be receiving payday loans. With the much lower default rate, the remaining borrowers could be charged lower rates. If we adopt a consequentialist ethic, the lenders do not need to be doing this intentionally, but the result is unethical to all legitimate borrowers. The dollar amount of the exploitation is quite small for a one-time borrower, but it is nonetheless unethical. The dollar amount overcharged to a frequent borrower is much higher.

The same issue of adverse selection and cross-subsidization can arise in any credit market, since information is never perfect and the lenders cannot assess the risk level of every borrower accurately. The problem is far more acute in the payday loan market because the lenders exercise so little control and charge only one rate.

We show in Chaps. 2, 3 and 4 that a great many loans are to repeat borrowers and repeat borrowing is essential for the success of payday lenders. The most serious harm for repeat borrowers is not the unfairly high interest rates that Mayer cites, but the debt trap of being unable to repay the loan. Chapter 3 recounts considerable evidence on the findings from interviews and surveys in Manitoba about the harmful effects of payday loans on many borrowers, though not all respondents expressed that they were being harmed. Chapter 1 cites US studies that recount similar evidence.

A different subset of borrowers may be being exploited on the second condition. If their emergency need for credit is in some sense caused by background conditions of injustice, then the payday lender charging a high price for credit amounts to taking advantage of an injustice done to them. This is increasingly plausible when one considers that many payday borrowers are members of otherwise disadvantaged groups. Chapter 2 notes that almost half of the respondents to a survey of payday borrowers were Aboriginal peoples, a group that is identified as seriously underprivileged in Canada.[3] US evidence shows a disproportionate number of African-American borrowers.[4]

Payday Lending and Market Failures

A different approach to assessing payday lending can be developed from the work of philosopher Joseph Heath who articulated the market failures

[3] For example, see Aboriginal Affairs Canada (2013) with respect to income disparity.

[4] African-American neighborhoods are allegedly being specifically targeted, with such neighborhoods having three times as many stores per capita as white neighborhoods (King et al. 2005), and with payday loans "…now specifically threatening students of historically Black colleges and universities" (Center for Responsible Lending 2005, p. 1).

approach to business ethics in his 2014 book. Heath's view can be summarized as follows:

1. Markets are an institution we use to organize cooperation around production.
2. Markets provide us with efficiency gains by generating price signals to allocate resources.
3. Just prices are conceptually distinct and in practice quite different from the market prices used to send price signals.
4. Markets are best assessed on their efficiency.
5. Markets ought to be regulated with an eye to preventing market failures.
6. Where markets cannot be regulated for pragmatic reasons, market actors have a moral responsibility to refrain from exploiting market failures and generating socially inefficient outcomes.

On this view the question of whether or not payday lending is ethical rests on whether or not payday lenders are taking advantage of a market failure. We have shown in Chap. 4 that payday lenders do not respond to competition properly by lowering prices. We cannot be certain why this is, but it likely is some combination of an information asymmetry between borrowers and lenders (many borrowers do not fully understand the loans) and an incomplete credit market at the low end because of the large transactions costs associated with very small loans. Thus the high rates that the payday lenders are able to charge are the result of a market failure and are unethical. This view also entails that not only should the government cap rates on payday loans, the payday lenders are being unethical by charging the excessive rates.

Payday Lending and Self-Control

Apart from the issues of exploitation and market efficiency raised by payday lending practices, the existence of people caught in debt traps points to a deeper issue about well-being and self-control. Many of those taking out payday loans know that they are paying interest rates they cannot afford but still take out the loan. Anyone trying to control their weight knows that keeping a bag of candy in the kitchen cupboard is a bad idea. The same applies to spending: access to a credit card, or worse, a payday lender makes it harder to limit spending. Self-control is not simply a function of internal willpower. As discoveries in behavioral economics have shown (see Chap. 1), our environment substantially structures how we think and behave. Easy access to overpriced credit can be as bad for our pocketbooks as candy is for our waistline.

A Corporate Social Responsibility Analysis

Corporate social responsibility is a somewhat broader concept than a specific theory of ethics. Heath (2014) is not stating the responsibility of business in quite those terms, but he is close to it when he asserts that when a business cannot be regulated effectively and efficiently, the business still has an ethical responsibility to treat the customers properly.

Schwartz and Carroll (2003) present a model of corporate social responsibility that depicts organizations as having three overlapping areas or domains of responsibility: economic, legal, and ethical. A socially responsible company or industry is one that strives to earn profits for its shareholders, meets its legal responsibilities both in form and in substance, and acts ethically towards its stakeholders. Robinson and Schwartz (2017) apply this model to the payday loan industry of Canada and the USA and conclude the industry does not meet reasonable standards in both the legal and ethical domains, though it does meet normal criteria in the economic domain.

Chapter 4 shows clearly that the industry operates as expected in the economic domain. Schwartz and Carroll (2003, pp. 509–510) define the legal domain as follows:

> [The legal domain] … pertains to the business firm's responsiveness to legal expectations mandated by and expected by society in the form of federal, state, and local jurisdictions, or through legal principles as developed in case law … *restrictive* compliance [with the law] occurs when a corporation is legally compelled to do something that it would not otherwise want to do … *opportunistic* compliance [occurs when] … a corporation … actively seek[s] out and take[s] advantage of loopholes in the legislation to be able to engage in certain activities. In such cases one typically finds that the corporation is abiding by the letter of the law but not the spirit of the law.…

As we have already reported in Chap. 5, quite a few Canadian and US payday lenders have violated laws, and many of them have engaged in opportunistic compliance. Under Section 347 of the Criminal Code, no interest in excess of 60% was allowed in Canada, until the federal government amended Section 347 in 2006 and the provinces subsequently enacted legislation governing payday lending. Despite that, payday lenders were well-established in every province with an estimated total of 1000 stores in 2006. Even much more recently we see the same legal non-compliance in New Brunswick, which has yet (at the time of writing) to enact its proposed legislation on payday lending and yet there are 35 payday lending outlets in operation. We could continue listing the violations, but for a corporate social responsibility analysis, the case that the industry as a whole is not operating completely in the legal domain is established.

According to Schwartz and Carroll (2003, p. 513), activities would fall outside of the ethical domain when they are:

> (i) amoral in nature (i.e., with an unawareness or indifference to the morality of the action); (ii) take place despite an awareness that the action conflicts with certain moral principles (i.e., are unethical); or (iii) are only intended to produce a net benefit for the corporation and not for the affected stakeholders.

In their analysis of payday lending, Robinson and Schwartz (2017) assess the ethical domain using three different ethical categories: conventional, consequentialist, and deontological. No common agreement exists that any one of these ways of defining "ethics" is "right." We investigate all three to show that we reach the same assessment with all of them.

Schwartz and Carroll (2003, p. 512) define the conventional standard as "those standards or norms which have been accepted by the organization, the industry, the profession, or society as necessary for the proper functioning of business." The evidence on adherence to a conventional standard is mixed, although it has been more often violated in Canada than in the USA. On the one hand, society has legitimized the payday lending industry in the majority of Canadian provinces and US states by enacting laws and regulations to govern it. The payday loan stores operate in visible locations open to everyone, with prominent signs and advertisements. We have documented considerable harm to the users, but the same is true of alcohol, tobacco, and gambling, yet these industries all operate openly under government regulation. Even when payday lending was illegal under Section 347 of the Criminal Code, the Attorneys General did not prosecute any cases.

Industry codes of conduct are part of evidence of meeting the conventional ethical standard. The Canadian Consumer Finance Association

(CCFA) is the industry association and about 60% of the total outlets in Canada belong to it. The CCFA is a very recent name change for the Canadian Payday Loan Association (CPLA). The CPLA did have a Code of Conduct that banned rollovers and abusive collection practices and introduced other measures to reduce some of the worst aspects of payday lending, but there is no code on the CCFA website,[5] which is evidence of a decrease in compliance with a conventional standard. The CPLA brought in its original Code of Ethics before the federal government changed Section 347 to allow the payday lenders to exist under provincial jurisdiction, if the provinces passed laws to regulate them. At the time, many payday lenders were still charging full fees on rollovers, which built up huge debt traps very quickly. The CPLA members realized this couldn't continue and so moved to ban it for the members several years before any province did so. The provincial laws that emerged all banned rollovers and repeat loans using a variety of forms of regulation, but in this instance the CPLA had met a conventional standard by enacting its own regulations first. The disappearance of the Code of Ethics is one signal that the industry is less compliant now with a conventional standard. Robinson and Schwartz (2017, p. 9) note that the USA has two payday loan industry associations, both with a Code of Ethics. One large US firm, Advance America, has published its own code. We do not know if the US firms are actually following the codes, and now in Canada there is no code, only the provincial laws and regulations.

The industry was not meeting the conventional standard when it originally allowed rollovers. Although rollovers are now banned and the industry says it does not allow them, the reality revealed in testimony to the Manitoba Public Utilities Board is different. A customer simply goes to another payday lender and borrows immediately to repay a loan. The staff members in the payday stores know this happens often, and the significant number of borrowers with many loans in a year could only occur if those borrowers are taking another loan to repay an existing loan and avoid a default. In addition, adhering to the conventional standards includes following the laws and regulations, and we have referred to the many examples of material violations.

Robinson and Schwartz (2017) are inquiring into the social responsibility of the industry, but our question is somewhat different. We are asking if there is a case for regulation. Measuring the industry's behavior

[5] http://canadiancfa.com/consumer-protection/, accessed June 1, 2017.

against the conventional ethical standard answers that question for us, because every Canadian provincial legislature, the Parliament of Canada, almost every US state, the US federal government (for military personnel), and the UK have all passed laws and implemented regulations to govern payday lending, including rates caps, bans on rollovers, and limits on the size of the loan. Thus, by a conventional ethical standard, society has already accepted that payday lending should be regulated strongly.

Robinson and Schwartz (2017) conclude the industry does not meet a consequentialist standard. We have already reached the same conclusion in the previous section. We use some of the same evidence and though our reasoning follows a somewhat different path, both strands are consistent.

Schwartz and Carroll (2003, pp. 512–513) define the deontological standard to reflect a consideration of duty or obligation to society and individual members of society. This ethical category embraces moral rights, justice, religious doctrine, Kant's categorical imperative, and core values such as trustworthiness (i.e., honesty, integrity, reliability, loyalty), responsibility (i.e., accountability), caring (i.e., avoid unnecessary harm), and citizenship (i.e., assist the community).

Kant states: "Act in such a way that you treat humanity, whether in your own person or in the person of any other, always at the same time as an end and never merely as a means to an end" (Kant 1964, p. 96). The exploitation of disadvantaged populations like African Americans in the USA and Aboriginal peoples in Canada, the inevitable devolution into debt traps that many borrowers experience, and the overcharging, all of which we have documented throughout the book, are clear evidence that the payday loan industry treats its customers solely as a means to a profit.

We can cite many other examples of failure to meet a deontological standard. For example, payday lenders have often stated their fees in formats that seek to hide the real cost and the harm done. The business model requires that clients borrow repeatedly and become stuck in a cycle of debt, and the payday lenders are fully aware of this reality, as disclosed even in industry-sponsored studies like Ernst & Young (2004). We do not need to continue; the evidence is already abundant in previous chapters.

Returning to the Industry's Justification

There are quite a few aspects of the payday borrower's situation that the industry avoids acknowledging in its characterization of "ALICE."

Canadian payday lenders initially loaned only on employment income. The image it tries to create is that payday lending supports the hard-working people. That situation has changed, and they now accept retirement pensions, disability pensions, welfare payments, employment insurance payments, and tax refunds as the basis for loans.[6] People on these fixed and sometimes limited duration payments do not have the ability to work harder or longer hours to earn more. If they cannot meet expenses this month, the payday loan will make the problem worse next month.

The industry tries to portray itself as lending to someone on an emergency basis. As we have seen, a large part of the loans are repeats, often very many repeats in a year. What they borrow for is not unexpected emergencies, but ordinary living costs.

The evidence in Canada shows that payday lenders overcharge everyone if they are not regulated tightly enough on the rate cap. They are not rendering a social service when they overcharge vulnerable borrowers.

The industry claims that it reduces the borrower's problems of NSF checks and has worsened credit rating. This claim is particularly disingenuous, since the industry requires checks or direct debit authorization, and hence forces repeat borrowers into either NSF charges or borrowing at another lender. Reliable customers who repay their loans on time do not get any improvement in their credit ratings because the payday lenders do not report to the credit rating agencies.

Finally, there is the claim from the storefront payday lenders that we need to ease off on regulation so that they can combat the worse problems that internet payday lenders create. We have established clearly that payday lending has serious ethical deficiencies, and the least onerous ethical benchmark, the conventional view, supports regulation. The logical answer to any greater evil posed by internet payday loans is regulation of those loans as well, not higher rate caps for storefront lenders. In any case, there is no reason to suppose that higher rate caps will have any effect on inter-

[6] Lenders vary as to which of these payments they will allow as security and there is no industry standard.

net lenders; to the contrary, if the storefronts charge higher rates, then the internet lenders can also raise their rates.

Should the Government Do Something About It?

It is important to recognize that the mere fact that something is going wrong—someone is being mistreated, a negative consequence is being imposed on some portion of the population—does not entail that the government ought to act. It must further be the case that:

1. Government action will positively impact the situation.
2. Government action (including enforcement) will not be more costly than the badness of the problem.
3. Government action will not create some other problem or undermine a different value.

Government action has improved the situation of payday loan customers when we compare the situation before and after regulation, and also look at jurisdictions where there is weaker regulation. Without regulation, the rates are higher than they need to be. The rate caps in Canada that the governments of Nova Scotia, Prince Edward Island, Ontario, Saskatchewan, Alberta, and British Columbia enacted in their initial regulations were all much too high, as we show in Chap. 4. The lenders responded by raising their existing rates to the maximum allowed in each province, which shows clearly that regulation needs to be preceded by proper research. Only Manitoba investigated properly and set reasonable rates at 17%. However, all the regulations ended the practice of rollovers, introduced clear and consistent disclosure rules and imposed limitations on the collection actions applied to overdue accounts. A few years after its initial regulated cap of 25% was enacted, Nova Scotia reduced its cap to 21%, which saved borrowers a lot money but did not end the payday loan industry there. In 2016–2017 three provinces seem to have paid attention to the research produced in Manitoba and lowered their rate caps a great deal.

Government action entails two costs: government administration and lender costs and response to the regulation. We observe that in the provinces that allow payday loans, there are still many payday lenders after regulation. The cost to the government is buried in the much larger consumer affairs ministries, but there are very few staff members involved and so it seems reasonable to conclude that the benefits outweigh the costs.

In the USA, the regulation was much more restrictive in almost all states, and rate caps vary from less than 15 to 17.6%. The rates in unregulated states are slightly higher and so regulation does have a benefit for consumers. We are unaware of any rigorous research that shows consumers in Québec, Newfoundland and Labrador, and the US states that banned payday lending have suffered serious harm because they cannot go to a payday loan store. We have seen no evidence that there is a group of citizens in those provinces and states who are requesting the government to reintroduce payday lending.

The third condition is not always obvious. Consider that we no longer forbid adultery. In part this is due to difficulty and cost of enforcement, combined with it being unclear whether anti-adultery laws actually reduce the behavior. However it is also because the process of enforcing adultery laws involves the state peering into people's lives in a way that is inconsistent with the degree to which we value privacy.

We have shown in a number of ways that payday lending operates unethically. It exploits vulnerable groups, harms many who get caught in debt traps, and overcharges every responsible borrower. Regulation has improved the situation of payday borrowers because it has ended the worst rollover practices and reduced the rates charged. Regulation is already a fact of the industry, and the question that remains is how to regulate. In the last chapter we will present our recommendations for regulation that will try to meet the three conditions.

References

Aboriginal Affairs and Northern Development Canada. 2013. *Aboriginal Income Disparity in Canada*. https://www.aadnc-aandc.gc.ca/eng/1378411773537/1378411859280. Accessed 24 April 2017.

Baradaran, M. 2015. *How the Other Half Banks*. Cambridge, MA: Harvard University Press.

Bruser, David. 2016. XCash Offers High Interest Loans to Toronto Nannies—But the Rates Are Sometimes Over the Legal Limits. *Toronto Star*. https://www.thestar.com/news/canada/2016/10/07/xcash-offers-high-interest-loans-to-toronto-nannies-but-the-rates-are-sometimes-over-the-legal-limit.htm. Accessed 27 February 2017.

Center for Responsible Lending. 2005. *Access Denied*. CRL Issue Brief, No. 23, January 5. http://www.responsiblelending.org/payday-lending/policy-legislation/states/ib023-Access_Denied_HBCU_Payday-0105.pdf. Accessed 22 January 2011.

Consumers Council of Canada. 2015. Consumer Experiences in Online Payday Loans. https://www.consumerscouncil.com/site/consumers_council_of_canada/assets/pdf/ccc_online_payday_loans_web.pdf

Ernst & Young. 2004. The Cost of Providing Payday Loans in Canada. Ernst & Young, Tax Policy Services Group.

Heath, J., ed. 2014. *Morality, Competition, and the Firm: The Market Failures Approach to Business Ethics.* Oxford University Press.

Kant, I. 1964. *Groundwork of the Metaphysics of Morals*, trans. H.J. Patron. New York: Harper & Row Publishers Inc.

King, U., W. Lei, D. Davis, and K. Ernst. 2005. *Race Matters: The Concentration of Payday Lenders in African-American Neighborhoods.* Center for Responsible Lending Research Report, March 22. http://www.responsiblelending.org/pdfs/rr006-Race_Matters_Payday_in_NC-0305.pdf. Accessed 22 January 2011.

Mayer, R. 2013. When and Why Usury Should Be Prohibited. *Journal of Business Ethics* 116 (3): 513–527.

Robinson, C., and M. Schwartz. 2017. *A Corporate Social Responsibility Analysis of Payday Lending.* http://ssrn.com/abstract=3044087, forthcoming in *Business and Society Review, 2018.*

Sample, Ruth J. 2003. *Exploitation: What It Is and Why It's Wrong.* Rowman and Littlefield.

Schwartz, M.S., and A.B. Carroll. 2003. Corporate Social Responsibility: A Three Domain Approach. *Business Ethics Quarterly* 13 (4): 503–530.

Wertheimer, Alan. 1996. *Exploitation.* Princeton University Press.

CHAPTER 6

Mainstream Financial Institution Alternatives to the Payday Loans

Brenda Spotton Visano

Introduction

A common definition of financial inclusion is one in which citizens have a checking account at a mainstream financial institution—a chartered bank or credit union in Canada. By this crudest of definitions, Canadians are among the highest banked and so most financially included in the world with estimates varying from 96% to 99%. While the World Bank cites 99% of Canadians have a bank account (Demirgüç-Kunt et al. 2015), the lower percentage appears in studies that ensure low-income Canadians are appropriately represented in the data and so may be the more accurate number (Buckland 2012b). Access to basic banking services is a "necessity of everyday life," and as the Federal Government of Canada acknowledges "it is critical that consumers be treated fairly in their dealings with financial institutions" (Department of Finance 1999, p. 46). The availability of a bank account to Canadians does not, however, assure the effective access to safe, sound, and affordable basic payments, savings, and consumer lending services. The question is what opportunities do Canadians have to use their bank account for everyday transactions and to meaningfully access other mainstream financial services, including short-term credit for managing cash flows over short

B. Spotton Visano (✉)
Department of Economics, School of Public Policy and Administration,
York University, Toronto, ON, Canada

J. Buckland et al. (eds.), *Payday Lending in Canada in a Global Context*,
https://doi.org/10.1007/978-3-319-71213-0_6

periods of time? While most Canadian adults hold a bank account, there exist some costly barriers to using a bank account for the most economically vulnerable among us.

The current chapter chronicles efforts designed to ensure that Canadian financial consumers are not excluded by force—that Canadians have the genuine opportunity of accessing financial services supplied by mainstream financial service providers. This chapter first reviews the barriers to effective use of the baseline bank account for measuring financial inclusion: checking accounts. It then highlights some of the ways by which policy-makers through federal legislation attempt to ensure access to basic banking services at federally regulated institutions. It chronicles pioneering efforts by some financial institutions, municipalities, and communities to design products and services intended to overcome critical barriers. The chapter ends with a brief assessment of an old idea for a new way forward: the reestablishment of the postal savings bank.

In addressing issues of financial inclusion at higher levels of abstraction, banks and credit unions are often considered together as mainstream banking institutions. They are, however, quite distinct institutions, each with a unique history shaping their response to the current challenge of financial exclusion. Canadian banks can trace their history back to the creation of the Bank of Montreal in 1817, when a group of businessmen operating in what was then Upper Canada established a business primarily to offer both a uniform medium of exchange and credit for stimulating local commerce. Over the course of history since that time, profit-oriented banks have evolved in both size and function and have been the primary focus of federal legislation intended to preserve and protect the Canadian financial system. Presently, the six largest domestic chartered banks in Canada (Royal Bank of Canada, TD Canada Trust, Scotiabank, Bank of Montreal, Canadian Imperial Bank of Commerce, and National Bank) hold most of the assets in the Canadian financial system, operate over 5500 branches nationwide, and are the principal suppliers of checking accounts and other sources of payments.

Credit unions appear later in Canada's history with the creation of the first successful *caisses populaires* in Quebec at the start of the 1900s. Responding to an earlier form of financial exclusion that saw a prevalence of loan sharking at usurious rates as the only borrowing option for many working-class French Canadians, Dorimène and Alphonse Desjardins opened the first credit union in Levis Quebec (Desjardins Group n.d.). As of 2015, Canada had 695 credit unions and *caisses populaires* with well over 10 million members and more than 2600 branches (World Council of Credit Unions n.d.; Canadian Credit Union Association n.d.). Ian Macpherson (2006, p. 584), a notable historian of credit unions, states, these organizations "were not only mutual self-help societies but a strong moral and spiritual force." Where chartered banks have been motivated to address financial exclusion by requirements to comply with federal legislation (see below), it is the cooperative financial institutions, grounded as they are more in a community-based banking model, that have initiated many of the experiments with services and products that offer Canadians innovative access to mainstream banking services (Hopper 2004).

Barriers to Banking in the Mainstream

Financial Literacy

Why Canadians do not use mainstream banking services and demand instead high-cost payday loans on offer at fringe financial firms is the question that concerns us. Some argue that such use is due to an inability on the part of the Canadian financial consumer to properly assess the full cost of the payday loan and so incompletely understand how financially better off they might be using their bank account instead. The Financial Consumer Agency of Canada (FCAC) reports in its study of Payday Loan use that "the higher respondents rated themselves [in areas of financial competency], the fewer payday loans they had taken out" (Financial Consumer Agency of Canada 2016b, p. 12).[1] From this, the FCAC concludes that "[s]elf-reported financial literacy therefore correlated with both successful budgeting and less frequent payday loan use. Together with our findings that payday loan borrowers were unaware of the relative costs, this highlights the role financial literacy plays in reducing payday loan use and strengthening Canadians' financial well-being (op. cit.)."

Where the FCAC and others point to low financial literacy preventing accurate financial comparisons (see Boisclair et al. 2017, as well), it remains unclear if low financial literacy is a significant reason for financial exclusion in Canada (see Buckland 2014; Buckland et al. 2013).

[1] Respondents were asked to rate their literacy by rating their personal financial knowledge and ability to keeping track of money, making ends meet, shopping around for the best financial product, and staying informed about financial issues (FCAC 2016b, p. 12).

There will be many benefits to improving consumer financial literacy, but if it is not a significant cause of or not the only cause of financial exclusion, improved financial literacy and other initiatives targeting the financial consumer's abilities and responsibilities will at best complement efforts to target reduction of the true barriers. One Canadian study suggests it is a welfare wall and other systemic obstacles instead that may better explain the reasons Canadians avoid mainstream banks, opting to use higher cost fringe financial services instead (Buckland 2011). In general, studies by the Law Commission of Ontario and others suggest the relevant barriers for economically vulnerable Canadians seem to be more in line with the industry-based barriers—rather than consumer-based barrier of low financial literacy—found in developing countries.

Common barriers to financial inclusion apparent in many developing countries may be classified into four main categories: difficulty opening a bank account, high cost of maintaining the account, distance to banking services, and lack of trust in the banking institution (Demirgüç-Kunt and Klapper 2013). A closer look at the Canadian consumer finance landscape reveals some of these same industry-based barriers, but with a distinctly Canadian flavor. In 2008, the Law Commission of Ontario (LCO) reported on its study of check-cashing polices in that province, identifying more specifically the reasons for why low-income Ontarians may resort to using the services of check-cashing services and other fringe financial service providers: attitudinal barriers and identification requirements (difficulty opening a bank account), check holding policies, garnishment and setoff (high cost of maintaining the account), hours of operation and location (distance to banking services), and a lack of appropriate products and accurate financial advice for people on a low-income (lack of trust in banking services).

Attitudinal Barriers

Attitudinal barriers are the disrespectful or discriminatory treatment and judgmental attitudes that create a negative experience for the client conducting an in-person banking transaction. "Low-income individuals have expressed concerns regarding negative or discriminatory treatment by staff of mainstream financial institutions, or have expressed the perception that they don't 'belong' in such institutions" (Law Commission of Ontario 2008, p. 3; Realini and Mehta 2015).

Prejudice against those among us who look or behave differently or who are depositing welfare checks seems to be key reason for the disrespectful treatment of some patrons. "Many odd-looking people are simply escorted from bank lines by security guards. Income stigma is another issue. I have seen this personally, when shadowing clients at the bank. Tellers often treat people badly when they recognize that they are cashing or depositing various types of benefits of which they disapprove, such as welfare checks" (Stapleton 2014, p. 9). Buckland and Thibault (2005, p. 24), too, report on those who "commented on feeling alienation and discrimination; they often expressed feeling mistreated and disregarded by the bank tellers because they received social assistance."

Difficulty Opening a Bank Account

For a variety of sound reasons, ensuring a secure process of obtaining identification creates complexities that can cause considerable difficulties for the economically marginalized Canadian or newcomer to Canada. Canadians and newcomers in transitional situations, precariously employed, living a more transient life, or living with a disability (or often some combination of the former) may all have difficulty acquiring the appropriate identification required to open a bank account. Buckland, McKay, and Reimer (2016a, p. 14) highlighted identification as a critical barrier to accessing not only basic banking services but a wider variety of entitled benefits and services, "one barrier to financial services faced by Indigenous People is a lack of personal identification (ID), which is necessary for many financial transactions such as opening a bank account, filing taxes, and accessing the Child Tax Benefit."

The process of obtaining appropriate identification can be complicated further if the acceptable payments options for the identification itself are limited to a credit card or check, that is, the very payments options to which the identification is intended to access. The cost of the identification document itself may pose something of a barrier (e.g. the cost of applying for a birth certificate in Ontario is equivalent to three days of the food allowance calculated in student assistance). Further, in a number of cases, there is a circularity of the requirements—acceptable identification supporting a health card application may include a birth certificate and acceptable identification for the birth certificate includes the health card, for example. While circularity in document requirements may be surmountable, contradictions such as these may create an additional "frustration barrier" on first encounter. At the very least, it means for some Canadians and newcomers that securing identification requires dedicated assistance, advocacy, and support.

Box 6.1 lists the identification required to open a bank account, as posted on the FCAC's website.[2]

Box 6.1 Identification required to open a bank account in Canada

As listed by the FCAC at http://www.fcac-acfc.gc.ca/eng/resources/publications/yourRights/Pages/OPENINGA-Ouvertur.aspx#types

What identification (ID) do you need?

Choice 1: Show two pieces of ID from List A:

List A

- Canadian driver's license
- Current Canadian passport
- Birth certificate issued in Canada
- Social Insurance Number (SIN) card
- Old Age Security Card with your Social Insurance Number (SIN) on it
- Certificate of Indian Status
- Provincial or territorial health insurance card that can be used as identification under provincial or territorial law
- Certificate of Canadian Citizenship or Certification of Naturalization
- Permanent Resident Card or a Citizenship and Immigration Canada Form IMM 1000, IMM 1442, or IMM 5292
- Document or card, with your picture and signature on it, issued by one of the following authorities:

[2]The Financial Consumer Agency of Canada (FCAC) created in 2001 is an independent agency of the federal government "working to protect and inform consumers of financial products and services." For a summary of the FCAC's mandate, see http://www.fcac-acfc.gc.ca/Eng/about/Pages/OurManda-Notreman.aspx

- Insurance Corporation of British Columbia
- Alberta Registries
- Saskatchewan Government Insurance
- Department of Service Nova Scotia and Municipal Relations
- Department of Transportation and Infrastructure of the province of Prince Edward Island
- Service New Brunswick
- Service NL of the province of Newfoundland and Labrador
- Department of Transportation of North West Territories
- Department of Community Government and Transportation of Nunavut

If you don't have two pieces of ID from List A above, you can:

Choice 2: Show one piece of ID from List A and one piece of ID from List B.

List B

- Employee ID card with your picture on it and issued by an employer who is well known in the community
- Debit card or bank card with your name and signature on it
- Canadian credit card with your name and signature on it
- Client card from the Canadian National Institute for the Blind with your picture and signature on it
- Current foreign passport

OR

Choice 3: Show one piece of ID from List A and have someone at the bank confirm that you are who you say you are.

Difficulty opening a bank account may arise for reasons other than a lack of appropriate identification. Even with the two pieces of List A identification, for example, banks may refuse to open account for an applicant if they are wary of the applicant's desirability as a client. "Low-income people often have bad credit histories. Many banks will not allow a person with such a history to open a bank account" (Stapleton 2014, p. 9). "Mystery shopping undertaken for the Task Force on the Future of the Canadian Services Sector showed that refusals [to open a bank account] continued to be a problem even after voluntary agreement had been reached with the banks…" (Kempson et al. 2004, p. 4).[3] A poor banking history or low credit rating may be reasons for caution, but one cannot be certain of the accuracy of any such assessment that results in banning a customer without fuller transparency.

High Cost of Using a Bank Account

The high cost of maintaining a bank account includes direct money costs associated with high bank fees and the indirect costs flowing from garnishment and setoff. Fees for maintaining a basic transactions (checking) account can be high and levied as a fee per transaction on counter transactions, Automatic Teller Machine (ATM) withdrawals, check processing, overdraft, and bounced checks. As a result of recent changes in public policy, however, banks and federally regulated credit unions are now required to offer some banking services at a much lower cost (see *Federal Regulatory Initiatives* discussed below).

The cost of borrowing to cover a shortfall of funds for a 2–3-week period is often cheapest through an overdraft facility with a mainstream banking institution. As Chris Robinson calculates in Table 6.1, a borrower will generally pay far less for access to an overdraft facility than for payday loans. The exception is where a customer pays for a standby plan but uses it only infrequently. In this case, the payday loan will be cheaper than but not as cheap as the pay-per-use overdraft plan. The standby plan only becomes cheaper than a payday loan for someone taking out ten loans or more per year. The table shows the TD Canada Trust plan, but all banks have similar overdraft plans. Using the TD plan of $4 per use plus interest at 21% per month would cost the borrower only a fraction (19%) of the cost of a payday loan, if the payday rate is 15% (the current rate in Alberta and in Ontario starting in 2018). The savings are even greater in other provinces with higher payday loan rate caps. Notably, however, where more than one check is posted in the same period, the order in which the financial institution posts withdrawals can affect the number of overdraft charges. Banks may design posting order policies to intentionally maximize bank fee revenue. "Some banks reorder transactions from high to low by dollar amount, depleting the funds in the account more quickly and maximizing fee revenue" (Pew Charitable Trusts 2016, p. 5).

[3] Notably, the lack of a checking account will eliminate the possibility of acquiring a payday loan since a post-dated check or debit authorization is one requirement of the loan contract.

Table 6.1 Comparing overdraft protection with payday loan

	Payday Ontario 2018	*TD Canada Trust overdraft plans*	
		$4/ mo. + interest	*$5 per use + interest*
Annual interest rate (APR)		21%	21%
Monthly interest rate		1.75%	1.75%
Fee	15.00%	$4.00	$5.00
Panel 1: A single loan during the year			
Loan size	$300.00	$300.00	$300.00
Loan period (days) per loan	20	20	20
Total interest payable		$3.49	$3.49
Fee	$45.00	$48.00	$5.00
Total cost undiscounted	$45.00	$51.49	$8.49
Panel 2: Six loans during the year			
Loan size	$300.00	$300.00	$300.00
Total loan amount	$1800.00	$1800.00	$1800.00
Loan period (days) per loan	20	20	20
Total interest payable		$20.94	$20.94
Fee	$270.00	$48.00	$30.00
Total cost undiscounted	$270.00	$68.94	$50.94

Calculated and compiled by Chris Robinson
The person is paid monthly and repays each loan 20 days after borrowing

Strong financial literacy skills and appropriate financial advice will help customers choose the most cost-effective solution for their needs. When overdraft protection is unavailable, however, other bank fees such as the $35–45 one-time only charge for non-sufficient funds (NSF), for example, can shift the financial advantage in favor of the payday loan for some consumers.

In a calculation of the fuller costs and benefits, one considers the invisible costs related to the inconvenience of delayed access to funds due to a bank's "hold" on the funds as well as the indirect time and additional money costs incurred when bank holds or garnishment result in cascading money shortfalls. A bank's decision to impose a hold on funds deposited by check is a security measure involving some degree of bank discretion. As the FCAC states, a financial institution *may* place a "hold" on the funds,[4]

[4] http://www.fcac-acfc.gc.ca/Eng/resources/faqs/answers/Pages/AE256.aspx

- to make sure that the person or company who wrote the check has enough funds to cover the check
- to make sure that the person or company who wrote the check has not put a stop payment on the check (a stop payment means that, for some reason, the person or company that issued the check does not want it to be cashed)
- to verify the check details with the person or company who wrote the check, to make sure that it has not been altered.

In addition to the inconvenience and potential cost of delayed access to one's funds, garnishment is another costly complication. Previous financial difficulties can result in a creditor registering a lien against a person. When it is Canada Revenue Agency which "freezes" funds in a person's bank account as part of process to obtain payment for overdue taxes, there is a clear, transparent process to its resolution and reinstatement of access to the funds as well as a transparent process for correcting any errors. A bank or collection agency that has obtained a court judgement for an unpaid debt may also obtain a lien on a bank account for repayment, but there is no parallel ease of access and no transparency in the process for resolution and restatement. As John Stapleton (2014, p. 12) notes, "garnishment and offset" are possibly "the main reasons that people go off the financial grid."

Altogether, there are considerable compounding effects of holds, visible and invisible liens, transactions fees, and penalty rates on the already precarious income situation of the low-income customer. "When a lien gets placed on an account, there is no requirement to notify the consumer .... through right of offset, the creditor empties it. The fees for executing the lien are all charged to her, the account holder. She goes into overdraft. The NSF fees are very high" (Stapleton 2014, p. 13). In situations such as these, a payday loan may be less costly, assuming the borrower avoids the much higher costs of rolling over the payday loan and the resulting debt trap.

Distance to Banking Services

Location as a barrier to accessing banking services has always been a problem for remote and many rural communities. "Many rural and remote communities have no local banks or credit unions. As a result, people have to travel to other communities to open a bank account (the law requires this be done in person). This can be expensive for people with low-incomes, particularly those living in fly-in communities" (Prosper Canada n.d.). In addition, the closure of many city bank branches and the coincident opening of fringe financial service providers have compounded the location problem. As Buckland and Guenther (2005), as well as others (Brennan et al. 2011; Simpson and Buckland 2016), have documented, the geographical barrier imposed by the distance to a mainstream banking institution now affects inner city communities. The national charity Prosper Canada (n.d.) echoed location as a barrier, in addition to the unexpected fees and penalties, poor access to affordable short-term small-dollar credit mentioned above.

Lack of Trust

There are longstanding regulations in place targeting financial system stability by promoting trust in Canadian financial institutions as a safe place to deposit one's funds. Most notably, since 1967, Canadian Deposit Insurance Corporation operates a nationwide system of deposit insurance guaranteeing deposits up to $100,000 in the event of insolvency in a federally regulated financial institution. Ensuring that one's funds are safe in the event of a bank collapse is, however, only one of many sources of trust building.

Trust that the advice one is receiving is accurate, appropriate, and respectful is equally important. For many Canadians, the financial products available and the advice received are appropriate and respect communicated in a variety of culturally appropriate ways; for some though, this is not yet the case. Financial savings or loan products and services such as financial planning advice will be effective only when they are appropriately conditioned on the specific situation of the customer. Advances in both financial education and information and communications technologies make possible the mass customization of a wide array of these products and services. The similarities among and easy distinctions between most financial consumers ensure the best-fit take-up of standardized products and communication of appropriate mix-and-match advice. For Canadians and Indigenous peoples whose situations do not fit within the parameters defined by the majority, however, the lack of appropriate products and advice can cause a significant barrier to accessing financial services. As some suggest, bank staff are "often unaware of the entitlements and circumstances of low-income individuals, and may provide inappropriate or inadequate advice to individuals seeking assistance" (Law Commission of Ontario 2008, p. 29).

As one example, Indigenous peoples living on reserves or in settlement communities are ineligible for traditional mortgage products but instead require a product that accounts for the fact that only the building but not the land is their private property. And because of the significantly different tax treatments, all investment advice will be inaccurate if not appropriately informed and conditioned.[5] As a second example, low-income Canadians whose anticipated retirement income may be *higher* than their pre-retirement income are ill-advised to invest funds in a Registered Retirement Savings Plan (RRSP). Most Canadians can anticipate a retirement income that is less than their pre-retirement income. In these most common of situations, a RRSP is appropriate since it allows one to exclude from current income tax calculations those funds deposited in the RRSP. Taxing these funds later when withdrawn in retirement at a lower income reduces one's lifetime average tax burden. If the reverse situation applies, however, and one's retirement income is, instead, higher, this tax averaging via the RRSP may actually increase one's lifetime average tax burden. Since this non-traditional situation is most likely to exist for those Canadians with the lowest of incomes, such inappropriate financial advice risks a significantly regressive tax penalty.

Alternatives: Expanding Choices and Overcoming Barriers

Many acknowledge that there may be barriers to accessing mainstream bank and credit union services and some agree that ensuring access to necessary financial services is a collective responsibility. The attempts to overcome the barriers have, in recent years, taken a variety of approaches. The federal government exercising its authority over federally regulated financial institutions has extracted voluntary agreements and enacted federal legislation, some credit unions are partnering with local community agencies to develop community-based delivery models designed to reach the hardest to reach, and there are interesting examples of novel financial products, some aided by the advances in payments technologies.

[5] Historically, and for a variety of reasons, Aboriginal communities have had difficulty accessing basic banking services and business capital; see Collins (2011).

Federal Regulatory Initiatives[6]

The principal focus of federal government initiatives over the past 20 years has been on ensuring access to low-cost bank accounts for everyday transactions. In recognition of its public policy responsibility in this arena, federal legislation and oversight has targeted the reduction of barriers that make it difficult to open a bank account and that result in high costs of maintaining one once it is opened. "In 1997 the federal bank negotiated a new indemnity agreement with the banks. This agreement covers banks for checks up to $1500 that are cashed pursuant to section 458.1(2)(b) of the Bank Act (Law Commission of Ontario 2008)." In its 1999 report to the government, the Task Force on the Future of the Canadian Financial Services Sector acknowledged the role government regulation has to play in ensuring accessibility to basic banking. "Promoting equitable access for the less well-off, for seniors and for people with disabilities is an important public policy objective. ...Given the importance of ensuring that all Canadians can obtain affordable basic banking services, the government intends to introduce legislation requiring banks to offer a standard low-cost account" (Department of Finance 1999, pp. 47–49). "In 2001, section 458.1(1) was added to the Act. This stipulates that a bank must cash a federal check of up to $1500 without a fee for anyone, including individuals that are not customers of the particular bank" (Law Commission of Ontario 2008). Since then, the federal government has gone some distance to first persuade and then require federally regulated financial institutions to improve access to basic financial services (op. cit.). Subsequent expansions of this accessibility framework include legislation mandating annual Public Accountability Statements in 2002, the Access to Basic Banking Services in 2003, and the most recent (2015) extraction of a voluntary agreement of the primary chartered banks to offer no-cost basic banking services to some segments of the low-income population.

Public Accountability Statements

The legislation designed to promote transparency and public accountability for efforts to promote accessibility to basic financial services appears in the 2002 Public Accountability Statements Regulations (SOR/2002-133)

[6] All banks operating in Canada are chartered under federal legislation. It is these federally regulated financial institutions that are within the reach of federal legislation. Where credit unions may be chartered either federally or provincially, only the federally chartered and regulated institutions are subject to the federal legislation discussed below.

affecting banks and federally regulated insurance and trust and loan companies. The legislation requires these institutions to report annually on such efforts as the following:

- their goals in the area of community development and of their participation during the period in activities for the purpose of community development, including the making of financial contributions for that purpose (3ci)
- activities undertaken on their behalf during the period by their employees on a voluntary basis for the purpose of community development (3cii)
- charitable donations that they made during the period (3ciii)
- their philanthropic activities, other than charitable donations, during the period, including their total value in money to the extent that the value of those activities can be expressed in money (3civ)
- any new initiatives or technical assistance programs that they undertook during the period in relation to (a) financing for small businesses and (b) investments or partnerships in micro-credit programs; ...(3cv)
- an overview of initiatives undertaken during the period, by the declarant and by the affiliates in respect of which the statement is published, to improve access to financial services for low-income individuals, senior citizens and disabled persons (3f)

A scan of these Public Accountability Statements suggests that reporting quality has improved over time. Significant shortcomings remain, however. There are no benchmarks for accessibility goals against which to assess progress and the tendency to blend together compliance reporting with reporting on modest additional efforts risks confusion at best.

> Discussion of initiatives to improve access for low-income individuals is generally limited to account opening and check cashing procedures, availability of low-cost accounts, consumer education, and branch bank closure statistics. But little data are provided to demonstrate activities here. A small number of local projects, and a few that are more national in scope, remain at the pilot stage but offer little formal evaluation. Thus the reports provide evidence to support the first hypothesis, that banks are relatively inactive in addressing financial exclusion. (Buckland 2012b, p. 8)

Access to Basic Banking Services Regulations
Where the 2001 revision of the Bank Act requires banks to cash federal government checks on demand, even if the presenter is not a depositor at the bank, other checks may still be held for a specified maximum period of time. The 2003 *Access to Basic Banking Services Regulations* (SOR/2003-184) sets out the conditions under which a federally regulated financial institution may delay cash payment on any other check. For undamaged paper checks in Canadian dollars presented at the bank in person and drawn on a Canadian financial institution, a bank must make $100 immediately available, and the rest available within four business days (for amounts of $1500 or less).[7] For higher amounts deposited in an Automated Banking Machine (ABM), the hold maximum is eight days; yet, with the advances in electronic funds transfer technology and the Automated Clearing Settlement System operated by the Canadian payments system, these checks only take 1–3 days to clear through the Canadian payments system (Deloitte Canada 2011).

In addition, the *Access to Basic Banking Services Regulations* provides a

- statutory obligation for banks to open retail deposit accounts for consumers (FCAC 2007)
- reduction in the number of pieces of identification needed to open an account and an accompanying increase in the types of identification that were acceptable (Law Commission of Ontario 2008)
- requirement for banks to provide low fee bank accounts and reduce the other requirements needed to open an account. Minimum balances, bad credit reports and bankruptcy can not be used as reasons to deny the opening of an account (op. cit.), and
- a requirement, through the *Cheque Holding Policy Disclosure (Banks) Regulations* (SOR/2002-39) [subsequently *Access to Funds Regulations* (SOR/2012-24)] that banks disclose their check holding policies to their customers (op. cit.).

January 2015 Extension of No-Cost Accounts for Targeted Populations
In the 2013 throne speech, the federal government committed to expanding low-cost banking, and in May of 2014, the Minister of Finance announced

[7] For plain language details, see the FCAC's summary at http://www.fcac-acfc.gc.ca/eng/forConsumers/topics/yourRights/Pages/Checkho-Retenues.aspx

> that voluntary commitments have been secured from Canada's eight largest banks to enhance low-cost bank accounts and offer no-cost accounts with the same features as low-cost accounts to a wider range of eligible consumers. No-cost accounts will be available to youth, students, seniors qualifying for the Guaranteed Income Supplement, and Registered Disability Savings Plan beneficiaries. Banks have committed to bringing the voluntary guidelines into force by January 15, 2015. (Canada 2014)

The lasting force of this voluntary agreement may, however, be limited, if history is any guide. Past attempts to persuade banks to open bank accounts, offer low-cost bank accounts, and advance other measures intended to improve access have gradually been replaced with legislation imposing a statutory obligation. Most recently, the Government of Canada explains the need for additional legislation to limit bank fees in its January 2015 news release: "while demand for low-cost accounts had increased since their introduction in 2003, several banks had reduced the maximum number of transactions allowed in these plans. The result was an indirect increase in monthly fees" (Canada 2015).

Today's Regulated Low-Cost Banking Opportunity

As a result of federal legislation, FCAC oversight, and bank compliance, Canadians now have more low-cost banking options available to them than they did in 1998 (Box 6.2) (Financial Consumer Agency of Canada 2016a). The FCAC's public website lists a useful *Account Selector Tool* to

Box 6.2 FCAC low-cost and no-cost bank accounts (Financial Consumer Agency of Canada 2016a)

At a minimum, low-cost accounts include the following services where these services are available to the financial institution's other retail customers:

- at least 12 debit transactions per month, including at least 2 in-branch transactions per month where available
- check writing privileges
- a debit card
- unlimited deposits
- monthly printed statements
- pre-authorized payment forms
- check image return or online check image viewing.

Service fees apply to all transactions you make that are over your monthly limit; contact the financial institution for details.

And eligible to receive low-cost account services at no cost.

You may be eligible to receive a low-cost account for no cost if you are a:

- youth
- student
- senior receiving the Guaranteed Income Supplement (GIS)
- Registered Disability Savings Plan (RDSP) beneficiary

compare and contrast the suitability of over 100 different low-cost accounts now on offer by a variety of banks and credit unions

Product Initiatives

There are a variety of initiatives in loan and payments products that reduce or have the potential of reducing reliance on high-cost non-bank financial services such as payday loans. Credit unions such as Vancity Credit Union in British Columbia, Connect First Credit Union in Alberta, Assiniboine Credit Union in Manitoba, and First Nations Bank of Canada are leaders in the design and delivery of effective alternatives to the payday loan. Vancity and Connect First Credit Unions are piloting convenient small-loan products. (Vancity and Assiniboine Credit Unions and the First Nations Bank are experimenting with more robust community banking models; see "Community Banking Models" below.) Emerging from closely networked communities and socially-minded groups pulling together to help each other, a few of these efforts are exemplars of how local efforts can formally ensure the provision of critical financial services. In a different sphere, advanced payments technology enable some government agencies to ensure that the check-cashing process does not impose inordinately high costs on the recipients of some income supports.

Credit Union Convenient Small-Loan Products

There are two credit union products designed intentionally to compete with the payday loan. Both Vancity's *Fair & Fast Loan*[8] and Connect First's *Cash*

[8] https://www.vancity.com/Loans/TypesOfLoans/FairAndFastLoan/

Crunch Loan[9] share many of the same application features of the payday loan, for a fraction of the cost. Both products offer a quick (60–90 minutes) and easy (personal identification and a pay statement) application process for a small loan—up to $1500 for a *Cash Crunch Loan* or up to $2500 for a *Fair & Fast Loan*. Unlike the payday loan, the repayment charges and terms are much more favorable to the borrower. Rates are no higher than the average credit card interest rate (12% APR—*Cash Crunch Loan*; 19% APR—*Fair & Fast Loan*) and may be repaid in installments over a period of up to 18 months (*Cash Crunch Loan*) or 24 months (*Fair & Fast Loan*).

These are relatively newer products and whether they will be effective and viable remains to be seen. At the time of writing however, there were plans to expand beyond the pilot phase suggesting a favorable early performance.

General Emergency Funding Assistance

The Desjardins Fédération Fonds d'entraide Desjardin is a fund available through the network of *caisses populaire* in Quebec designed to provide small emergency loans of up to $1000. These small loans are interest-free, available on application for such emergency expenses as car repairs or dental costs, with the borrowed funds paid directly by the *caisse* to the merchant who owed the debt (Buckland et al. 2016b). Partnering closely with community agencies to deliver financial literacy and budget counseling services to borrowers means this product contains some elements of the more robust community banking model discussed below.

> The project involves the federation, a local caisse populaire and a credit counselling agency. The federation and local caisse provide the capital and contribute to the financial counsellor's salary. The local caisse agrees to maintain the loan fund by replenishing any loan losses. The budget counselling agency refers clients to the program, does pre-lending counselling and monitors repayment. As of December 2007, approximately $1.3 million in loans were made in 2,421 loans with an average loan size of $549 and a repayment rate of 89%. The typical borrower is between 25 and 54 years of age, often female relying on social assistance and with annual income less than $10,000. The Mutual Assistance Fund was operating in 28 locations involving 299 out of 536 caisses populaires across 15 of the total 17 regions of Québec. (Buckland 2008, p. 8; see as well, Marsh et al. 2010)

[9] https://www.connectfirstcu.com/news-events/media-releases/cash-crunch-loan-now-offers-first-alternative-payday-lending-southern-albertans

Dedicated Emergency Funding Assistance: Rent Banks

Rent Banks operate in several Canadian cities as part of a homelessness prevention strategy. The Rent Bank model pioneered by Neighbourhood Information Post (http://www.nipost.org/) in downtown Toronto offers interest-free rental arrears for anyone facing eviction and rental deposit loans for anyone having difficulty coming up with first and last month's rent. In a similar effort, the Network of Inner City Community Services Society operating the Vancouver Rent Bank reports (http://www.niccss.ca/VRB) issued 137 loans with an average loan of just over $900 in 2012–2013, its first year of operation.

Prepaid Benefits Cards: Toronto City Services Benefits Card

Reloadable debit cards eliminate barriers related to the use of checks. The debit card operates as user-owned payments medium; as such, it bypasses the recipient's need to convert the check into cash or bank deposit balances, thus avoiding altogether the check-cashing fees and check holding barrier. To the extent that it eliminates the need to open a bank account, it may avoid the very need to hold a bank account altogether, which then may increase rather than decrease financial exclusion, by definition (see Ricketts 2016; Monsebraaten 2016).

In 2012, the City of Toronto, in partnership with Mastercard©, introduced a Benefits Card for Ontarians receiving income supports. "The City Services Benefits Card is for Ontario Works clients living in Toronto who cannot access their monthly funds through direct bank deposit. Clients who receive checks often pay expensive check cashing service fees. The City Services Benefit Card is a new payments method that will help you avoid paying expensive fees. Once issued to you, payments will be loaded onto your City Services Benefit Card."[10] According to the City's promotion of it, the benefits of using the City Services Benefit Card include (City of Toronto n.d.):

- as convenient as carrying cash
- eliminates check cashing fees

[10] City of Toronto, The City Services Benefit Card. Ontario Works. Retrieved from http://www1.toronto.ca/wps/portal/contentonly?vgnextoid=95baa81204bc0410VgnVCM10000071d60f89RCRD&vgnextchannel=36b2d08099380410VgnVCM10000071d60f89RCRD

- protects privacy by not identifying cardholders as Ontario Works clients
- Personal Identification Number (PIN) and chip technology provides security
- works like a debit card but does not require a bank account
- can be used at ATMS and anywhere a MasterCard® is accepted
- online support for card balances and transaction history
- 24 hour automated and live customer care

The costs associated with this replacement option include some transactions fees, valid only for a limited period (with expiration after three months but can be replaced through the client's case worker), and cash withdrawal fees for withdrawals in excess of four per month. It will be interesting to follow this development and we look forward to seeing an assessment of its effectiveness now that it has been in operation for more than four years. Notably, it is attracting some promising attention, since the Ontario Government is seeking to eliminate paper checks for recipients of Ontario Disability Support Program. As with the City of Toronto initiative, it too is planning to introduce reloadable debit cards for recipients who do not have bank accounts.

Credit Union Community Banking Models

Where the banks are now statutorily required to offer low-cost basic bank accounts, credit unions have long offered free accounts and other breaks for financially vulnerable Canadians.[11] Some credit union initiatives designed to address financial exclusion have taken a fuller customer-centered, community banking approach.

> Community banks generally are relationship banks; their competitive advantage is a knowledge and history of their customers and a willingness to be flexible. (This is sometimes a problem, particularly in a regulatory system that reflects big bank processes, which are transactional, quantitative and dependent on standardization and mark-to-market accounting practices.) Their financials are different than those of the bigger banks, with less leverage and less—robust returns, and they tend to use less technology. (Lux and Greene 2015, p. 2)

[11] Credit Union Central of Canada https://www.central1.com/news/providing-accessible-financial-services-core-credit-unions

Partnering with local community-development agencies, store-front initiatives by credit unions such as Assiniboine Credit Union in north end Winnipeg, Manitoba, and Vancity Credit Union partnering in the operation of Pigeon Park Savings in downtown Vancouver, British Columbia, are two lasting examples.[12]

Both Assiniboine and Pigeon Park Savings offer low-income residents and underserved households with financial services and products tailored to their needs, designed specifically to overcome some of the key barriers to basic banking listed above, including and perhaps most importantly the attitudinal barrier.[13] In addition to offering low-cost basic checking services, low- or no-cost overdraft protection for small-dollar overages, and free savings accounts, thus removing the barrier of high money costs, dedicated attention is given to the fuller banking experience by working closely with community agency partners. At Assiniboine Credit Union, identification documents from a welfare office or generated in-house may be accepted (Buckland 2008), and the employees at Pigeon Park Savings, for example, are community workers from the PHS Community Services Society trained as tellers and branch managers.[14]

Financial consumers would be financially better off if there were effective lower cost savings alternatives to the high cost of forced income smoothing through the use of payday loans products and services for meeting unexpected and even expected expenses such as utilities. To address this need, Assiniboine Credit Union created the AssetBuilders Partnership with SEED (Supporting Employment and Economic Development) Winnipeg and the United Way of Winnipeg.

[12] Both have been in operation for more than ten years. The literature is sprinkled with references to other shorter-lived attempts to establish a store-front operation for serving the financial needs of traditionally underserved populations. For example, RBC operated Cash & Save in the low-income neighborhood of Parkdale and Regent Park (Toronto, Ontario) from 2002 until 2005. The Provincial Alliance Credit Union (PACU) was partnering with the Centre for Addiction and Mental Health (CAMH) in 2008 to extend check-cashing services to CAMH clients but was no longer operating after the amalgamation of PACU with two other credit unions in 2014.

[13] Assiniboine Credit Union https://www.assiniboine.mb.ca/PigeonParkSavings and https://www.phs.ca/index.php/project/pigeon-park-savings/

[14] PHS Community Services Society "strives to develop, maintain and promote affordable housing for adult individuals who are poorly served elsewhere in the community due to their physical health, mental health, behavioural issues, substance dependencies, forensic history, and for those who are homeless. All of our operations aim to foster a sense of community, encouraging members to accept and support one another while empowering them to determine their own course of recovery." https://www.phs.ca/

"Asset-building" is given an income-appropriate interpretation and includes education, computers, "or even a pair of eye glasses" in its list of supported assets. Further, participants in the Asset-builders program are eligible for the Matched Saving Account Program, a program that helps participants grow their savings by matching every dollar saved three to one with funds from organizations such as the United Way.[15] Since the program's inception in 2007, "more than 3,300 Manitobans have benefitted from the Asset Building Program. Collectively, participants have saved $1.2 million dollars, bolstered by $2.9 million in matching funds. Assiniboine employees embraced their supporting roles and in 2014 alone, 75% of employees raised $80,000 for Asset Building programs through the United Way campaign" (Canadian Credit Union Association 2015, p. 19).

Addressing a number of barriers simultaneously, the First Nations Bank of Canada (FNBC) adopts a community banking approach in its eight full service branches and two community centers. Chartered in 1996, FNBC operates in remote communities in Saskatchewan, Quebec, Ontario, Manitoba, Nunavut, Yukon, and the Northwest Territories. The FNBC addresses directly the specific needs of the Aboriginal and Indigenous peoples with products and services designed to fit the financial needs of people living in remote locations. "Our focus is the Aboriginal market in Canada. We are a leader in the provision of financial services to Aboriginal People and an advocate for the growth of the Aboriginal economy and the economic well-being of Aboriginal People. We increase shareholder value by participating in and promoting the development of the Aboriginal Economy."[16]

Government Postal Savings Bank

Postal banking has had a long history in Canada as elsewhere (Bickerton and Steinhoff 2013). Operating for 100 years from 1868 to 1968, Canada's postal savings banks offered Canadians a range of basic transactions and small savings options (Bunbury 1997). Closed in 1968 as part of the financial restructuring that saw banks move to compete more actively in the consumer banking markets, the possibility of resurrecting postal

[15] https://www.mtroyal.ca/cs/groups/public/documents/pdf/icp_caseletsassiniboine.pdf

[16] https://www.fnbc.ca/AboutUs/WhoWeAre/VisionPurposeValues/

banking emerges in the current financial landscape as a means of increasing access to basic banking services. For Canadians and Indigenous peoples living in rural and remote locations, banking services offered at postal outlets would allow greater physical access to in-person financial services. For those living in urban centers, affordable small-dollar "postal loans" could be an alternative product to the payday loan.[17]

With approximately 3700 rural corporate postal outlets servicing 4.6 million rural and remote addresses, post offices are significantly more widespread and wider reaching than the current branch network of banks and credit unions.[18] Consistent with its Universal Service Obligation, proponents argue that an expansion of the limited financial products and services currently available through Canada Post (money orders, prepaid payments cards, for example) together with an upskilling of employees in these outlets would significantly reduce the location barriers to basic banking services created by "bank deserts." "If Canada were to start a postal bank tomorrow, it would instantly become the most accessible bank in the country, with more outlets than all other banks combined. In roughly 2000 small communities which have a post office but no bank branch, it would revolutionize access to financial services, as it would for Canada's notoriously underserved First Nations population"(Cox 2013).

With a similar interest emerging in the United States for similar reasons, proponents of an American postal banking system see the possibilities of reaching the unbanked and underbanked through the offer of such services as bill payments, prepaid payments cards, check cashing, savings, identity authentication, and postal loans (US Postal Service Office of Inspector General 2014).

> The existing post office framework represents the most promising path forward for effectuating such a public option [of providing credit to the poor].

[17] The impetus for renewed interest in Postal Banking comes largely from a need to provide Canada Post with an alternative revenue stream to replace the lost revenue from declining letter mail services. See Anderson (2013), Canadian Union of Postal Workers (n.d.), and Le Goff (2005), all suggest that resurrecting postal banking could help "stabilize Canada Post revenue and services." "Postal Savings Bank is not to change the banking landscape but rather to 'breathe new life' into Canada Post" (Le Goff 2005, p. 20).

[18] Canada's postal system is now a blend of corporate (government-owned) and dealer (franchised) outlets. Dealer outlets are located primarily in urban areas (Canada Post 2015, p. 36).

> American banks long ago deserted their most impoverished communities, but post offices, even two centuries later, have remained still rooted in an egalitarian mission. There have never been barriers to entry at post offices, and their services have been available to all, regardless of income. (Baradaran 2015, p. 211)

Despite the growth of online and mobile banking as an alternative solution to the absence of branches in many rural and remote locations, there are a number of reasons why in-person financial services may be periodically needed in addition to opening the bank account itself. Face-to-face meetings and consultation still offer some important education, guidance, and advocacy access benefits, particularly for the underserved. The Task Force for the Review of the Canada Post Corporation (2016) recently acknowledged the potential benefit of expanding basic banking services as part of a "community hub" of essential services centered in the post offices in remote and rural communities. For those communities currently underserved by basic financial services as well as high-speed broadband access, basic office services (such as printing), and the like, the community hub solution is recommended by the Task Force.[19] More generally though, the Task Force (2016, p. 81) did not support the return of a full-scale postal banking system. Citing a third party expert, "market structures and macroeconomic conditions in Canada are unfavorable for a traditional postal banking model in which Canada Post would compete against Canadian banks and credit unions."[20]

[19] "In essence, the post office could become a community 'hub' since it would become a community resource center. Internet 'bridging services' would allow residents to connect to the rest of Canada, including businesses and various services at all levels of government. Where residents are not familiar with the use of the Internet, the local post mistress or post master would serve as a resource person, assisting residents with their connections to the wider world. The availability of Internet would also permit residents to engage in online banking as do most other Canadians. Credit unions and some banks (such as the First Nations Bank and many of the chartered banks that offer online services to rural, remote and Aboriginal communities) would undoubtedly welcome the opportunity to provide services to currently under-served rural and remote residents. Contacts could be identified at such financial institutions that would assist residents with their banking needs" (Task Force 2016, p. 76).

[20] The Task Force (2016, p. 81) reviewing Canada Post states, "[t]he overall finding by third-party experts was that Canada Post would be entering a well-established banking market that serves Canadians well, and in which a new player would have to earn its market share through fair competition. The basic pre-requisites are significant and include substantial investments in infrastructure, IT, security, acquiring new skill sets, and complying with increasingly complex regulatory requirements both domestic and international."

Remaining Barriers

Elements in each of the four categories of barriers to basic banking in Canada have been variously addressed by a variety of measures over the past 20 years. Federal legislation, with its national scope, explicitly targets the barriers related to opening a bank account and to the high costs of using it once it is opened. Additional efforts to introduce prepaid cards as the means of delivering benefits payments obviate the need to use the bank account altogether. The additional barriers addressed by creative delivery models piloted in specific communities have, to date, reached only a small, local segment of the wider population.

Receiving considerably less federal attention are the cost barriers stemming from garnishment and setoff as well as the high cost of non-sufficient funds (NSF), overdraft fees, and associated posting order policies. Federal solutions leave unaddressed as well distance barriers to the provision of in-person financial services in remote and rural communities. Finally, ensuring situation-appropriate advice and respectful treatment, as challenging as they may be for federal regulators and overseers to address, means both trust and attitudinal barriers remain.

Conclusion

This chapter reviewed products and services on offer at mainstream banks and credit unions designed to overcome some of the key barriers to accessing basic banking services. By virtue of the federal government's decision to enact legislation requiring banks to ensure accessibility to low-income clients on the heels of almost every prior voluntary agreement technically adhered to by the banks but deftly skirted in practice, these institutions are not otherwise willing to ensure accessibility in the absence of legislation. The question then is, from a public policy perspective, has the legislation gone far enough? The expanded use of high-cost non-bank financial services such as payday loans targeting financially marginalized clients suggests it has not.

While there are admirable attempts by some banks and credit unions in some communities to reduce the access barriers, there remain critical gaps in the availability of these barrier-free financial services to Canadians nationwide. Where pockets of access initiatives have gained considerable traction, the question remains for our purpose whether these efforts have resulted in any significant reduction in the use of high cost non-bank financial services such as payday loans by local residents. Such a patchwork of solutions, even if successful in reducing effective financial exclusion, remains ad hoc.

Resurrecting postal banking could be a structural alternative to the repeated attempts by the federal government to legislate access via federally regulated for-profit financial institutions. For meeting our public policy objective of "ensuring that all Canadians can obtain affordable basic banking services," an expanded mandate for Canada Post could be straightforward to implement, building as it would on both a rich history and a moderate enhancement of services already on offer at postal outlets located in bank "deserts." As with other well-established state-provided financial services designed to close gaps left by the for-profit financial sector, federally provided basic banking services in underserved urban, rural, and remote communities may be an old idea whose time has come again.[21]

References

Anderson, J. 2013. *Why Canada Needs Postal Banking*. Ottawa: Canadian Centre for Policy Alternatives. https://www.policyalternatives.ca/sites/default/files/uploads/publications/National%20Office/2013/10/Why_Canada_Needs_PostalBanking.pdf

Baradaran, M. 2015. *How the Other Half Banks: Exclusion, Exploitation, and the Threat to Democracy*. Cambridge, MA: Harvard University Press.

Bickerton, G., and K. Steinhoff. 2013. *Banking on a Future for Posts? A Financial Assessment of Postal Banking and Financial Services at Various Postal Administrations*. http://www.academia.edu/download/43548668/2013_Bickerton_Steinhoff_Banking_on_a_Future_for_Posts_Rutgers_2013_PDF_E-1.pdf

Boisclair, D., A. Lusardi, and P.C. Michaud. 2017. Financial Literacy and Retirement Planning in Canada. *Journal of Pension Economics & Finance* 16 (3): 277–296.

Brennan, M., B. McGregor, and J. Buckland. 2011. The Changing Structure of Inner-City Retail Banking: Examining Bank Branch and Payday Loan Outlet Locations in Winnipeg, 1980–2009. *Canadian Journal of Urban Research* 20 (1): 1–32.

[21] There is a well-established and widely supported practice of federal, provincial, and territorial governments providing a variety of financial services deemed too risky, too unprofitable, or otherwise too much in the national interest to be left to the private financial sector. Canada Mortgage and Housing Corporation, the Canadian Business Development Bank, the Bank of Canada, and the Canadian Pension Plan are but a few high-profile federal government examples.

Buckland, J. 2008. Community Banking Projects for Low-Income Canadians: A Report Examining Four Projects to Promote Financial Inclusion. *SSRN*, October 29. https://papers.ssrn.com/sol3/papers.cfm?abstract_id=1585804

———. 2011. *Money Management on a Shoestring: A Critical Literature Review of Financial Literacy & Low-Income People*. http://financialliteracyincanada.com/documents/consultation-2/Buckland-09-02-2011-eng.pdf

———. 2012a. *Hard Choices: Financial Exclusion, Fringe Banks, and Poverty in Urban Canada*. Toronto: University of Toronto Press.

———. 2012b. *Passing the Buck? Examining Canadian Banks Approaches to Financial Exclusion*. Research and Working Paper No. 49, Institute of Urban Studies.

———. 2014. Structural Barriers, Financial Exclusion, and the Possibilities of Situated Learning for Financial Education. *New Directions for Adult and Continuing Education* 2014 (141): 15–24.

Buckland, J., and B. Guenther. 2005. *"There Are No Banks Here": Financial and Insurance Exclusion in Winnipeg's North End*. Winnipeg, Canada: Winnipeg Inner-City Research Alliance.

Buckland, J., and M. Thibault. 2005. *Fringe Banking in Winnipeg's North End*. Winnipeg, MB: Canadian Centre for Policy Alternatives.

Buckland, J., A. Fikkert, and J. Gonske. 2013. Struggling to Make Ends Meet: Using Financial Diaries to Examine Financial Literacy among Low-Income Canadians. *Journal of Poverty* 17 (3): 331–355.

Buckland, J., D. McKay, and N. Reimer. 2016a. *Financial Inclusion and Manitoba Indigenous Peoples Results from an Urban and a Rural Case Study*. Winnipeg, MB: Canadian Centre for Policy Alternatives. https://seedwinnipeg.ca/files/Financial_Inclusion.pdf

Buckland, J., E. Sinclair, and K. Martin. 2016b. *Small Loan Workshop: Summary of Proceedings and Recommendations*. Unpublished manuscript.

Bunbury, D. 1997. The Public Purse and State Finance: Government Savings Banks in the Era of Nation Building, 1867–1900. *Canadian Historical Review* 78 (4): 566–599.

Canada. 2014. *Harper Government Secures Commitment from Largest Banks to Offer No-Cost Accounts for Financially Vulnerable Canadians*. May 27. http://www.fin.gc.ca/n14/14-073-eng.asp

———. 2015. *Enhanced Low-Cost and No-Cost Banking Services Now Available to Canadians*. January 15. http://news.gc.ca/web/article-en.do?nid=921119

Canada Post. 2015. *Annual Report 2015*. https://www.canadapost.ca/assets/pdf/aboutus/financialreports/2015_ar_complete_en.pdf

Canadian Credit Union Association. 2015. *Credit Union Community and Economic Impact Report*. https://www.ccua.com/~/media/CCUA/member_corner/CUSR/2015%20Credit%20Union%20Community%20and%20Economic%20Impact%20Report%20FINAL.pdf?la=en

———. n.d. *Credit Unions in Canada*. https://www.ccua.com/credit_unions_in_canada

Canadian Union of Postal Workers. n.d. *Postal Banking*. http://www.cupw.ca/en/campaign/resources/postal-banking

City of Toronto. n.d. *The City Services Benefit Card*. Ontario Works. http://www1.toronto.ca/wps/portal/contentonly?vgnextoid=95baa81204bc0410VgnVCM10000071d60f89RCRD&vgnextchannel=36b2d08099380410VgnVCM10000071d60f89RCRD

Collins, D. 2011. *Aboriginal Financial Literacy in Canada: Issues and Directions*. http://epe.lac-bac.gc.ca/100/200/301/taskforce_fin_literacy/aboriginal_financial-e/F2-201-2011-eng.pdf

Cox, E. 2013. How to Save Canada Post. *National Post*, December 16. http://news.nationalpost.com/full-comment/ethan-cox-how-to-save-canada-post

Deloitte Canada. 2011. *The Canadian Payments Landscape*. Report submitted to the Federal Task Force on Payments System Review. http://paymentsystemreview.ca/wp-content/uploads/Payments-Landscape-Main-Report.pdf

Demirgüç-Kunt, A., and L. Klapper. 2013. Measuring Financial Inclusion: Explaining Variation in Use of Financial Services Across and Within Countries. *Brookings Papers on Economic Activity* 2013 (1): 279–321.

Demirgüç-Kunt, A., L.F. Klapper, D. Singer, and P. van Oudheusden. 2015. *The Global Findex Database 2014: Measuring Financial Inclusion around the World*. World Bank Policy Research Working Paper, No. 7255. https://www.responsiblefinanceforum.org/wp-content/uploads/Global_Findex_2014.pdf

Department of Finance. 1999. *Reforming Canada's Financial Services Sector – A Framework for the Future*. Ottawa: Supply and Services Canada. http://publications.gc.ca/collections/Collection/F2-136-1999E.pdf

Desjardins Group. n.d. *Our History, Our Museum*. https://www.desjardins.com/ca/about-us/desjardins/who-we-are/our-history-museum/?navigMW=ari&

Financial Consumer Agency of Canada. 2007. *CG-2 Access to Basic Banking Services Regulations: Refusal to Open an Account*. http://www.fcac-acfc.gc.ca/Eng/forIndustry/publications/commissionerGuidance/Pages/CG2AccesDC2Regra.aspx

———. 2016a. *Low Cost Bank Accounts*. http://www.fcac-acfc.gc.ca/Eng/forConsumers/topics/banking/Pages/LowCostA-Comptesa.aspx

———. 2016b. *Payday Loans: Market Trends*. https://www.canada.ca/en/financial-consumer-agency/programs/research/payday-loans-market-trends.html

Hopper, J. 2004. *'Credit Union Firsts' Commemorate a Strong History of Innovation*. http://www.woccu.org/newsroom/releases/Credit_Union_Firsts_commemorate_a_strong_history_of_innovation

Kempson, E., A. Atkinson, and O. Pilley. 2004. *Policy Level Response to Financial Exclusion in Developed Economies: Lessons for Developing Countries*. Report of Personal Finance Research Centre, University of Bristol. https://www.researchgate.net/profile/Adele_Atkinson/publication/241102753_Policy_level_response_to_financial_exclusion_in_developed_economies_lessons_for_developing_countries/links/0a85e52d653a4ad542000000.pdf

Law Commission of Ontario. 2008. *Appendix C: Federal Initiatives*. http://www.lco-cdo.org/fees/Fees-Cashing-Government-Checks-Final-Report.pdf

Le Goff, P. 2005. *Canada Post Corporation as a Provider of Financial and Government Services: The Way of the Future?* Parliamentary Information and Research Service. http://publications.gc.ca/Collection-R/LoPBdP/PRB-e/PRB0514-e.pdf

Lux, M., and R. Greene. 2015. *The State and Fate of Community Banking*. M-RCBG Associate Working Paper, No. 37. https://www.communitybanking.org/documents/Session3_Paper1_Lux.pdf

MacPherson, I. 2006. *Credit Unions*. The Canadian Encyclopedia. http://www.thecanadianencyclopedia.ca/en/article/credit-unions/

Marsh, S., Y. Dildar, and R. Janzen. 2010. *Payday Lending: In Search of a Local Alternative*. Centre for Community Based Research.

Monsebraaten, L. 2016. Ontario Trades Checks for Debit Cards for Disabled People. *The Toronto Star*. https://www.thestar.com/news/gta/2016/05/16/ontario-trades-checks-for-debit-cards-for-disabled-people-on-welfare.html

Pew Charitable Trusts. 2016. *How a Set of Small Banks Compares on Overdraft: An Analysis of Programs, Fees, and Terms at 45 Financial Institutions*. http://www.pewtrusts.org/en/research-and-analysis/reports/2016/12/how-a-set-of-small-banks-compares-on-overdraft

Prosper Canada. n.d. *Barriers to Safe and Affordable Financial Products and Services for People on Low Incomes*. http://prospercanada.org/prospercanada/media/PDF/News/Barriers-safefinancialproducts-PDF.pdf

Realini, C., and K. Mehta. 2015. *Financial Inclusion at the Bottom of the Pyramid*. Victoria, BC: FriesenPress.

Ricketts, J. 2016. *The Impact of Financial Exclusion on Vulnerable Groups Accessing Check Cashing Services*. Unpublished manuscript, York University.

Simpson, W., and J. Buckland. 2016. Dynamics of the Location of Financial Institutions: Who Is Serving the Inner City? *Economic Development Quarterly* 30 (4): 358–370.

Stapleton, J. 2014. *Welcome to the Financial Mainstream? The Hazards Facing Low Income People When Navigating the Financial World*. Prepared by John Stapleton for Houselink (with Max Wallace), Edited by Sally McBeth, Clear Language and Design. http://openpolicyontario.com/wp/wp-content/uploads/2012/02/jsbb-report-v2-R9.pdf

Task Force for the Review of the Canada Post Corporation. 2016. *Canada Post in the Digital Age*. https://www.tpsgc-pwgsc.gc.ca/examendepostescanada-canadapostreview/rapport-report/consult-eng.html

U.S. Postal Service Office of Inspector General. 2014. *Providing Non-Bank Financial Services for the Underserved*. https://www.uspsoig.gov/document/providing-non-bank-financial-services-underserved

World Council of Credit Unions. n.d. *Our Global Reach*. https://www.woccu.org/impact/global_reach

CHAPTER 7

Payday Lending Regulations

Katrine Dilay and Byron Williams

Overview

Payday lenders offer relatively short-term smaller dollar loans to consumers whose needs are not fully met by mainstream banks and credit unions. While payday loans may be particularly attractive for vulnerable consumers with a bad credit history who do not have sufficient access to credit cards or bank loans, the charges on these loans can represent an Annual Percentage Rate (APR) upwards of 500%—a rate well in excess of the 60% usury limit identified in Canada's Criminal Code.[1]

In 2007, faced with a legislative vacuum flowing from the gap in regulation for a rapidly growing credit product during the 1990s and challenges in enforcing the *Criminal Code* prohibition on usury,[2] the federal government chose to create an exemption for payday lenders in those

[1] For example, in Manitoba, the maximum allowable cost of credit is 17% of the amount borrowed regardless of term, which yields an Annual Percentage Rate of 621% for a ten-day loan.

[2] The lack of enforcement of usury laws was likely due to the laws being meant to apply to loan sharking.

K. Dilay (✉) • B. Williams
Public Interest Law Centre, Winnipeg, MB, Canada

J. Buckland et al. (eds.), *Payday Lending in Canada in a Global Context*,
https://doi.org/10.1007/978-3-319-71213-0_7

provinces where the government would regulate payday lenders. The creation of this exemption represented recognition by the federal government of the role for payday lenders in the modern Canadian marketplace, notwithstanding certain features of payday loans, such as their high fees, that are often criticized by consumer advocates.

Left with some discretion on how to regulate the payday lending market, provincial governments initiated a regulatory response in an attempt to protect consumers through regulation while allowing the payday lending market to continue operating. The different approaches in legislation regulating payday lenders in Canadian provinces and in the United States (US) demonstrate that governments and regulators have not agreed on a unified regulatory model.

Introduction: The Rationale for Government Intervention

While markets play an important role in Western economies, governments, to varying extents, will choose to intervene in and regulate the marketplace. Efficiency, ethical, and political rationales are often cited in support of government intervention in the economy (Iacobucci and Trebilcock 2012):

> Many of the rationales for regulating can be described as instances of 'market failure'. Regulation in such cases is argued to be justified because the uncontrolled marketplace will, for some reason, fail to produce behavior or results in accordance with the public interest. (Baldwin et al. 2011)

Critics, such as consumer organizations and advocates, argue that the payday lending marketplace is characterized by market failure associated with both an absence of effective price competition and a disproportionate number of vulnerable consumers and so requires government intervention. Such intervention can be in the form of regulations setting price caps, limiting the number of loans one customer can take out, or licensing payday lending outlets.

Once a government decides to intervene in a market, there are a number of levels and forms of intervention (Iacobucci and Trebilcock 2012). Economic regulation is a form of government intervention designed to influence the behavior of firms and individuals in the private sector. "Regulation consists of rules administered by a government agency to influence economic activity by determining prices, product standards and types, and the conditions upon which new firms may enter an industry" (Parkin and Bade 2006).

There are various approaches taken by government intervention in this industry. A few provinces and territories have chosen not to set price caps but to rely on the *Criminal Code* usury law, which criminalizes interest rates higher than 60% (Government of Canada 1985). Québec, based on pre-existing legislation, effectively prohibits payday lenders by setting the maximum allowable annual interest rate in the province at 35%.

Many provinces have chosen to enact legislation and regulations establishing price caps—maximum prices that payday lenders are allowed to charge—and additional restrictions and prohibitions applying to the payday lending industry. The price caps ranged from relatively high, with the objective of allowing all existing firms in the marketplace to continue operating, while others were set lower, to disallow higher fees.

Government regulation in Canada has been a key tool in responding to and driving change in the payday lending marketplace. While provinces began regulating the industry after amendments to the *Criminal Code* a decade ago, governments still appear to be adjusting their regulations. Recent developments in Alberta, Ontario, and British Columbia suggest a trend toward lower price caps.

Usury Laws

While opinions about the ethics of charging interest have changed as commerce expanded and credit became an important part of doing business, throughout much of recorded history, many governments around the world have limited the interest rate that a lender can charge in order to prevent lenders from taking advantage of borrowers (Ellis 1998; Kitching 2006). These limits are known as laws against usury. "Usury" is defined in the *Oxford Dictionary* as the "action or practice of lending money at unreasonably high rates of interest" (Oxford 1884). As noted by Bellam and Talai:

> The antecedents of modern usury law can be traced all the way back to the Babylonian code of Hammurabi, the Book of Deuteronomy of the Old Testament, and the Koran. The breadth and significance of these sources demonstrates a remarkably universal moral and social condemnation of excessive interest rates. (Bellam and Talai 2012)

The biblical origins of the prohibition on usury appear to derive from the principle that charging interest is taking advantage of the debtor (Ellis 1998). The Greek philosopher Plato condemned charging interest because "he felt that it produced an inequality of wealth and destroyed the harmony between citizens of the state" (Ellis 1998). Plato suggested that some members of society need to be protected from lenders, a concept which still appears in today's interest rate laws (Ellis 1998).

In the modern financial landscape, usury laws or similar laws are still present in many countries, although, in some of the earlier cases, the rationale appeared to be geared less toward universal disallowance and more toward disallowing the practice of loan sharking and related activities.

Legislative History of Usury Laws in Canada

Sometimes a distinction is made between the continental (European) and the Anglo-American approaches to usury regulations. The continental approach, which has informed the approach currently in place in the province of Québec, places the usury rate relatively low; for instance, the rate is set at 35% in Quebec. The Anglo-American approach has tended to allow a higher rate for usury ceilings or has left regulation under the jurisdiction of the state or the province.

Canadian legislative efforts to combat predatory lending practices have traversed an uneven pendulum ranging from very restrictive limits under national small loans legislation, to criminalization under the *Criminal Code* (Government of Canada 1985), to a focus on product-based provincial regulatory interventions through price caps. A useful overview of this history can be found in a 2008 report of the Manitoba Public Utilities Board (PUB 2008). While this chapter focuses on the regulation of payday loans, regulation also exists for other types of financial products, such as government check cashing and rates for income tax returns (at the federal level).

Section 347 of the *Criminal Code* replaced the *Small Loans Act*, which had been enacted in 1939 to replace an earlier version from 1907 (PUB 2008).[3] The intention of the *Small Loans Act* in 1939 was to set an acceptable rate of the costs of small loans such that companies would still be able to give out small loans and be profitable, as opposed to people having to turn to loan sharks (Act 1939). The interest rate limits of the 1907 and

[3]The 1907 and 1939 laws represented Parliament's exercise of its constitutional right to regulate national interest rates. The *Small Loans Act* defined a small loan as a loan at or below $1500, with legislated maximum rates of interest being 24% to $300, 12% on sums between $301 and $1000, and 6% on sums between $1001 and $1500.

1939 laws were much stricter than the current 60% established by Section 347 and they specifically targeted small consumer loans (Act 1939).

The limits under the *Small Loans Act* of 1939 were 2% per month for loans of 15 months or less and 1% for loans of more than 15 months (Act 1939).[4] It appears that the main motivation for the repeal of the *Small Loans Act* and for limits to small loans to be included under the *Criminal Code* was its adverse effects on credit unions and *caisses populaires*, which were not as common in 1930. This is largely because the restrictions on small loans applied to them, as opposed to federal chartered banks, and rendered them unable to turn a profit on their loans. Many financial institutions would not give out loans of less than $1500 because of the differing regulations. The 1980 changes were to maintain the originally intended protections against loan sharks through added provisions in the *Criminal Code* (Government of Canada 1980a,b,c).

The repeal of the *Small Loans Act* in 1981 meant that all loans became covered by the *Criminal Code*. Section 347 of the *Criminal Code* went far beyond the scope of the previous legislation both by "criminalizing a particular interest rate for the first time, and by imposing a generally applicable ceiling on all types of credit arrangements without regard to the sophistication of the parties or the amount in issue."[5] The higher allowable maximum interest rates applying to all loans represented a new reliance on

[4] Section 3(2) stated that: The cost of the loan mentioned in subsection one of this section shall, for a loan for a period of fifteen months or less, not exceed two per centum per month on the amount actually advanced to the borrower and monthly balances thereof from time to time outstanding, and, for a loan for a period greater than fifteen months, the cost of the loan shall not exceed one per centum per month on the amount actually advanced to the borrower and monthly balances thereof from time to time outstanding and in addition thereto such proportion of one per centum per month on said amount and balances thereof from time to time outstanding and in addition thereto such proportion of one per centum per month on the said amount and balances as fifteen is of the period of the loan expressed in months.

[5] Section 347(1) provides that: Despite any other Act of Parliament, everyone who enters into an agreement or arrangement to receive interest at a criminal rate, or receives a payment or partial payment of interest at a criminal rate, is

- guilty of an indictable offence and liable to imprisonment for a term not exceeding five years; or
- guilty of an offence punishable on summary conviction and liable to a fine not exceeding $25,000 or to imprisonment for a term not exceeding six months or to both.

Section 347(2) provides the following definition:

> criminal rate means an effective annual rate of interest calculated in accordance with generally accepted actuarial practices and principles that exceeds <u>sixty per cent</u> on the credit advanced under an agreement or arrangement. [emphasis added]

the marketplace to provide fair rates for consumers, rather than the federally determined market maximum rates (PUB 2008).

It appears that section 347 of the *Criminal Code* was designed to criminalize loan sharking, which has been described as "unlicensed street-lenders offering credit at exorbitant rates and employing intimidation and violence to enforce their contracts" (Uniform Law Conference 2008; Garland 1998). Prior to the changes made in 1980, loan sharks had been prosecuted under various criminal offenses and under the *Small Loans Act*, which required lenders to be licensed. When the decision was made to repeal the *Small Loans Act*, there was a concern that illicit lenders would be left unchecked and the *Criminal Code* provisions were created in part to address these concerns (Uniform Law Conference 2008). There were some concerns regarding the *Criminal Code* interest rate:

> The decision to tackle the problem of loan sharking by way of a criminal interest rate was questioned by some, including members of the Senate Standing Committee on Banking, Trade and Commerce. Some Senators questioned whether sixty percent was too high; other Senators were concerned that setting a fixed rate at 60 percent would send a message that loans with interest rates of 60 percent or less would be given legitimacy. (Uniform Law Conference 2008)

Some of the reasons for using a fixed rate in the *Criminal Code* have been argued to be certainty and the importance of having the elements of the criminal offense clearly defined (Uniform Law Conference 2008). Another stated reason was for practicality: it would be easier to prove the offense of loan sharking through evidence of an agreement in violation of an objectively determined criminal interest rate rather than proving the violence or intimidation associated with the act of loan sharking (Uniform Law Conference 2008).

While the Department of Justice initially considered setting the criminal interest rate at lower than 60%, bankers and investors expressed concerns that a lower rate could interfere with legitimate financial transactions, such as short-term lending and the funding of high-risk ventures (Uniform Law Conference 2008).

While section 347 was enacted to address problems associated with the void in statutory response to loan sharking, the provision has rarely been used for that effect (Uniform Law Conference 2008). It has been applied "to a very broad range of commercial and consumer transactions involving the advancement of credit, including secured and unsecured loans, mortgages and commercial financing agreements" (Uniform Law Conference 2008; Garland 1998).

The Regulation of Payday Loans in Canada

Criminal Code Exemption

Payday lenders began offering their services in Canada in the late 1990s/early 2000s, approximately ten years after the practice became prominent in the United States, following a court decision allowing banks to circumvent state anti-usury laws (PUB 2008). While sub-prime consumer loans existed in Canada before the entrance of payday lenders in the marketplace, finance companies usually respected anti-usury laws by offering loans with interest rates below the *Criminal Code*'s 60% cap (PUB 2008).

Prior to the entrance of payday lenders in the marketplace, borrowers typically relied on banks, credit unions, finance companies, employers, family, and pawnshops (PUB 2008). Before direct payroll deposit and the out-sourcing of payroll became common practice, some employers offered payroll advances to employees, often with no interest charges (PUB 2008). Anecdotes find that in some industrial settings and factories, employees had access to short-term loans through "lunch-box" lending, where a fellow employee would make a short-term loan to the next payday to colleagues (PUB 2008).

While section 347 of the *Criminal Code* would appear to make unlawful practices associated with payday lending, most lenders had a different perspective. The Manitoba Public Utilities Board explained in 2008 that most lenders had structured their products to avoid the *Criminal Code* prohibition (PUB 2008). Before the changes to the *Criminal Code*, most payday lenders charged both interest, at no more than the allowable 60%, and non-interest charges, such as brokerage, check cashing, administration, and/or other fees (PUB 2008). When both the interest and other charges and fees were taken into account, payday lenders were charging borrowers ten times and more the maximum specified in section 347 of the *Criminal Code* (PUB 2008).

For example, National Money Mart charged interest just below the 60% *Criminal Code* limit, and allowed borrowers to pay only the interest if they repaid the loan in cash prior to the due date (PUB 2008). If prepayment did not occur, the borrower's payment included the principal and interest, as well as a check cashing fee, comprising the majority of the cost of credit to the borrower (PUB 2008).

Despite this apparent separation of "interest' from check cashing fee, National Money Mart was the subject of at least one major class action suit claiming the check cashing fee was a component of the overall "interest" being charged and that the overall cost of credit exceeded the legal maximum of 60% under the *Criminal Code* (PUB 2008).

Other payday lenders also took the view that section 347 did not preclude them from separately assessing and charging fees other than interest, and that only the interest rate could be no higher than 60% (PUB 2008). Rentcash, a Canadian company operating as Instaloans and The Cash Store, developed a large national chain based on a broker model, which had Rentcash operating as a broker and service agent and not as a direct lender—the lender was a third party not owned by Rentcash (PUB 2008).

Notwithstanding the mechanisms chosen to avoid the application of section 347 to their practices, payday lenders, including the largest of the firms, were the defendants of several class action suits, some of which were ongoing when the changes to the *Criminal Code* were enacted (PUB 2008). In addition, a number of court decisions in the civil realm in Manitoba and elsewhere in Canada upheld the rate of section 347, resulting in cancelled consumers' obligations to lenders (PUB 2008).

While courts in the civil realm tended to find that payday lenders were in violation of section 347 of the *Criminal Code*, there was a lack of enforcement of the criminal law. As stated by the Honorable Greg Selinger, Minister of Finance in Manitoba, when the province began regulating payday lenders, "[t]he *Criminal Code* wasn't being enforced, it is as simple as that" (Selinger 2017). It is likely that payday lenders were never prosecuted through the *Criminal Code* because their product was not anticipated when section 347 was crafted (Garland 1998).

In view of the legal challenges against payday lenders, the high costs being charged to consumers and the lack of enforcement of section 347 of the *Criminal Code*, the federal government decided to step in. The Legislative Summary from Parliamentary Information and Research Services (LS-541E) stated that shared federal-provincial jurisdiction over payday lenders meant that they had been left essentially unregulated (Kitching and Starky 2006). Provinces were unable to regulate the price of a loan since it would bring them in conflict with section 347 and could be challenged as beyond their jurisdiction. Section 347 had rarely been used in a criminal context to prosecute and convict payday lenders. The Legislative Summary notes that provincial governments may have feared that the absence of payday lenders in the marketplace could result in consumers turning to illegal alternatives, such as loan sharks (Kitching and Starky 2006).

Faced with jurisdictional challenges in addressing the high fees charged by payday lenders, federal and provincial/territorial governments negotiated a regulatory regime. The *Consumer Measures Committee (CMC) Working Group on the Alternative Consumer Credit Market* was established by Industry Canada and the provinces to explore ways to provide standard levels of consumer protection across Canada (Kitching and Starky 2006). In December 2004, the CMC published a consultation document containing a proposed consumer protection framework and a number of possible measures for discussion, which led to consultations with stakeholders (Kitching and Starky 2006).

Bill C-26 ultimately came out of the consultations, amending the *Criminal Code* to allow provinces to regulate the operations of payday lenders. Bill C-26 created a new provision in the *Criminal Code*, which amounted to an exemption to criminal prosecution for payday lenders under section 347 (Kitching and Starky 2006).[6]

In approving the revisions to section 347 of the *Criminal Code*, Parliament decided to allow payday lending, as it had been practiced, including fees and interest rates well in excess of 60%, to continue to operate, providing that provinces enacted the required legislative consumer protection measures (PUB 2008). Parliament acted to allow the industry to continue operating because the disappearance of payday lenders was perceived as being potentially damaging to consumers, with mainstream lenders not serving the short-term and small-dollar loan needs of a growing component of the borrowing community (PUB 2008). If payday lenders were restricted to the 60% maximum of section 347, with no other charges or levies permissible, the industry alleged that it would be "out of business" (PUB 2008).

[6] Payday loans are defined as "...an advancement of money in exchange for a post-dated cheque, a preauthorized debit or a future payment of similar nature but not for any guarantee, suretyship, overdraft protection or security on property and not through a margin loan, pawn broking, a line of credit or a credit card."

The revisions to the *Criminal Code* consisted of the addition of section 347.1, which states that section 347 does not apply to a person, other than a financial institution within the meaning of paragraphs (a) to (d) of the definition of "financial institution" in section 2 of the *Bank Act*, in respect of a payday loan agreement entered into by the person to receive interest, or in respect of interest received by that person under the agreement, if:

- the amount of money advanced under the agreement is $1500 or less, and the term of the agreement is 62 days or less;
- the person is licensed or otherwise specifically authorized under the laws of a province to enter into the agreement; and
- the province is designated under subsection (3) (Government of Canada 1985).

Under section 347.1(3), the Governor in Council shall designate the province for the purposes of this section if the province has legislative measures that protect recipients of payday loans and that provide for limits on the total cost of borrowing under the agreements (Government of Canada 1985).

Achieving the Balance

Where the overall goal in payday lending regulation is to achieve a delicate balance between consumer protection and allowing reasonably efficient payday lenders to operate, the differences in approaches and tools used by regulators illustrate the challenges in achieving this objective.

The Objective of Regulating Payday Loans

Since the development of the payday loan industry, governments have struggled with the conundrum of regulating a popular product that is very expensive. From legislative debates and decisions relating to the regulation of payday lending, it appears that *the goal of payday lending regulation is to achieve a delicate balance between adequate consumer protection and allowing relatively efficient payday lenders to remain in business.*

On the one hand, governments and regulators have noted the apprehended concerns of eliminating the payday lending industry, such as consumers turning to dangerous loan sharking or unregulated online lending. On the other hand, governments and regulators have also noted the risks of allowing payday lenders to operate by charging exorbitant interest rates, resulting in money being taken away from disproportionately vulnerable consumers. As stated by the Honorable Greg Selinger, Minister of Finance in Manitoba, regarding the introduction of payday lending legislation in Manitoba and the goal of regulation, "[a]t the end of the day, it was to keep more money in the hands of Manitobans, their families and the community" (Selinger 2017).

Manitoba was one of the first provinces to enact legislation regulating payday loans, pursuant to section 347.1 of the *Criminal Code*.[7] The Honorable Greg Selinger has stated that "[g]overnment role is to use the policy tools we have to protect the public, legislation, regulation, education, consumer protection" (Selinger 2017). The Manitoba payday lending regulatory regime has reflected the balance sought to be achieved in regulating the payday lending market.

The Manitoba legislation gave jurisdiction to the Public Utilities Board to conduct hearings relating to the maximum cost of credit charged by payday lenders. The Public Utilities Board issued an Order in 2008 premised on the view that the federal government had not sought to abolish the industry but desired lower charges than were currently prevalent.

Recognizing the legislative intent to protect consumers in the absence of effective price competition, the Manitoba Public Utilities Board concluded there was no public interest basis for supporting inefficient payday lending (PUB 2008). As a result, the Manitoba Public Utilities Board sought to achieve balance between consumer protection and industry health by setting rates enabling a reasonable return for an efficient payday lender. The Public Utilities Board recognized that the maximum charges proposed would lead some payday lenders to exit the marketplace unless they became more efficient. The Public Utilities Board also understood that relatively efficient payday lenders would continue to operate at the authorized rate and those surviving firms would assume a portion of the market becoming available as a result (PUB 2008).

The Public Utilities Board concluded that "the maximum charges to be set for payday loans should be such as to reduce the cost of credit for consumers while promoting **increased efficiency** within the industry" (PUB

[7]While Manitoba was the first province to amend its *Consumer Protection Act* to include provisions regarding payday loans, which were assented to in 2007, regulations on price caps for payday loans came into effect in 2010. Nova Scotia's *Consumer Protection Act* was amended in 2006 to include provisions relating to payday lending, which were proclaimed and took effect in 2007 and 2009. Payday lending regulation in Nova Scotia came into effect in 2009.

2008; emphasis added). It explicitly rejected the alternatives presented by the industry interveners as being too costly for consumers and concluded that the maximums set would allow for the survival and continuance of business of efficient payday lenders. The Public Utilities Board acknowledged the possibility of considerable consolidation in the industry and the exit of several firms and outlets (PUB 2008).

A Patchwork of Regulation

The current exemption for payday loans under the *Criminal Code* has led to a patchwork of regulation across the country, with some provinces choosing not to regulate payday loans, other provinces opting for different degrees of regulation, and one province choosing to effectively outlaw payday loans. Under this decentralized legislative framework, Canadian consumers do not all benefit from the same level of protection across the country, and the industry has to be familiar with and adapt to different jurisdictions in which it operates.

While it appears that giving the provinces jurisdiction to regulate payday loans has led to significant research into the industry and the impact of payday loans on consumers, a federal regulatory framework in addition to or as a substitute to provincial regulations, such as under the *Small Loans Act*, could be a way to ensure that all Canadians benefit from the same level of protection and could provide more predictability for the industry.

Payday Lending Regulation Across Canada

In response to the exemption created in the *Criminal Code* for payday lenders, provinces began enacting legislation and regulation to protect consumers, while still allowing the industry to operate.

The package of regulatory tools used by legislators range from significant interventions in the marketplace and business model, such as price caps and limits on the amount borrowed, to less interventionist, such as education and disclosure of information to consumers. The particular common elements of regulation found in Canadian provinces include: price caps on rates charged for loans, limits on the amount borrowed, limits on the number of loans that a customer can take out at once, enforcement of regulation, provisions relating to installment loan options, data requirements, and disclosure of information to borrowers (Table 7.1).

Table 7.1 Summary of Canadian payday lending regulations[a]

Province	*Price cap*	*APR disclosure*	*Borrowing limit*
BC	17	Yes	50% net pay
Alberta	15	Yes	$1500
Saskatchewan	23	No	50% net pay
Manitoba	17	Yes	30% net pay
Ontario	15[b]	No	$1500
Nova Scotia	22	Yes	$1500
New Brunswick[c]	15	Yes	30% net pay
PEI	25	No	$1500

Source: Barrett Consulting Services Inc. (2015, p. 18), and modified to reflect recent changes to payday lending regulation, including changes to the price cap for payday loans in Alberta, Nova Scotia, British Columbia, and Ontario.

[a]Quebec, Newfoundland and Labrador, Yukon, the Northwest Territories, and Nunavut are not included in this table given that payday lending regulations are not in effect in these jurisdictions.

[b]In Ontario, section 23 of the *General* regulation pursuant to the *Payday Loans Act* (Government of Ontario 2008a) sets out the maximum allowable cost of borrowing (Government of Ontario 2008b). Effective January 1, 2017, section 23 of the regulation lowered the cost of borrowing to $21 per $100 borrowed for agreements entered into before January 1, 2017; $18 per $100 borrowed for agreements entered into between January 1, 2017, and January 1, 2018; and $15 per $100 borrowed for agreements entered into on or after January 1, 2018.

[c]Effective January 1 2018, the *Cost of Credit Disclosure and Payday Loans Act*, the *Payday Lending Regulation* (Government of New Brunswick 2008), and Rules PDL-001 *Payday Loans Licensing and Ongoing Obligations* and PDL-002 *Fees* came into force in New Brunswick (FCNB 2017).

In some Canadian provinces, the payday lending market is not yet regulated:

- In 2010, the provincial government of Newfoundland and Labrador announced that it would not regulate payday loan companies operating in the province and that it would rather uphold the maximum interest rate set out in the *Criminal Code* (Government of Newfoundland 2010). The government's rationale for not regulating payday lenders was that putting in place regulations permitting interest charges above 60% would not protect consumers' best interests and would be counter-protective to the provincial Poverty Reduction Strategy (Government of Newfoundland 2010). However, Newfoundland and Labrador's House of Assembly passed *An Act to Amend The Consumer Protection and Business Practices Act* on December 16, 2016 that would make payday lending legal in Newfoundland and Labrador (Government of Newfoundland and Labrador House of Assembly 2016). The Act does not come into force until proclaimed by the Lieutenant Governor in

Council (Government of Newfoundland and Labrador 2016). The Act is not in force at the date of writing and the proposed Regulations have not been made public.

- Before the issue of regulating payday lending arose, Québec chose to limit interest on all loans to 35% annual interest, which has effectively banned the industry from the province (Lo 2011). This capped interest rate makes it unprofitable for the payday loan industry to provide its conventional services in the province.
- Yukon, the Northwest Territories, and Nunavut do not currently regulate payday loans and therefore section 347 of the *Criminal Code* applies.

In addition to provincial regulation, some cities have also begun to enact by-laws to regulate some aspects of payday lenders. For example, the City of Calgary has a by-law which prohibits payday lenders from being located within 400 meters from another payday lending outlet (Calgary 2007). Another example is the City of Hamilton which enacted a by-law that regulates the licensing of payday lending outlets, the information provided to customers about the products, and that credit counseling information be provided to customers (Hamilton 2016). While we note the existence of such municipal by-laws, the focus of this chapter is on provincial regulation.

Price Caps

Price caps have been a primary tool used by provincial governments in Canada to protect consumers from very expensive payday loans. Under economic regulatory theory, the creation of price caps is one way to regulate a market:

> A price cap regulation is a price ceiling—a rule that specifies the highest price the firm is permitted to set. This type of regulation gives a firm an incentive to operate efficiently and keep costs under control. (Parkin and Bade 2006)

Regarding the Manitoba government's amendment to its *Consumer Protection Act*, the Honorable Greg Selinger, then Minister of Finance, stated that the government's purpose "…was not to drive the companies out of business, because people are showing an interest in having this service, but to make sure that when they offer the service they do it in a way that's **just and reasonable**" (PUB 2008).

The first "just and reasonable" rates for payday lenders were set by regulation in 2010 based upon a 2008 Manitoba Public Utilities Board Order. The price cap is set in section 147(1) of the *Consumer Protection*

Act, which states that a payday lender cannot charge more than the maximum cost of credit allowed by regulation. The *Payday Loan Regulation* at section 13.1(1) indicates that the total cost of credit for a payday loan must not be greater than 17% of the principal amount of the payday loan (Government of Manitoba 2007).

The price caps enacted in 2010 are still in effect today and the Public Utilities Board has most recently recommended to the provincial government in June 2016 that price caps should remain unchanged (PUB 2016).

The price cap set by Manitoba in 2010 was initially significantly lower than the price cap selected by other provinces and was subject to industry criticism. According to the Honorable Greg Selinger, "[w]e were able to lead in Manitoba and most other provinces followed us" (Selinger 2017). Recent legislative developments in provinces such as Alberta, British Columbia, New Brunswick, and Ontario suggest an emerging consensus that consumers would be better protected and the industry would continue to be sustainable at price caps in the range of $15–$17 per $100 borrowed.

While he notes that a national regulatory regime could have ensured uniformity across the country, the Honorable Greg Selinger has also noted the advantage of having provinces regulate the payday lending industry: "[i]t allows for more innovation and every time there is a breakthrough, it is an obvious example for other jurisdictions to follow" (Selinger 2017).

In Alberta, effective August 2016, rates for payday loans became the lowest in Canada, for provinces that allow payday loans. Section 124.61(1) of the *Fair Trading Act* sets the maximum cost of borrowing at 15% of the principal amount of the payday loan, including fees for all mandatory and optional services and any other fees or charges set out in the regulation (Government of Alberta 2000).

In Ontario, section 23 of the *General* regulation pursuant to the *Payday Loans Act* (Government of Ontario 2008a) sets out the maximum allowable cost of borrowing (Government of Ontario 2008b). Effective January 1, 2017, section 23 of the regulation lowered the cost of borrowing to:

- $21 per $100 borrowed for agreements entered into before January 1, 2017;
- $18 per $100 borrowed for agreements entered into between January 1, 2017, and January 1, 2018; and
- $15 per $100 borrowed for agreements entered into on or after January 1, 2018 (Government of Ontario 2008b).

In British Columbia, section 112.02 of part 6.1 of the *Business Practices and Consumer Protection Act* establishes that the Lieutenant Governor in Council may set the maximum amount that may be charged for a payday lender in the regulation (Government of BC 2004). As of January 1, 2017, section 17 of the *Payday Loan Regulation* lowered the maximum allowable cost of credit from 23 to 17% of the principal borrowed (BC Gov News 2016; Government of BC 2009).

In addition to lowering the rates, in September 2016, the British Columbia provincial government announced that it was undertaking a consultation with stakeholders to "help determine how best to further strengthen consumer protection for British Columbians who use high-cost alternative financial services, and whether more affordable options exist" (BC Gov News 2016).

In Nova Scotia, the Nova Scotia Utility and Review Board most recently reviewed payday loans in 2015. In its March 2015 decision, the market approach was retained to determine the maximum cost of borrowing and the price cap was reduced from $25 to $22 per $100 borrowed (NSUARB 2015).

In Saskatchewan, the maximum cost of credit is set out in section 14(1) of the *Payday Loans Regulations*, pursuant to the *Payday Loans Act*, and is currently set at 23% of the principal amount as set out in the payday loan agreement (Government of Saskatchewan 2007, 2012a,b).

In Prince Edward Island, section 24 of the *Payday Loans Act Regulations* pursuant to subsection 30(2) of the *Payday Loans Act* (Government of PEI 1988) provides that the prescribed limit on the cost of borrowing under a payday loan agreement is $25 per $100 advanced under the agreement (Government of PEI 2015).

Borrowing Limit

As another tool to achieve consumer protection, some jurisdictions have enacted limits on the amount that consumers can borrow through a payday loan. As was noted by the Manitoba Public Utilities Board, the debt spiral for payday loan users is a known phenomenon and "limiting the level of borrowing to a portion of the net pay of the individual reduces the likelihood that they will further overextend their credit obligations" (PUB Order 2013).

In Manitoba, section 151.1(1) of the *Consumer Protection Act* provides that the loan agreement cannot exceed the proportion of the borrower's net pay set out in the regulation. Section 15.2(1) of the regulation indicates that the prescribed proportion of the borrower's net pay is 30%

(Government of Manitoba 2007).[8] In June 2016, the Manitoba Public Utilities Board recommended that the borrowing limit remain unchanged.

In British Columbia, section 18 indicates that a payday lender must not issue a payday loan in excess of 50% of the borrower's net pay or other net income to be received during the term of the payday loan (Government of BC 2009). In Saskatchewan, payday lenders may not enter into a payday loan agreement with a borrower that is in excess of 50% of the borrower's net pay during the term of the payday loan (Government of Saskatchewan 2012b).

Multiple Loans/Repeat Loans

Many jurisdictions have legislated provisions regarding the number of loans that consumers can borrow at once or during a specified period of time. These types of provisions attempt to address the cycle of debt that has been observed in many payday loan consumers.

For example, in Manitoba, concurrent loans are prohibited by sections 154(1) and 137 of the *Consumer Protection Act*, meaning that a payday lender shall not offer, arrange, or provide a payday loan to a borrower who is indebted to the lender under an existing payday loan, unless the new loan is a replacement loan,[9] and immediately after the initial advance under the new loan is made, the borrower is no longer indebted under the existing loan (Government of Manitoba 1987). The regulation at section 13.1 sets out that the total cost of credit for a replacement loan must not be greater than 5% of the principal amount (Government of Manitoba 2007).

The regulation states that the total cost of credit for a payday loan must not be greater than 5% of the principal amount of the payday loan if the payday loan is an extension or renewal of a payday loan previously arranged or provided, or if the payday loan is arranged or provided by a payday

[8] The formula to determine a borrower's net pay is found in section 2.2(1) of the Regulation: Net pay = (MNI × 12)/26, where MNI consists of the person's net income for the most recent previous calendar month where the person received income. This is calculated by adding all incomes received by a person from all sources during that month, minus all compulsory and voluntary deductions.

[9] See the *Consumer Protection Act* at section 137 and the *Payday Loan Regulation* at section 2.1: A replacement loan is defined as "a payday loan arranged or provided by a payday lender as part of a series of transactions or events that results in the borrower's debt under another payday loan previously arranged or provided by that payday lender being repaid in whole or in part" and "a transaction or series of transactions specified in the regulation." The Regulation specifies that in addition to what is stipulated under the Act, a replacement loan is a payday loan "that advances an amount in excess of the borrower's debt under the payday loan previously arranged or provided by that payday lender."

lender within seven days after the borrower repaid in full another payday loan previously arranged or provided by that payday lender (Government of Manitoba 2007). This seven-day period is referred to informally as a "cooling-off period."

In June 2016, the Manitoba Public Utilities Board recommended that the 5% "cooling-off period" rate cap imposed in the regulations be amended to only apply for a one-day period, after which the client would be able to take out another loan at the regular rate of 17%. The one-day cooling-off period would delineate the issuance of a replacement loan which is used to repay the initial loan and a completely new loan. The Board found that the seven-day "cooling-off period" was not preventing borrowers from getting stuck in a debt trap spiral given that consumers could simply go "across the street" to another lender if they needed another loan during the seven-day period (PUB 2016).

In its June 2016 report, the Manitoba Public Utilities Board also recommended that lenders be prohibited from making more than 10 payday loans to a customer in a consecutive 12-month period. The Board concluded that some lenders are making an excessive number of payday loans to individual customers such that these customers are stuck in a debt trap (PUB 2016).

Another example of this regulatory tool is in Nova Scotia where the Utility and Review Board has recommended that the Minister consider placing restrictions on repeat and concurrent loans, such as (1) a requirement that payday lenders report all loans to a central database; (2) a requirement that a payday lender, before agreeing to lend money, must first check with the central database to see if the prospective borrower has any outstanding payday loans; and (3) that where a borrower takes out more than two loans in a 62-day period, the third loan and any subsequent loan should be extended over a minimum of three pay periods if the borrower is paid bi-weekly, or a minimum of two pay periods if the borrower is paid less frequently (NSUARB 2015).

Data Requirements

Some jurisdictions require payday lenders to provide annual data to a central agency, which is especially useful in tracking the effect of regulation on consumer trends and assisting regulators in making decisions based on evidence. The governments of Nova Scotia and British Columbia have been Canadian leaders on the requirement to provide annual data to regulators.

In British Columbia, sections 4(2)(b) and 4(3) of the *Payday Loans Regulation* require all payday lenders licensed in the province to annually report aggregated loan data. According to the *Regulation*, the aggregate data must include data respecting the number of loans, number of transactions, loan amounts, loan duration, and number of default charges (Government of BC 2009).

Consumer Protection BC, an arm's length not-for-profit corporation that protects consumers and encourages a fair marketplace in British Columbia, regulates and licenses payday lenders. An Aggregate Data Form is available on its website that is filled out by payday lender licensees to provide information on the most recently completed fiscal year (CPBC 2016). Aggregate data are then reported publicly on the regulator's website.

In Nova Scotia, section 5 of the *Payday Lenders Regulations* stipulates that payday lenders must provide information on loans granted from the location specified in their permit for the 12-month period from July 1 to June 30 immediately before the date of the permit renewal (Government of Nova Scotia 2015). Form A, attached to the Regulations, must be filled out by the payday lender and collects information regarding the number of loans granted, the average size of loans granted, the number of defaults on loans granted, the average size of loans defaulted, the number of borrowers who have been granted more than one loan, the number of repeat loans granted, the total number of borrowers who have been granted repeat loans, and the number of borrowers who have been granted repeat loans 1, 2, 3, 4, 5, 6, 7, and 8 or more times in one year (Government of Nova Scotia 2015). This information in aggregate form is available from the regulator upon request.

In June 2016, the Manitoba Public Utilities Board recommended that data collection provisions for the receipt of detailed information from lenders should be included in payday lending regulation (PUB 2016).

Installment Loans

Some have argued that converting payday loans into installment loans, either universally or where certain conditions occur, is one way to address the repeat loan cycle. As a result of the traditional payday loan paid in full on the next payday, many consumers have no choice but to take out another payday loan in order to meet all their expenses, resulting in significant difficulties in getting out of the loan cycle.

In June 2016, the Manitoba Public Utilities Board recommended that a mandatory installment loan option or a loan extension option should be made available to payday loan consumers to assist them in paying back their loans in a manner which is manageable, potentially avoiding the start of a "debt spiral" (PUB 2016). The Manitoba Public Utilities Board suggested that, at the request of a borrower, a lender be required to extend the loan for at least another pay period or to convert the loan to an installment loan, provided that the borrower has successfully paid off three previous payday loans during the preceding 12-month period. If an installment loan is issued, the cap on the rate for the loan should be set at 7%. The installment loan repayment terms should allow repayment over at least the next four pay periods, where no payment exceeds 35% of the sum of the principal and cost of borrowing (PUB 2016).

In Alberta, as of 2016, the government has mandated installment payments for payday loans. Section 124.3(1) states that a payday lender shall ensure that a payday loan agreement contains a term requiring the borrower to repay the loan through an installment plan over a period of at least 42 days and no more than 62 days (Government of Alberta 2000). The payday lender must ensure that if the borrower receives income on a semi-monthly, bi-weekly, or more frequent basis, the agreement specifies that repayment is to be spread over at least three pay periods or if the borrower receives income less frequently, the payday loan agreement specifies that repayment is to be spread over at least two pay periods (Government of Alberta 2000). Finally, a borrower may pay all or part of the outstanding balance under the loan agreement at any time without incurring any prepayment charge or penalty (Government of Alberta 2000).

Disclosure to Borrowers

Most jurisdictions legislate specific information that must be presented to consumers in a specific format by payday lenders. These provisions aim at ensuring that consumers have all the information required to make financial decisions in an accessible format. As stated by the Honorable Greg Selinger, it is an "[a]ttempt to show [consumers] that they may wish to choose another way to get credit" (Selinger 2017).

For example, in Manitoba the legislation specifies that payday lenders must post signs at each location providing information regarding the payday loan products they provide (Government of Manitoba 1987). The Regulation articulates the information to be posted at each physical licensed location as well as for Internet payday loans (Government of Manitoba 2007). The Act and the Regulation also set out the information to be provided in both physical and online payday loan agreements (Government of Manitoba 1987, 2007).

In Nova Scotia, in March 2015, the Utility and Review Board recommended that the Minister consider mandating that lenders display comparisons of borrowing costs of alternative financial products in dollar terms (NSUARB 2015).

Enforcement

Most payday lending legislation includes provisions relating to the enforcement of obligations faced by payday lenders and, in many cases, a consumer protection body is designated to enforce the legislation and regulation.

In Manitoba, the Act and Regulations establish that a notice of administrative penalty may be issued if a person fails to comply with provisions of the Act or the Regulations (Government of Manitoba 1987, 2007).

One example of a regulator enforcing the provisions found in the payday lending legislation is demonstrated in a decision by the Ontario Superior Court of Justice in 2014. In that matter, an action was brought by the Director designated under the *Ministry of Consumer and Business Services Act* and authorized under section 54(1) of the *Payday Loans Act* to apply for an order "if it appears to the Director that a person or entity is not complying with this Act or the regulations" (Director v The Cash Store 2014). The action was brought against The Cash Store, a company that previously offered payday loans in Ontario but whose license had lapsed in 2013. The company had restructured its business and began offering a newly fashioned financial product called a "Basic Line of Credit" to its customers (Director v The Cash Store 2014).

In that case, the Director alleged that The Cash Store's new product was in substance a payday loan and that it was subject to the numerous consumer protection provisions built into the provincial regulatory regime for payday loans. The Court found that the "Basic Line of Credit" amounted to a payday loan and stated that "the persistent regulatory cat has caught the clever business mouse" (Director v The Cash Store 2014). In addition to declaring that the company's new product was subject to the provisions under the *Payday Loans Act*, the Court ordered the Respondent prohibited from acting as a loan broker of the product without a license under the *Act* and the Respondents were ordered to pay costs in the amount of $50,000.

Education and Financial Literacy

While government regulation of payday lending has been a primary tool in responding to and driving change in the payday lending marketplace in Canada, laws and regulation by themselves cannot resolve broader issues relating to financial exclusion. Government investments in education and financial literacy are vitally important to achieving financial well-being for all consumers.

Recent thinking in the field of financial literacy has been linking literacy with well-being, such as in the Financial Consumer Agency of Canada's "National Financial Strategy for Financial Literacy" released in 2015 (FCAC 2015). Another example is the work of the US Consumer Financial Protection Bureau (CFPB), which has defined financial well-being as:

> ...a state of being wherein a person can fully meet current and ongoing financial obligations, can feel secure in their financial future, and is able to make choices that allow enjoyment of life. (CFPB 2015)

The CFPB further specifies that the concept of financial well-being has four central elements:

- Control over day-to-day, month-to-month finances;
- Capacity to absorb a financial shock;
- Being on track to meet financial goals; and
- Having the financial freedom to make choices to enjoy life (CFPB 2015).

In Canada, in an effort to encourage and support financial literacy, the ultimate measure of success being individual financial well-being (CFPB 2015; FCAC 2015), some jurisdictions have legislated requirements for contributions by payday lenders to a financial literacy fund.

For example, in Manitoba, the Financial Literacy Fund was established in 2011 under section 161.6(1) of the *Consumer Protection Act*. Since its implementation, each licensed payday lender has had to pay an annual financial literacy support levy to the Fund.[10] In the past number of years, the Fund has contributed to community organizations supporting financial literacy programming, to a study on financial literacy in Manitoba and to support financial literacy tools (Government of Manitoba 2014–2015 and 2015–2016).

Regulation of Payday Loans in Other Jurisdictions

Canada is not the only country that has decided to address payday lending through legislation and regulation. In this section, we have chosen to focus on the United Kingdom (UK), Australia, and the United States (US) given that there exist some similarities to the approach taken in Canada. However, the differences in the tools used in these jurisdictions provide a further example that regulators are still struggling with finding the appropriate balance between consumer protection and allowing the industry to operate. In reviewing the effectiveness of payday lending regulation, it can be beneficial to look to other jurisdictions to learn from best practices, where possible.

Regulation of Payday Lending in the United Kingdom and Australia

In the United Kingdom, the Financial Conduct Authority began regulating payday loans in 2014 and implemented Policy Statement PS14/16 in 2015 (FCA 2015). Under this policy statement, the following caps and rules were implemented:

- Initial cost cap of 0.8% per day—lowers the cost for most borrowers. For all high-cost short-term credit loans, interest and fees must not exceed 0.8% per day of the amount borrowed.
- Fixed default fees capped at £15—protects borrowers struggling to repay. If borrowers do not repay their loans on time, default charges must not exceed £15. Interest on unpaid balances and default charges must not exceed the initial rate.

[10] Tourism, Culture, Heritage, Sport and Consumer Protection Annual Reports 2014–2015 and 2013–2014: In the past two years, the Fund has contributed to the following projects: the Legal Help Centre received a grant toward financial literacy programming; the Manitoba Financial Literacy Forum received a grant to conduct a baseline study on financial literacy in Manitoba; a grant was provided toward the financial literacy calendar through the Manitoba Financial Literacy Forum.

- Total cost cap of 100%—protects borrowers from escalating debts. Borrowers must never have to pay back more in fees and interest than the amount borrowed (FCA 2014).

The caps established by the Financial Conduct Authority are to be reviewed in the first half of 2017. In addition, under UK law, the enforcement of debts through harassment, deception, or threats is prohibited (Uniform Law Conference 2008; Government of UK 1970). The civil law provides for relief from the court where there exist unfair relationships between creditors and debtors (Uniform Law Conference 2008; Government of UK 1974).

In Australia, under the National Credit Act, the Australian Securities and Investments Commission (ASIC) regulates and licenses any entity that engages into credit activities, including lenders, lessors, and brokers (ASIC 2015b). Under this law, credit providers must:

- Make reasonable inquiries about your financial situation, requirements, and objectives;
- Take reasonable steps to verify your financial situation; and
- Decide whether the credit contract you are asking for is "not unsuitable" for you (ASIC 2015b).

As of March 1, 2013, new laws came into effect affecting loans of $2000 or less. Under the law, the following is established:

- "Short-term" loans of $2000 or less that you must repay in 15 days or less are prohibited.
- Credit providers are required to display a warning that notifies you of your options before you borrow money when they offer a "small amount" loan of $2000 or less that is to be repaid between 16 days and 1 year.

Fee limits on small amount loans ($2000 or less): from July 1, 2013, fees charged on small amount loans are capped (i.e., limited to a maximum amount). Credit providers can only charge the following fees:

- A one-off establishment fee (of not more than 20% of the loan amount);

- A monthly account keeping fee (of not more than 4% of the loan amount);
- A government fee or charge;
- Default fees or charges (the credit provider cannot collect more than 200% of the amount loaned if you default—i.e., fail to pay back the loan); and
- Enforcement expenses (if you fail to pay back the loan, these are the costs incurred by the credit provider going to court to recover the money owed under your credit contract) (ASIC 2015b).

This cap on fees and ban on short-term loans described above does not apply to loans offered by Authorized Deposit-taking Institutions (ADIs) such as banks, building societies, and credit unions, or to continuing credit contracts such as credit cards (ASIC 2015b).

In 2015, the ASIC published a report which found that "payday lenders need to improve compliance with some of the key consumer protection laws operating in the industry" (ASIC 2015a). While it found that payday lenders were complying with some of the rules put in place in 2013, it also found that they were falling short of meeting some of the important regulations. It found particular compliance risk around the test for loan suitability established in the law. In this report, ASIC noted the 2013 small amount credit reforms would be independently reviewed after July 1, 2015, and that it would continue its focus on enforcing the current provisions and raising industry standards (ASIC 2015a).

In addition in Australia, the law provides relief for credit transactions that may be deemed unjust or unconscionable (Uniform Law Conference 2008; Government of Australia 2009).

Regulation of Payday Lending in the United States

Active debate about usury in the United States focuses currently on the regulation of the costs of payday loans. This section will review the regulation of payday lending in the United States, especially where recent developments are relevant to the Canada regulatory landscape. We have chosen to include the United States as the principal comparator for the purposes of this analysis given the significant research on payday lending in the United States, and some similarities between the United States and Canada in regulation at the state level. A further discussion of the United States as a comparator country is found in the introduction to this book.

Permissive, Hybrid, and Restrictive

An important source of the research on payday lending from the United States comes from the Pew Charitable Trusts (Pew), which is an independent, non-profit global research and public policy organization (Pew 1946).[11] Since 2011, Pew has conducted extensive research on payday, auto title, and similar loans in its Small-Dollar Loan Project, which included a large-scale omnibus survey, leading to a series of four comprehensive reports on payday lending practices in the United States and, in the face of identified problems, policy recommendations.

Similar to Canada, different states have taken different approaches to regulating the industry, ranging from less to more restrictive (refer to Appendix 4 in Chap. 4). In order to analyze the impact of different regulatory schemes and to compare the consequences of policies in states with different policy regimes, Pew has categorized state payday loans regulation into three categories: Permissive, Hybrid, and Restrictive (Pew Trusts 2012).

Under Pew's categorization, Permissive states "are the least regulated and allow initial fees of 15 percent of the borrowed principal or higher" (Pew Trusts 2012). While most of these states have some type of regulation, they allow for payday loans due in full on a borrower's next payday with Annual Percentage Rates usually in the range of 391–521% ($15–$20 per $100 borrowed per two weeks). Payday loan storefronts are readily available to borrowers located in these states, and 55% of Americans live in the 28 Permissive states (Pew Trusts 2012).

Hybrid states have relatively more exacting requirements than Permissive states with at least one of the following three forms of regulation: (1) rate caps, usually around 10% of the borrowed principal, which are lower than most states but still permit loans to be issued with triple-digit APRs; (2) restrictions on the number of loans per borrower, such as a maximum of eight loans per borrower per year; or (3) allowing borrowers multiple pay periods to repay loans (Pew Trusts 2012). While storefronts that offer payday loans exist in substantial numbers in these states, the market may be more consolidated and per-store loan volume may be higher than in less restrictive states. Sixteen percent of Americans live in the eight Hybrid states (Pew Trusts 2012).

[11] Given its status as a charitable trust, it may be argued that it has a stronger level of objectivity as compared with industry associations and advocacy agencies.

Restrictive states either do not permit payday lending or have price caps low enough to eliminate payday lending in the state (Pew Trusts 2012). This rate cap is often 36% APR. Generally, payday loan storefronts are not found in these states. Twenty-nine percent of Americans live in the 14 states and the District of Columbia that have a Restrictive payday loan regulatory structure (Pew Trusts 2012).

Pew's categorization of policy regimes can be applied to the Canadian regulatory framework in order to compare the policy choices made by provinces. In Canada, if Pew's categorization is applied, most jurisdictions that currently regulate payday loans would initially have been considered Permissive when regulations were first introduced in 2009 and shortly thereafter. In more recent years, however, and especially since 2016, additional consumer protection provisions have been implemented or have been recommended to provincial governments, and many more jurisdictions may be moving toward the Hybrid category. The province of Québec, however, would be categorized as Restrictive given that payday loans are effectively illegal. Provinces that do not yet regulate payday lending and where the Criminal Code limits operate, such as the territories, Newfoundland and Labrador, would also be considered Restrictive as payday lenders are unable to profitably operate at 60% interest rate or less but some do operate, nevertheless.

Colorado

The state of Colorado has particularly interesting payday loan regulations that relate to the movement toward installment repayment plans. Colorado's payday lending regulatory scheme is very different than the rest of the United States and Canada. Lump-sum payday lending came into use in 1992 in that state, making it an early adopter (Pew Trusts 2013). In 2010, state lawmakers agreed that the payday loan market had failed and decided to act to correct it. As indicated by Pew, legislators "forged a compromise designed to make the loans more affordable while granting the state's existing nonbank lenders a new way to provide small-dollar loans to those with damaged credit histories" (Pew Trusts 2013). The law changed the terms for payday loans from a single, lump-sum payment to a series of installment payments stretched over six months and lowered the maximum allowable interest rate (Pew Trusts 2013).

While payday loans remain costly in Colorado compared to mainstream borrowing options, borrowers now pay an average of 4% of their paychecks to pay back the loan, compared with 36% under a conventional lump-sum payday loan model (Pew Trusts 2013). The average Annual Percentage Rate in Colorado is 129%, and Pew reports that individual borrowers are spending 42% less money than they did under the old law (Pew Trusts 2013).

According to Pew, short-term credit remains widely available in Colorado despite considerable storefront consolidation. "The Colorado law has transformed a payday lending business with low-volume stores into one that serves more customers at each location, with borrowers spending less on loans annually" (Pew Trusts 2013).

Pew finds that "small-dollar lending can fit better into a borrower's budget when the loans are due in installment based on ability to repay—that is, to make required loan payments and meet other financial obligations without having to borrow again or draw from savings" (Pew Trusts 2013).

Notwithstanding the advantages with the Colorado mode, Pew reports it has its shortcomings. It allows interest rates that may be substantially higher than those needed for small-dollar lending to be profitable and the fee structure is complicated, making comparison shopping difficult and price competition unlikely (Pew Trusts 2013). Pew adds that it is possible that eliminating high-cost lending entirely would have been better for consumers (Pew Trusts 2013).

According to Pew, simply adding installment payment plans to payday loans is not sufficient. Pew suggests that small-dollar loan markets generally lack price competition so that the cost of borrowing can become unnecessarily high in states that do not limit interest rates (Pew Trusts 2013). In addition, Pew notes that when the law allows installment loans to include fees and charges that are front-loaded, data shows that lenders encourage borrowers to refinance repeatedly, a concept known as loan flipping (Pew Trusts 2013). Finally, Pew observes that consumers can be put at risk of losing control over their checking accounts and being harmed by unscrupulous lenders where postdated checks and electronic access are used as loan collateral (Pew Trusts 2013).

Washington

The state of Washington has introduced another approach to installment loans. This approach is to allow a borrower to take out a traditional payday loan with the fixed fee and loan repayment due on the next payday, while also providing the customer the option to convert the loan to an installment loan on or before the due date.

Under the state of Washington's regulation, the regular payday fee is 15% on the first \$500 and 10% on any additional amount, with a maximum of the lower of \$700 and 30% of income (Washington 2015). A borrower may not take out more than eight loans in a 12-month period (Washington 2015).

The borrower also has the right to an installment loan:

> BORROWERS' RIGHTS TO INSTALLMENT PLANS Borrowers are entitled to an installment loan at any time prior to default. Borrowers do not have to pay a fee for the installment plan and have from 90 to 180 days (depending on the original loan amount) to repay the loan in a series of installments. (Washington 2015)

There is still an active payday loan industry in Washington state, even with several regulations that reduce fees substantially below those in Manitoba. The option to convert to an installment does not entail any further cost to the borrower.

Consumer Financial Protection Bureau Proposed Rule

The Consumer Financial Protection is a federal agency that "helps consumer finance markets work by making rules more effective, by consistently and fairly enforcing those rules, and by empowering consumers to take more control over their economic lives" (Government of US 2008).

In recognition that there remain challenges in the regulation of payday lending in the United States, in June 2016, the CFPB proposed a rule "aimed at ending payday debt traps by requiring lenders to take steps to make sure consumer have the ability to repay their loans" (Government of US 2016). This proposed rule was open for comments until October 2016. The Rule, entitled *Payday, Vehicle Title, and Certain High-Cost Installment Loans*, was issued on November 17, 2017 and is effective January 16, 2018 (Government of US 2017).

Under this rule, the protections cover payday loans, auto title loans, deposit advance products, and certain high-cost installment and open-end loans as a result of serious concerns by the CFPB that risk lender practices were pushing borrowers into debt traps (CFPB 2016).

The rule includes an ability to pay test, requiring lenders to determine upfront that consumers can afford to repay their loans without further borrowing (Government of US 2016, 2017). The rule identifies it as "unfair and abusive practice for a lender to make covered short-term or long-term balloon-payment loans, including payday and vehicle title loans, without reasonably determining that consumers have the ability to repay the loans according to their terms" (Government of US 2017).

The rule limits attempts by lenders to debit the client's bank account that can result in multiple fees and make it difficult for consumers to get out of the cycle of debt (Government of US 2016, 2017). Lenders are required to provide certain notices to consumers before attempting to debit the consumer's account and after two straight unsuccessful attempts, the lender is prohibited from debiting the account again unless specifically authorized by the borrower (Government of US 2016, 2017).

In addition to the proposed rule, the CFPB has launched an inquiry into other products and practices that may harm consumers facing cash shortfalls.

Regulating for Effectiveness in a Dynamic Marketplace

In order to remain effective in their regulations, governments and regulators must acknowledge that the marketplace is constantly changing. Industries and companies constantly develop new products or find new ways to provide existing products, which may differ from traditional products covered by laws and regulations. To achieve effective consumer protection, laws and regulations should change alongside the marketplace.

Dynamic Marketplace

In the payday lending marketplace, online loans are a product that has proven difficult to regulate. As demonstrated in a 2015 report by the Consumer Council of Canada, the chance of finding an unlicensed lender online is greater than the chance of finding a licensed lender (C.C. 2015). The danger to consumers is that unlicensed lenders are more likely not to comply with applicable laws around payday lending (C.C. 2015). While many Canadian provinces have enacted provisions regulating online payday lenders, enforcing the regulation can be challenging, in part due to the presence of lead generators, "firms that present themselves to consumers as companies that can arrange payday loans, but, in fact, collect the consumer's information and pass it along (i.e., sell it) to lenders anywhere in the world" (C.C. 2015). Significant challenges relating to jurisdiction and enforcement of legislation arise when lenders are located outside the province or the country.

In recognition of the changing marketplace, Manitoba has recently enacted a new regulation under the *Consumer Protection Act*, which came into force on September 1, 2016, as per the *Consumer Protection Amendment Act (High-Cost Credit Products)* (Government of Manitoba 2013). This regulation supports recommendations made by the Manitoba Public Utilities Board in 2013 to regulate payday loan-like products, such as high-cost credit products (News Release – Manitoba 2013).

The *High-Cost Credit Products Regulation* (Government of Manitoba 2016) applies to loans of money and lines of credit where the annual interest rate exceeds 32%, as well as loans of money and lines of credit that are no more than $5000 and where the high-cost credit agreement terms include the payment of interest at a rate of up to 32% and one or more high-cost credit fees, and where the repayment of the loan is over a term not exceeding two years (Government of Manitoba 2016).

Under this regulation, the creditor requires a license to provide high-cost credit products. The regulation ensures that an information disclosure document be provided to consumers and sets out what must be included in high-cost credit agreements, such as the grantor's business name, the principal amount of the loan, the terms of the agreement, as well as the forms that should accompany this agreement (Government of Manitoba 2016). The regulation specifies requirements for the entrance signs for each type of high-cost credit product at their licensed locations. The name and license of the high-cost credit grantor must be prominently displayed (Government of Manitoba 2016).

There exist specific design requirements to provide information for Internet high-cost credit products. A high-cost credit grantor must ensure that the borrower has consented to entering into the Internet high-cost agreement (Government of Manitoba 2016).

The regulation specifies that discounting the principal amount of the high-cost credit product by deducting or withholding from any advance or drawing an amount representing any portion of the cost of credit or any component of the cost of credit is prohibited (Government of Manitoba 2016). The regulation also restricts other high-cost credit product lending activities (Government of Manitoba 2016).[12] The regulation specifies that

[12] This includes, for example, accepting a check or pre-authorized or other negotiable instrument unless it is made payable to the high-cost credit grantor, making any unauthorized withdrawal from a borrower's account, disclosing information about the agreement, and giving inaccurate information about improving the borrower's personal credit rating.

there cannot be repeated attempts to process repayment if the borrower is charged a fee, penalty, or other amount (Government of Manitoba 2016).

The regulation provides for an administrative penalty if a person fails to comply with specific provisions of the legislation and the regulation (Government of Manitoba 2016).

While this law focuses on disclosure requirements for lenders and prohibits certain conducts, it does not limit the interest rates charged by lenders on their products, making it less interventionist than the payday lending legislation.

Monitoring and Accountability

Regulating to achieve the desired balance between sufficient consumer protection and allowing efficient payday lenders to operate requires regular monitoring given that the market for payday loans is dynamic. To ensure regulations best address this tension requires active public participation in periodic reviews that inform the decision-making process.

In Manitoba, the Minister is legislatively mandated to review the effectiveness of the legislation and regulation every three years, and to decide whether the Public Utilities Board should conduct a further review. This demonstrates one type of effort by government in assessing the success of the legislation in achieving its objectives. The Honorable Greg Selinger stated the following:

> The reason we put it into PUB, because it is a quasi-judicial body, arms-length from government, and they can play a strong role in monitoring and reviewing the legislation on a proactive basis. They have a requirement to review every three years, I thought that was quite innovative[…] We gave them a proactive role to stay in front of this issue.
>
> […]
>
> By putting [the PUB] in charge, it would endure any government, [and be a] sort of a permanent mechanism. (Selinger 2017)

In order to make periodic review of legislation and regulation effective, a determination may be necessary of how to measure success and against which benchmarks. One example of measuring success can be found in the intervention by a coalition of consumer groups to the Manitoba Public Utilities Board hearings on payday loans, where evidence has been filed showing changes and trends in statistics and data relating to payday lending outlets and payday lending use over the years since regulation has been enacted.

Public Participation

Public participation in decision-making "actualizes fundamental principles of democracy and strengthens the democratic fabric of society" and contributes to both individual and community empowerment and learning (Stewart and Sinclair 2007). Practically speaking, there are many advantages associated with public participation.[13] While much of the literature on public participation relates to environmental assessment, the findings are transferable to other policy and legislative decisions affecting the public. While there is no one superior format for meaningful public participation, best practices have been established in the literature:

- the process should reflect integrity, accountability, and transparency;
- participants should have a genuine opportunity to be heard and influence decisions;
- the process should be inclusive and provide for adequate representation of affected groups;
- the dialogue should be fair and open;
- there should be multiple and appropriate methods of public participation rather than a one-size-fits-all process;
- provision should be made for participant assistance;
- participation should be early and ongoing; and
- adequate and accessible information should be available to participants.

Additionally and importantly, given the current Canadian context in which the federal government has committed to a "renewed relationship with Indigenous peoples, based on the recognition of rights, respect, co-

[13] Practical benefits associated with public participation in decision-making include, but are not limited to, enhancing the credibility and legitimacy of proposed projects by increasing the transparency of decision-making, helping define problems and identify solutions, helping identify alternative options, permuting a more comprehensive consideration of factors upon which decisions are based, ensuring that projects meet the needs of the public in terms of both purpose and design, bringing alternative ethical perspectives into the decision-making process, increasing accountability for decisions made, facilitating challenges to illegal or invalid decisions before they are implemented, assisting in developing public expertise and creativity, assisting in gaining public support for a particular decision, increasing ease of implementation, providing avenues for conflict resolution for affected parties and stakeholders helping to avoid costly and time-consuming litigation, and reducing the level of controversy associated with a problem or issue.

operation, and partnership" (Rt Hon Justin Trudeau 2017), public participation mechanisms should allow for Indigenous peoples to participate in *their* environments and respect should be given to Indigenous legal traditions and worldviews.

Laws enacted by governments should be a mechanism to give meaning to the best policies for consumers. Meaningful public participation should become an essential part of decision-making relating to payday loans to better ensure that laws meet the needs and circumstances of consumers and that the decision-making process is accountable, transparent, and legitimate.

Decision-Making

Many jurisdictions in Canada, such as Manitoba, Nova Scotia, Alberta, Ontario, and British Columbia, have already incorporated public participation in their decision-making processes relating to payday lending, whether in a public hearing or public consultation format.

In Manitoba, the *Consumer Protection Act* states that the Public Utilities Board holds hearings in relation to payday lending. Under section 164(3) of the *Consumer Protection Act*, within three years after the first regulation regarding the maximum cost of credit for payday loans came into the force, the Public Utilities Board was directed to conduct a review, including public consultation (Government of Manitoba 1987). Every subsequent third year, the Minister must review the effectiveness of the legislation and the regulations and decide whether to require a further review by the Public Utilities Board and whether to recommend changes to the legislation or to the regulation (Government of Manitoba 1987).[14]

The Honorable Greg Selinger recognizes the importance of public participation and the decision-making process established in the legislation:

> I think the PUB review is very innovative, I think that was very positive and has shown results because they have improved the regulations.
>
> [...]
>
> It also gave a venue for the public to have a hearing on a regular basis, in a proactive way, and there is the possibility of intervener funding[....] That

[14] This review had to consider the meaning of "cost of credit" for the purposes of the Act, the maximum cost of credit that may be charged, required, or accepted in respect of a payday loan and the maximum amounts, or the rates, tariffs, or formulas for determining the maximum amounts, that may be charged, required, or accepted for any component of the cost of credit for a payday loan, for the extension of renewal of a payday loan, for a replacement loan, or for a default by the borrower under a payday loan.

> makes the legislation much more of a living piece of legislation that stays in touch with current trends and what's happening to people (Selinger 2017).

Since the amendments to the Manitoba legislation in 2006, the Public Utilities Board has held three public hearings, in 2008, 2013, and 2016, on issues relating to payday lending, including the maximum cost of credit. Giving jurisdiction to the Public Utilities Board to conduct public hearings has allowed any interested organization or individual to participate in the process, whether by applying for formal intervener status or by making an oral presentation or submitting written comments to the Board.

In Manitoba, interveners who fulfill a set of criteria can apply for costs from the Public Utilities Board for their participation in the hearing (PUB Rules). Parties who are granted intervener status can present expert evidence through the submission of written reports and oral witness evidence during the hearing.

The oral hearing represents an essential element of the decision-making process in Manitoba allowing parties to cross-examine witnesses who may be adverse in interest. Cross-examination allows for parties to question the accuracy and the credibility of the evidence adduced by other parties, while direct examination of a witness and closing arguments allow a party to demonstrate to the Board why their evidence should be given more weight in making findings and recommendations.

A coalition of consumer groups has participated in each Public Utilities Board hearing relating to payday loans.[15] This coalition has focused on evidence-based advocacy and has been represented by legal counsel from the Public Interest Law Centre, an independent office of Legal Aid Manitoba. In each hearing, the coalition has retained a team of experts to conduct extensive research and file evidence with the Public Utilities Board in support of their arguments and submissions. The research filed by the coalition has been undertaken by an interdisciplinary team of experts, bringing together different analytical and methodological tools. Interdisciplinary research enables in-depth disciplinary analysis and broad-based interdisciplinary examination. The main methods used in the research undertaken for the coalition have been from the fields of eco-

[15] The organizations involved in the intervention in 2016 were Winnipeg Harvest, Community Financial Counselling Services, and the Manitoba Branch of the Consumers' Association of Canada.

nomics, finance, and social sciences. Methodologies used have included econometric analyses, financial analyses, and field research and analyses.

For the first time in 2016, the Manitoba Public Utilities Board heard directly from a panel of payday loans consumers during the hearing. The panel answered questions from interveners' legal counsel and directly from the Board on their payday loan practices.

Nova Scotia has also taken the approach of holding public hearings, with the most recent hearing being held in February 2015 (NSUARB 2015). The hearing allowed for formal interveners to participate, as well as groups and individuals to make presentations at an evening session.

Ontario and Alberta provide a different example of a decision-making process where public consultations have assisted governments in making decision regarding payday loan regulation (Government of Alberta 2016; Government of Ontario 2016). British Columbia also recently announced a public consultation to review its payday lending regulation (CPBC 2016). In public consultations, governments have invited comments from the public on payday lending regulation and interested organization or individual can participate by sending in their submissions.

Conclusion

The history of payday lending legislation and regulation in Canada and in the United States demonstrates the recognition by governments that payday lenders fill a gap in the marketplace but that payday loan consumers must be protected from high fees and the cycle of debt often associated with payday loans. In these jurisdictions the objective of payday lending regulation appears to be a delicate balance between protecting consumers and allowing reasonably efficient companies to continue operating. However, as demonstrated by governments constantly evolving and reviewing regulatory tools and that the marketplace remains dynamic, regulators are still struggling to achieve the desired delicate balance.

The Manitoba Public Utilities Board has recognized in each of its reports on payday lending that the industry exists because a significant segment of consumers cannot access the products they require through mainstream financial institutions, such as banks and credit unions. The Manitoba Public Utilities Board has consistently recommended that mainstream banks and credit unions begin offering small balance short-term credit options for consumers who rely on payday lenders (PUB 2008).

While some credit unions have recognized this gap in the market and have begun offering products with similar characteristics to payday loans (Buckland et al. 2016),[16] it is likely that until more banks and credit union begin offering products that meet the needs of all consumers, payday lenders will continue to fill a gap in the marketplace. Given this reality, governments will likely continue to strive to achieve the balance between protecting consumers and allowing efficient payday lenders to operate, while remaining vigilant of payday loan-like products developing in a constantly evolving marketplace.

Works Cited

Australian Securities and Investments Commission (ASIC). 2015a, March. *15-056MR ASIC Puts Payday Lending Industry on Notice to Lift Standards.* Australia. Accessed on July 25, 2017. http://www.asic.gov.au/about-asic/media-centre/find-a-media-release/2015-releases/15-056mr-asic-puts-payday-lending-industry-on-notice-to-lift-standards/

———. 2015b. Australia. Accessed on July 25, 2017. https://www.moneysmart.gov.au/borrowing-and-credit/consumer-credit-regulation

Baldwin, R., M. Cave, and M. Lodge. 2011. *Understanding Regulation: Theory, Strategy, and Practice.* 2nd ed. New York: Oxford University Press.

BC Gov News. 2016, September 21. *Cost of Payday Loans to Drop Amid Look at All High-Cost Financial Services.* (P. S. General, Producer). Accessed on July 24, 2017. https://news.gov.bc.ca/releases/2016PSSG0193-001751?WT.cg_n=Hootsuite

Bellam, J., and A. Talai. 2012. Short-Term Emergency Lending: Examining Usury Law in the United States and Canada. *Western. Journal of Legal Studies* 2 (1).

Buckland, J., E. Sinclair, and K. Martin. 2016. *Small Loan Workshop: Summary of Proceedings and Recommendations.* Accessed on July 27, 2017. http://www.pubmanitoba.ca/v1/payday_loan_review2016/cac_12_tab_9_small_loans_workshop_j_buckland_e_sinclair_k_martin.pdf

CBC News. 2016. http://www.cbc.ca/news/canada/newfoundland-labrador/payday-loan-regulations-1.3876186

City of Hamilton. 2016. *By-Law No. 07-170, a By-Law to License and Regulate Various Businesses.* Accessed on July 27, 2017. https://d3fpllf1m7bbt3.cloudfront.net/sites/default/files/media/browser/2016-02-25/16-053.pdf

[16] One example is Vancity Credit Union out of Vancouver, British Columbia, offers a Fair and Fast Loan, which shares some characteristics with payday loans, such as convenience and the ability to borrow small amounts, but charges an interest rate of 19% APR, online: https://www.vancity.com/Loans/TypesOfLoans/FairAndFastLoan/?xcid=pers_mega-menu_fairfast

Consumer Financial Protection Bureau (CFPB). 2015. *Financial Well-Being: The Goal of Financial Education*. January. Accessed on July 25, 2017. http://files.consumerfinance.gov/f/201501_cfpb_report_financial-well-being.pdf

Consumer Protection BC. 2016. Accessed on July 24, 2017. https://www.consumerprotectionbc.ca/component/search/?searchword=aggregate%20data%20form&searchphrase=all&Itemid=1325; https://www.consumerprotectionbc.ca/news/payday-lending/1348-cost-of-payday-loans-to-drop-from-23-to-17-per-100-borrowed

Consumers Council of Canada. 2015. *Consumer Experiences in Online Payday Loans*. Denise Barrett Consulting. Accessed on July 25, 2017. http://www.consumerscouncil.com/site/consumers_council_of_canada/assets/pdf/ccc_online_payday_loans_web.pdf

Ellis, D. 1998. *The Effect of Consumer Rate Deregulation on Credit Card Volumes, Charge-Offs, and the Personal Bankruptcy Rate*. Federal Deposit Insurance Corporation. Accessed on July 24, 2017. https://www.fdic.gov/bank/analytical/bank/bt_9805.html

Financial Conduct Authority. 2014. *FCA Confirms Price Cap Rules for Payday Lenders*. Australia. Accessed on July 25, 2017. https://www.fca.org.uk/search-results?search_term=Borrowers%20must%20never%20have%20to%20pay%20back%20more%20in%20fees%20and%20interest%20than%20the%20amount%20borrowed

Financial Conduct Authority (FCA). 2015. *PS14/16: Detailed Rules for the Price Cap on High-Cost Short-Term Credit – Including Feedback on CP14/10 and Final Rules*. Australia. Accessed on July 25, 2017. https://www.fca.org.uk/publications/policy-statements/ps14-16-detailed-rules-price-cap-high-cost-short-term-credit

Financial Consumer Agency of Canada (FCAC). 2015. *National Strategy for Financial Literacy: Count Me In, Canada*. Government of Canada. Accessed on July 25, 2017. https://www.canada.ca/content/dam/canada/financial-consumer-agency/migration/eng/financialliteracy/financialliteracycanada/strategy/documents/nationalstrategyforfinancialliteracycountmeincanada.pdf

Government of Alberta. 2000. *Fair Trading Act*. RSA 2000, c F-2, at s 124.61(1). Legislative Assembly of Alberta. Accessed on July 24, 2017. http://www.qp.alberta.ca/documents/Acts/F02.pdf

———. 2016. *Payday Loan Regulation Review*. Service Alberta. Accessed on July 27, 2017. http://www.servicealberta.ca/3154.cfm

Government of Australia. 2009. *National Consumer Credit Protection Act, No 134. (2009)*. In *National Consumer Credit Code* (pp. Schedule 1, ss 72–81). Australia: Commonwealth Consolidated Acts. Accessed on July 25, 2017. http://www.austlii.edu.au/au/legis/cth/consol_act/nccpa2009377/sch1.html

Government of British Columbia. 2004. *Business Practices and Consumer Protection Act, [SBC 2004] Chapter 2, at s 112.02*. Victoria. Accessed on July 24, 2017. http://www.bclaws.ca/civix/document/id/complete/statreg/04002_00

———. 2009. *Payday Loans Regulation, BC Reg 57/2009, at s. 17(1)*. Accessed on July 24, 2017. http://www.bclaws.ca/Recon/document/ID/freeside/16_57_2009
Government of Canada. 1939. *Small Loans Act of 1939, George VI c 23 SC 1939 c 23*.
———. 1980a. *32nd Parliament 1st Session Vol 1, 752*. May 6.
———. 1980b. *32nd Parliament 1st Session Vol 4, 4642*. Nov. 13.
———. 1980c. *SENATE 32nd Parliament 1st Session Vol 1, 816*. Oct. 7.
———. 1985. *Criminal Code R.C.C., c. C-46*. Accessed on July 24, 2017. http://laws-lois.justice.gc.ca/eng/acts/C-46/
Government of Manitoba. 1987. *Consumer Protection Act, CCSM c C200, RSM 1987. (Payday Loans Act)*. Legislative Assembly of Manitoba. Accessed on July 25, 2017. http://web2.gov.mb.ca/laws/statutes/ccsm/c200e.php
———. 2007. *Payday Loans Regulation, 99/2007*. Accessed on July 24, 2017. https://web2.gov.mb.ca/laws/regs/current/_pdf-regs.php?reg=99/2007
———. 2013. *The Consumer Protection Amendment Act (High-Cost Credit Products) Bill 34, 3rd Session, 40th Legislature*. The Legislative Assembly of Manitoba. Accessed on July 27, 2017. https://web2.gov.mb.ca/bills/40-3/b034e.php
———. 2014–2015 and 2015–2016. *Manitoba Tourism, Culture, Heritage, Sport and Consumer Protection Annual Reports 2014–2015 and 2015–2016*. Accessed on July 25, 2017. https://www.gov.mb.ca/chc/reports/pdf/annual_report_2014-15_tchscp.pdf; http://www.gov.mb.ca/chc/reports/pdf/annual_report_2015-16_tchscp.pdf
———. 2016. *High-Cost Credit Products Regulation, Pursuant to the Consumer Protection Act CCSM c. C200*. Accessed on July 27, 2017. https://web2.gov.mb.ca/laws/regs/current/_pdf-regs.php?reg=7/2016
Government of New Brunswick. 2008. *An Act Respecting Payday Loans, SNB 2008 c3*. Legislative Assembly of New Brunswick.
Government of Newfoundland and Labrador – Canada. 2010. *Provincial Government Will Not Regulate Payday Loan Companies*. Government Services. Accessed on June 16, 2010. http://www.releases.gov.nl.ca/releases/2010/gs/0616n11.htm
Government of Newfoundland and Labrador. 2016. An Act to Amend The Consumer Protection and Business Practices Act. http://www.assembly.nl.ca/business/bills/bill1652.htm
Government of Newfoundland and Labrador House of Assembly. 2016. Progress of Bills. http://www.assembly.nl.ca/business/bills/ga48session1.htm
Government of Nova Scotia. 2015. *Payday Lenders Regulations, NS Reg 84/2015, s 5*. Accessed on July 25, 2017. https://novascotia.ca/just/regulations/regs/cppayday.htm
Government of Ontario. 2008a. *Payday Loans Act, 2008, S.O. 2008, c. 9*. Accessed on July 24, 2017. https://www.ontario.ca/laws/statute/08p09

———. 2008b. *O. Reg. 98/09: General, at s. 23, (*under *Payday Loans Act, 2008, S.O. 2008, c. 9)*. Accessed on July 24, 2017. https://www.ontario.ca/laws/regulation/090098

———. 2016. *Ontario Seeking Input on Lower Rates for Payday Loans.* Ontario Newsroom. Accessed on July 27, 2017. https://news.ontario.ca/mgs/en/2016/04/ontario-seeking-input-on-lower-rates-for-payday-loans.html

Government of Prince Edward Island. 1988. *Payday Loans Act, RSPEI, c P-2.1.* Accessed on July 24, 2017. https://www.princeedwardisland.ca/sites/default/files/legislation/p-02_1.pdf

———. 2015. *Payday Loans Act Regulations, Chapter P-2.1, at s 24.* Accessed on July 24, 2017. https://www.princeedwardisland.ca/sites/default/files/legislation/p02-1g.pdf

Government of Saskatchewan. 2007. *The Payday Loans Act, SS 2007, c P-4.3.* Accessed on July 24, 2017. http://www.qp.gov.sk.ca/documents/English/Statutes/Statutes/P4-3.pdf

———. 2012a. *The Payday Loans Act, SS 2007, c P-4.3.* The Statutes of Saskatchewan. Accessed on July 24, 2017. http://www.qp.gov.sk.ca/documents/English/Statutes/Statutes/P4-3.pdf

———. 2012b. *The Payday Loans Regulations, c P-4.3, Reg 1, at s. 23(1).* Accessed on July 24, 2017. http://www.qp.gov.sk.ca/documents/English/Regulations/Regulations/P4-3R1.pdf

Government of the United Kingdom. 1970. *Administration of Justice Act 1970, c. 31.* Accessed on July 25, 2017. http://www.legislation.gov.uk/ukpga/1970/31/introduction

———. 1974. *Consumer Credit Act 1974, c 39, Part IX.* Accessed on July 25, 2017. http://www.legislation.gov.uk/cy/ukpga/1974/39/part/IX/data.xht?wrap=true

Government of the United States. 2008. *Consumer Financial Protection Bureau.* Accessed on July 25, 2017. https://www.consumerfinance.gov/about-us/the-bureau/

Government of the United States (CFPB). 2016. *Consumer Financial Protection Bureau Proposes Rules to End Payday Debt Traps.* June 2. Accessed on July 25, 2017. http://files.consumerfinance.gov/f/documents/CFPB_Proposes_Rule_End_Payday_Debt_Traps.pdf

Government of the United States. 2017. Payday, Vehicle Title, and Certain High-Cost Installment Loans. November 11, 2017. https://www.gpo.gov/fdsys/pkg/FR-2017-11-17/pdf/2017-21808.pdf. Accessed 27 December 2017.

Iacobucci, E., and M. Trebilcock. 2012. *The Role of Crown Corporates in the Canadian Economy.* 5:9 The School of Public Policy Research Papers 1. Toronto: Faculty of Law, University of Toronto.

Kitching, A. 2006. *Bill C-26: An Act to Amend the Criminal Code (Criminal Interest Rate).* Legislative Summary LS-541 E. (Revised on September 28,

2007). Library of Parliament. Accessed on July 24, 2017. http://www.lop.parl.gc.ca/Content/LOP/LegislativeSummaries/39/1/c26-e.pdf

Kitching, A., and S. Starky, 2006. *Payday Loan Companies on Canada: Determining the Public Interest.* Legislative Summary (PRB 05-81E), Parliamentary Information and Research Service, Library of Parliament of Canada. Accessed on July 24, 2017. http://www.lop.parl.gc.ca/contents/lop/researchpublications/prb0581-e.pdf

Lo, J. 2011. *A Criminal Rate of Interest: Updating Garland for Consumers.* Ottawa: Public Interest Advocacy Centre. Accessed on July 24, 2017. https://www.piac.ca/wp-content/uploads/2014/11/GarlandUpdate_FINAL

Manitoba Public Utilities Board. 2008. *Public Utilities Board Rules of Practice.* Accessed on July 27, 2017. http://www.pubmanitoba.ca/v1/pdf/pandp/rules_pandp_mar07.pdf

News Release – Manitoba. 2013. *New Rules Would Add Protections for Consumers Using High-Interest Loans.* Accessed on July 27, 2017. http://news.gov.mb.ca/news/?item=19831&posted=2013-12-04

Nova Scotia Utility and Review Board. 2015. *NSUARB 64.* Accessed on July 24, 2017. https://nsuarb.novascotia.ca/sites/default/files/m06084_payday_loans_decision.pdf

Ontario Superior Court of Justice. 2014. *The Director v The Cash Store, 2014 ONSC 980.*

Oxford Dictionary. 1884. Usury. In *Oxford Dictionary.* Accessed on July 21, 2017. https://en.oxforddictionaries.com/definitions/usury

Parkin, M., and R. Bade. 2006. *Micro Economics: Canada in the Global Environment.* 6th ed. Toronto: Pearson Addison Wesley.

Pew, N. 1946. *The Pew Charitable Trusts.* Accessed on July 25, 2017. http://www.pewtrusts.org/en/about/mission-and-values

Public Utilities Board. 2008. *Maximum Charges for Payday Loans, PUB Order No. 39/08.* Manitoba. Accessed on July 24, 2017. http://www.pubmanitoba.ca/v1/proceedings-decisions/orders/misc07on.html

———. 2013. *Payday Loans Review, PUB Order No. 38/13.* Manitoba. Accessed July 25, 2017. http://www.pubmanitoba.ca/v1/pdf/misc/38_13.pdf

———. 2016. *Report on Payday Loans Review.* Manitoba, June 17. Accessed on July 25, 2017. http://www.pubmanitoba.ca/v1/payday_loan/2016_payday_loans_review_report.pdf

Rt Hon Justin Trudeau. 2017. *New Ministers to support the renewed relationship with Indigenous Peoples.* Accessed on February 4, 2018. https://pm.gc.ca/eng/news/2017/08/28/new-ministers-support-renewed-relationship-indigenous-peoples

Selinger, G. 2017. *Conversation on the Origin and Development of Payday Lending Regulations in Manitoba.* Interviewer K. Dilay, Winnipeg, January 27.

Stewart, J., and J. Sinclair. 2007. *Meaningful Public Participation in Environmental Assessment: Perspectives from Canadian Participants, Proponents, and*

Government. 9:2 *Journal of Environmental Assessment Policy and Management* 161, 162.
Supreme Court Judgments. 1998. *Garland v Consumers' Gas Co., 3 SCR 112.* Ontario. Accessed on July 24, 2017. https://scc-csc.lexum.com/scc-csc/scc-csc/en/item/2138/index.do
The City of Calgary, City Council. 2007. *Land Use Bylaw – 1P2007, at s 254.1(c)*. Land Use Bylaw Sustaining Team, Development and Building Approvals, Planning Implementation. Accessed on July 27, 2017. http://www.calgary.ca/PDA/pd/Documents/Calgary-Land-Use-bylaw-1P2007/bylaw_1p2007.pdf
The Financial and Consumer Services Commission of New Brunswick. 2017. Saint John. http://0104.nccdn.net/1_5/046/09d/2c6/Bulletin---2017-006---Payday-Loan-Implementation.pdf. Accessed 27 December 2017.
The Pew Charitable Trusts. 2012, July. *Payday Lending in America: Who Borrows, Where They Borrow, and Why*. Washington, D.C.: Pew Safe Small-Dollar Loans Research Project. Accessed on July 25, 2017. http://www.pewtrusts.org/~/media/legacy/uploadedfiles/pcs_assets/2012/pewpaydaylendingreportpdf.pdf
———. 2013, October. *Payday Lending in America: Policy Solutions. Report 3 in the Payday Lending in America Series*. Accessed on July 25, 2017. http://www.pewtrusts.org/~/media/legacy/uploadedfiles/pcs_assets/2013/pewpayday-policysolutionsoct2013pdf.pdf
Uniform Law Conference of Canada. 2008. *Report of the Criminal Section Working Group on Criminal Interest Rate: A Discussion Paper Section 347 of the Criminal Code in Need of Reform*. Quebec City. Accessed on July 24, 2017. http://www.ulcc.ca/en/annual-meetings/229-2008-quebec-city-qc/criminal-section-documents/854-criminal-interest-rate
Washington State Department of Financial Institutions. 2015. *2015 Payday Lending Report*. Accessed on July 25, 2017. http://www.dfi.wa.gov/sites/default/files/reports/2015-payday-lending-report.pdf

CHAPTER 8

Conclusion

Jerry Buckland, Chris Robinson,
and Brenda Spotton Visano

Introduction

Payday lending is a growing sector in terms of geographic reach and in terms of the number of products it offers. It is a highly contentious industry and a part of a 'second tier' of banking directed at income- and asset-constrained consumers. Yet books on payday lending are few in number and focus primarily on the United States. This book has uniquely completed an in-depth and inter-disciplinary analysis of payday lending in Canada. Its scope of analysis included examination of payday lending in the United States, and so the book has examined two countries with a relatively long history of payday lending. Thus its analysis has important implications for countries where payday lending has more recently been established. The analysis is based on a large-scale mixed methodology research and

J. Buckland (✉)
Menno Simons College, Canadian Mennonite University,
Affiliated with the University of Winnipeg, Winnipeg, MB, Canada

C. Robinson
Faculty of Liberal Arts and Professional Studies, School of Administrative Studies, York University, Toronto, ON, Canada

B. Spotton Visano
Department of Economics, School of Public Policy and Administration, York University, Toronto, ON, Canada

J. Buckland et al. (eds.), *Payday Lending in Canada in a Global Context*,
https://doi.org/10.1007/978-3-319-71213-0_8

includes socio-economic, financial, econometric, and legal components. It fills a major gap in terms of comprehensive studies of payday lending.

The motivation in writing the book was that payday lending is an important example of financialization, a process that increases the supply and demand for financial products. This study is important because payday loans are largely used by people with limited income or who are credit-constrained, and a certain share of these people take out many loans in one year. Indeed, there is evidence that for the payday lender to improve their efficiencies, they require customers to borrow repeatedly. Payday lending is a controversial industry with proponents and opponents arguing pros and cons, often with limited evidence. This book has provided up-to-date financial, econometric, and socio-economic analysis using evidence from a number of sources. And the objective of the book is to present evidence, theory, and argument that demonstrate the complex impact of payday lending on their clients and the need for careful regulation of payday lending to minimize these harmful consequences.

By Chapter

The literature has found that payday lending has reached a mature period in the sense that its growth has slowed from the 1990s and 2000s period. Corporatization and proliferation of additional and related services is a part of the industry dynamics today. Finally, payday lending is expanding beyond its Anglo-American roots into Eastern Europe and South Africa. Online payday lending is also new, but there is very little evidence about its size and so forecasting its future is difficult.

The overall evidence is limited and somewhat mixed about whether payday lending benefits consumers. What is clear is that some consumers who rely on multiple loans really need a different type of product or approach and they are not benefiting—and are possibly being harmed—from excessive use of payday loans. Behavioral theorists argue that this type of short-sighted use of payday lending is consistent with what they call tunneling, or 'borrowing from Peter (or tomorrow's income) to pay Paul (today's expenses).' With few options and bills to pay, some people opt for payday loans even though they are likely unable to pay them off. This behavior might be promoted through the marketing actions of payday lenders.

Studies on the impact of regulations find that price caps at $10 per $100 borrowed might lead to a substantial reduction in storefronts but caps at $15 per $100 borrowed are sufficient to maintain payday loan volumes. Restrictions on amount borrowed tend to be less successful as consumers find other ways to borrow money. One study found that in US states that effectively disallow payday loans consumers are able to 'make ends meet' by either reducing spending or finding other sources of credit such as family and friends.

Insights from the Econometric Analysis

Statistical analysis of the most recent Canadian national surveys find that, while there are important exceptions, payday loan clients continue to come from lower-income categories. Moreover, a growing share of payday loans clients are getting a loan levered not on their paycheck but on another source of income such as social assistance or child benefit payments. The evidence finds that payday loan clients are younger, less educated, and more likely to be supporting children, on average, as compared with the general population. Canadian national data on repeat borrowing are limited. The rates of repeat borrowing are highest among people in the second and third (from the bottom) income quintile of the population. And the evidence finds that people receiving social assistance or pension payments are becoming more common repeat borrowers. Only British Columbia and Nova Scotia have data regarding loan volumes per customer, and the evidence from the former is that repeat borrowing is a major problem for a subset of payday loan customers.

The more sophisticated econometric analysis that allows for the better control of certain variables finds similar if somewhat different results than the statistical analysis. This analysis finds that the typical client is poor but not the poorest and lacking assets; less educated as compared to the general population; relatively young but aging; likely to be working, but this factor is declining as relying on social payments for a payday loan is rising.

Insights from the Socio-economic Analysis

Analysis of a small sample mixed methods research project revealed interesting results about the reasons for using payday loans and payday loan borrowers' thoughts on comparing the standard Canadian payday loan with two alternatives. Borrowers discussed factors that led them to rely on payday loans, and these factors come from a 'push side' and a 'pull side.'

Push side factors include factors that prevent borrowers from using alternatives and so include things such as deteriorating income, an absence of locally available bank branches, and/or an inability to access bank credit products. Pull side factors include things that attract borrowers to payday lenders, and this includes factors such as learning from one's community of practice (e.g., frequenting payday lenders because they are used by friends and family members), accessibility of local payday loan outlets, and the invitational nature of payday lender staff. Respondents reinforced insight from the national survey analysis in that several of them used their payday loan not in anticipation of a paycheck but in anticipation of a social assistance or pension payment. Respondents were confused about what the annual interest rate is for a two-week payday loan, and many respondents thought that the price cap of $17 per $100 borrowed represented an APR.

Respondents' experiences with repeat borrowing varied. Respondents generally agreed that payday loans are easy to get and, for some, hard to repay. Some engaged in borrowing several payday loans in one year and others did not. Those that borrowed repeatedly described falling into a debt cycle, feeling a sense of loss of control, and finding it difficult to recover. Respondents that limited their borrowing were better able to repay the loan and in fact were quite strategic with their use of payday loans.

In the case of repeat borrowing, some respondents described how they would borrow from one payday lending company to pay off another payday lending company. In some cases people relied on payday loans sporadically, while other respondents were chronically relying on them. Respondents noted that in some cases occasional use of payday loans could grow into a chronic reliance.

Respondents of a focus group were asked to compare a typical Canadian payday loan with two alternatives, and the results were interesting. After the three products—a typical Canadian payday loan, the Vancity Fair and Fast loan, and the US state of Colorado's installment payday loan—were explained to them, respondents were asked about their preferences about the different products and why (Table 4.2). The Canadian payday loan is a maximum $1500 two-week loan with APRs that start around 500% and is repaid in one installment. The Vancity Fair and Fast loan is up to $2500 1–2-year loan with a 19% APR that involves installment repayments. The Colorado model loan is up to USD 500 with a 129% APR with installment repayments.

Focus group participants were largely in favor of the Vancity Fair and Fast loan because of its lower interest fees, but two strategic users of payday loans preferred the Canadian payday loan. Some respondents preferred the installment repayment of the Colorado state product, and some of these also like the Vancity Fair and Fast loan. However, some of these people felt the term of the Vancity Fair and Fast loan was too long. However, some respondents were unwavering that they preferred to pay off their loan within the two-week period. The larger loan which is available through the Vancity Fair and Fast loan was appealing to some of the participants, but others saw it as a weakness as they felt that it led to excessive borrowing that could not be repaid. The opportunity to build one's credit rating, associated with the Vancity Fair and Fast loan, appealed to some participants who expressed support for this feature. Other respondents did not find this feature attractive.

Payday Lender Finances and Economics

Robinson undertook a careful financial and economic analysis of payday lending to present important insights about the characteristics of the industry that policy makers and consumer advocates must understand. He finds that the average payday loan store handles 11 loans per day for an average volume of $5000 and revenue of $1000 and concludes that this is a relatively inefficient way to deliver small loans. He argues that payday lenders rely on repeat borrowers to remain in business as there are insufficient one-time payday loan users. His analysis includes a comparison of the industry in Canada, the United States, and the United Kingdom. Robinson also considers how to formulate regulation to enable efficient payday lenders to offer relatively lower-priced payday loans. Robinson argues that the industry is earning excessive profits in provinces where rate caps are above the efficient price level, which he estimates to be around $15 per $100 loaned. He also finds that limiting loan size will not assist consumers and that internet lending is, until now, highly unprofitable.

Ethical Issues and Payday Lending

Robinson and Robinson examined ethical aspects of payday lending. They begin by defining what it means to undertake an ethical or an unethical act. An unethical act, they argued, is an exploitative act that harms the borrower. They argue that there is strong consensus that the relationship is unethical in the case of the repeat borrower who is unable to repay her loan. In this case the borrower is harmed either deliberately or not. But they challenge the notion, promoted by industry proponents, that argues that lending to the one-time borrower is not unethical, and argue that in some cases it can be. They argue that unethical behavior occurs, for the one-time and repeat borrower, when the lender takes the lion's share of the mutual benefit that flows from the transaction. Chris and Denys Robinson also argue that since payday lenders do not underwrite their loans, that they tend to lend to risky borrowers and that there is a cross-subsidization from the less risky who default less to the more risky who default more, and this is unethical. Finally, the authors used a corporate social responsibility framework to assess the ethics of payday lenders and find evidence of payday lender violations. The authors concluded that payday lenders charge unethical rates if they are not effectively regulated and that payday loans often do not benefit consumers sufficiently—as compared with the benefit to the firm—to justify their operations. They conclude that there is a strong ethical case to effectively regulate payday lenders in order to minimize human harm.

Mainstream FI Alternatives

Spotton Visano begins her analysis by discussing the barriers un-banked and under-banked people face to accessing mainstream financial institution (FI) services. She noted that without a bank account, people lack a means to facilitate transactions, let alone access credit, savings, and investment services. These barriers include issues such as lack of personal identification, difficulty accessing a mainstream FI branch location, and unhelpful bank staff. Spotton Visano notes that for some people the cost of maintaining a bank account is high or unknown so that fees are charged to the account without knowledge of the types of fees or even that the fees will be charged. Moreover, sometimes funds are 'held' by the bank, before the client can access them, in order to fully process them. This delay can cause a 'cash crunch' for vulnerable people on a tight budget.

In the next section, Spotton Visano investigated various alternatives to payday loans that mainstream FIs have pursued or could pursue. In the late 1990s/early 2000s, the federal government introduced a number of initiatives intended to improve access to banking for un-banked and under-banked Canadians. This included negotiating with banks to create low-cost accounts, clarifying and simplifying the personal identification requirements to set up a bank account, completing indemnification agreements with the major banks with respect to the cashing of certain federal government checks, and establishing annual bank reporting requirements with respect to community contributions. This process culminated in the establishment of the 2003 Access to Basic Banking Regulations. Since that time some other minor initiatives have been made by the federal government in this area.

Other levels of government have taken initiatives to address financial exclusion. For instance, some jurisdictions have introduced prepaid benefits cards as an alternative to checks. This enables the un-banked recipient to access her money immediately. Some mainstream FIs have taken initiatives to address financial exclusion such as credit schemes (e.g., Vancity Fair and Fast loan and the Desjardins Federation small loan project) and the establishment of community banking projects (e.g., Pigeon Park Savings, a Vancity Credit Union's partnership with PHS Community Services; Assiniboine Credit Union's 'mini branch' system in inner-city Winnipeg). Finally, Spotton Visano identifies critical gaps in financial service access, most notably remote rural access.

Payday Lending Regulations

The chapter on regulations, by Dilay and Williams, examines the full range of regulations used to control the payday lending industry in Canada, and they spend considerable time looking at the situation in the United States. Their chapter begins by considering the concept of market failure which is the common justification for government intervention. They argue that proponents of regulating the payday loan industry justify the regulation on the basis of it lacking effective competition and that there is a power differential between firms and vulnerable consumers. The authors note that in Canada the regulation of payday lending has been handed to the provinces and their (the provinces') response has varied from effectively outlawing, through ignoring, to establishing a package of regulations that generally include fair disclosure requirements and price caps.

Dilay and Williams then examine the foundation of usury laws, usury laws around the world, and consider a brief history of usury laws in Canada. They note the movement from more active federal government regulations in the mid-twentieth century that was later substituted with criminalization of usurious interest, but they note that this criminalization is understood to have been directed at credit from organized crime. They note that continental European nations and Australia are more active in regulating high-interest credit. The authors then discuss the development of payday loan regulations that began with the federal government creating an exemption to the Criminal Rate of Interest and requiring the provinces to establish a package of regulations for payday lending. Dilay and Williams argue that the objective of most Canadian jurisdictions, with the notable exception of Quebec, has been to regulate 'excessive' payday lender fees and practices while enabling 'efficient' payday lenders to continue to operate. Today each province has separate payday loan regulations, but the majority of provinces have a package of regulations that include fair disclosure requirements and price caps. Quebec effectively outlaws payday loans through its usury ceiling of 35%, and Newfoundland and Labrador and New Brunswick have either not regulated payday lending or are in the process of regulating the sector. Dilay and Williams then consider the regulatory regime in the United States and find some parallels to Canadian regulations. They note the pioneering approach by regulators in Colorado to transform payday loans into installment loans and the current efforts on the part of the US Consumer Financial Protection Bureau to require lenders to underwrite their loans.

Dilay and Williams conclude their discussion by considering the success of regulation in Manitoba. They argue that the regulations have been successful in that they have enabled the most efficient firms to offer payday loans to consumers in Manitoba. Moreover, the regulatory process in the province has engaged with stakeholders, involved expert analysis, and heard from payday loan consumers.

By Theme

The objective of the book is to present evidence, theory, and argument that demonstrate the complex impact of payday lending on their clients and the need for careful regulation of payday lending to minimize these harmful consequences. The data and evidence provided here enable us to point to four areas in which we can make strong conclusions. These include: Do payday loans help its clients? Are payday loan characteristics well-aligned with its clients' interests? Are there mainstream FI alternatives to payday loans? And, do regulations help payday loan consumers?

Do Payday Loans Help the Clients?

Caskey (2010) finds that there is little empirical evidence that definitively finds that payday lending helps or harms the clients. But through this we see evidence of a variety of client experiences that include clients who are helped and those who are not helped and/or harmed. Some studies find benefits for consumers and some find a lack of benefits and/or costs for consumers. What we argue is, while the overall effect of payday lending on its clientele may be ambiguous, there is evidence of groups of people who benefit, the 'strategic borrower,' and people who do not benefit and/or are harmed by using payday loans, the 'debtor.' Let us characterize each of these groups as follows:

- Customers who benefit from a payday loan

  Payday lenders sometimes justify their product by painting anecdotal pictures of their clients who are employed and have a temporary income shortfall/expenditure overage that can be addressed through the occasional use of a payday loan. This client is able to strategically use the payday loan in order to meet the temporary deficit in her net income. Statistical and econometric analysis of Canadian national surveys finds that while most clients come from a modest income background, some come from a less modest income background. These relatively better-off clients are less likely to be overwhelmed by one or two payday loans in one year. The socio-economic research found some respondents in this situation: they had savings but strategically used payday loans to achieve a financial goal. In this case it would appear that the payday loan is benefiting the client.

- Clients who are not helped and/or harmed by using a payday loan

  Statistical and econometric analysis found that the lion's share of payday loans continue to be used by modest income Canadians and that a growing share of payday loans clients are getting a loan levered not on their paycheck but on another source of income such as social assistance or pension payment. The socio-economic research identified push and pull factors leading these people to use payday loans. Push side factors include deteriorating income, an absence of bank branches, and/or an inability to access bank credit products. Pull factors include having friends and family members that regularly use payday loans, the availability of payday loan outlets in one's neighborhood, and the invitational nature of payday lender staff. The socio-economic research found that clients in this situation were sometimes drawn into a payday loan cycle that they found hard to get out of. The problem lies in the misalignment between the payday loan structure (short term and expensive) as compared to these clients' needs (long term and not expensive) and the lack of payday lender underwriting of their clients' loans. Without the filter of underwriting, some clients gain access to payday loans to address longer-term credit issues and are therefore not helped by the payday loan and in some cases are harmed. The question of how to reduce the harms and increase the benefits of payday lending will be dealt with below.

Are Payday Loan Characteristics Well-Aligned with Its Clients' Interests?

Payday loans are popular with payday lenders and a variety of borrowers because of a confluence of interests. On the one hand, the lender finds that leveraging the loan on a source of income like a paycheck improves repayment. Since they are a relatively expensive product to supply, the payday lender charges a very high fee. Since most Canadians receive some type of regular payment and some modest incomer recipients lack sufficient credit, they are also interested in the payday loan. Some common payday loan consumers include low-income unemployed, low-income employed, and modest middle-income employed. Our limited evidence suggests that payday loans are more useful for people who use credit strategically. This is more likely to be associated with people who are earning above minimum wage and are employed or temporarily unemployed. For at least some of these people they use payday loans strategically. A payday loan seems to be aligned with their short-term needs, and their short-term needs do not seem to be entirely in conflict with their longer-term needs.

In some cases payday loan borrowers become entangled in a debt cycle. For instance, some clients who are more permanently unemployed or earning minimum wage are more likely to face more chronically lower income. These clients are more likely to experience a misalignment of their financial needs in using a payday loan. They require a longer-term solution that they are attempting to deal with through a short-term credit product. For these vulnerable people, a payday loan is not a helpful solution and instead they need some combination of increased income, decreased spending. This might be the result of a longer-term financial product, new employment, improved employment, improved social supports, and/or improved financial literacy. None of these options are available at a payday lender. A mainstream FI could provide longer-term financial products (see discussion below) and, possibly, financial literacy related to these products. Improved employment and/or social supports are outside of the realm of the financial service sector.

Are There Mainstream FI Alternatives to Payday Loans?

Most mainstream FIs offer a variety of products that can partly compete with payday loans. They are not perfect substitutes but, together, they can offer many payday loan clients the products they need to meet most of their financial needs. But part of the issue here, as discussed in Chap. 6, is that mainstream FIs have closed down branches in low-income neighborhoods, they do not market their basic banking services in a deliberate fashion, and their staff are not trained to work with low-income clients. Thus the barriers to this set of services substituting for payday loans are at an 'institutional' level that requires a holistic institutional change and not simply the creation of a payday loan substitute. While Canadian basic banking regulations address opening an account or cashing certain federal government checks, they do not address these barriers.

The set of mainstream FI products that can meet many of these financial needs include basic bank accounts with automatic deposit and debit features, overdraft protection, free federal government check cashing with immediate release of some funds, and community banking projects that provide bricks and mortar branches into low-income neighborhoods.

Overdraft protection is the closest substitute, among present mainstream FI offerings, to a payday loan. It is also a product that mainstream FIs can and do offer in a way that is viable (i.e., profitable) for them (the FI). By expanding (through marketing and increased capital allocation) overdraft protection to payday loan clients, mainstream FIs could assist in reducing people's reliance on payday loans. However, it is not clear that this particular product has the same features that will make it attractive to all payday loan customers. Interestingly one small community banking project in a very poor neighborhood in Vancouver, Pigeon Park Savings, has created an overdraft product for its clients. But generally speaking, overdraft is something that is not widely available for un-banked and under-banked people. Along with basic bank accounts, overdraft could be an important part of addressing financial exclusion in Canada.

In some cases payday loan customers are looking for a loan that has a 'structured' repayment process, like a standard installment loan, whether one-time repayment like a payday loan or multiple repayment like an installment loan. Consistent with behavioral economics insights, at times people look for products that might be more expensive but that will 'nudge' them into a desired outcome, for example, require them to repay their loan through installments. In some cases mainstream FIs such as Vancity Credit Union and the Desjardins Federation have created credit products to compete with a payday loan, but these products, so far, are small in scope. Most mainstream FIs shy away from offering these products because they anticipate high costs associated with delivering a labor-intensive credit product. Vancity Credit Union's product is the closest to a substitute for payday loans, but it may be too soon to determine if the credit union can viably provide this product into the future.

Community banking projects offer a holistic means to addressing financial exclusion: they offer a variety of financial services such as a basic bank account and overdraft protection. Examples of community banking projects include Pigeon Park Savings in Vancouver and Assiniboine Credit Union's 'mini' branches in Winnipeg's inner city. These projects are not directly competing with payday loans; however, they are offering a set of services that address financial exclusion, which may indirectly reduce the demand on payday loans. They are a low-cost version of an FI branch and something that is needed in many inner-cities given the branch closures that hit those communities from the 1980s. The challenge with these projects is that they are expensive to run, they are often seen by FI management as short-term projects, and therefore fairly uncommon and/or short-lived.

Postal banking was also considered as an alternative to payday lending, offered by the postal system that might be owned by the state or the private sector. Because of the privatization of much of Canada's postal branches, it is not clear how practical this would be in Canada. However, where the state owns the postal system and if branches are located in regions of financial exclusion, then the postal system may be a means to reduce financial exclusion, in a blunt way, and that might partly reduce reliance on payday loans.

Do Regulations Help Payday Loan Consumers?

Most provinces regulate payday lending using price caps, fair disclosure, and disallowance of repeat loans, to name the most important components of these regulations.

With respect to price caps, only the province of Quebec proactively disallows payday loans through its usury cap of 35%. Newfoundland and Labrador disallow payday loans, not through their own regulations, but through the federal Criminal Rate of Interest. Since they have not prosecuted payday lenders, it does not seem to be an effective form of regulation. Remaining provincial regulators, until recently, have placed the price caps quite high, ranging from $17 to $23 per $100 loaned when there is quite substantial evidence that payday lenders can operate efficiently at $15 per $100 loaned. Alberta and Ontario have moved to a price cap of $15 per $100 loaned.

Data on the impact of regulations on payday lending and payday loan clients are limited and so, for the Canadian context, it is difficult to say much definitively what the impact of regulations is on the consumer. Only two jurisdictions (BC and Nova Scotia) monitor the industry, and since they do not collect adequate information about payday lending, it is hard to evaluate the outcome of the regulations. It is hard to conclude whether customers are being harmed or helped by payday loans or by the regulations. There is a clear need for the regulators and the federal government to monitor and evaluate the payday loan sector—and other fringe banking sectors for that matter—more carefully.

Regulators ban rollovers and seek to control repeat borrowing, but there is evidence that not enough is being done to control this problem. It is a problem, as discussed above, because some customers need a longer-term solution to their financial challenges and taking out a two-week expensive payday loan does not help them, and in these cases, it can harm them. The issue needs to be addressed, and regulators might consider carefully the US Consumer Financial Protection Bureau's plan to require payday lenders to underwrite their loans in order to provide credit to clients with the ability to repay the loan.

Recommendations for Action

The payday loan industry is situated in a broader social problem of financial exclusion from the mainstream financial institutions and services that most Canadians take for granted. We recommend several actions that financial regulators, banks, and credit unions could implement to provide all Canadians with access to the financial services they need at reasonable cost. These recommendations overlap each other and the implementation of some would supersede others. In view of the evidence provided in this book, we offer a set of preferred policy recommendations. In default of the political will needed to implement these preferred policies, we offer a set of secondary recommendations that, as a minimum, are required to restore some measure of fairness in access to essential financial services.

Preferred Policy Recommendations

Our preferred set of recommendations is a threefold approach that sees the enhanced access to mainstream banking, the banning of payday loans, and a nationwide guarantee of minimum overdraft protection on all bank and credit union checking accounts.

Enhance Access to Mainstream Banking

A key recommendation flowing from the research in this book is that payday loan consumers need better access to financial services and the mainstream financial institutions—banks and credit unions—are best placed to provide this access. Credit unions have taken the lead in developing financial inclusion and credit products that can reduce reliance on payday loans. But their smaller size restricts the scope of these efforts. Mainstream banks must step up to offer more accessible financial products in more accessible locations by staff that are trained to work with people who have only modest financial means.

There is considerable evidence that shows that many payday loan borrowers feel banks do not respect them or treat them fairly. This claim appears to be the feeling across a wide spectrum of different payday loan customers in Canada and the US. Canadian banks enjoy a privileged position in a protected oligopoly that has rendered them very profitable. As a return for the advantages they enjoy, banks should offer their services and their respect to the entire Canadian population.

Postal banking offers another way to enhance access to basic financial services by using the existing network of postal outlets to deliver basic banking services to virtually the entire Canadian population. Thousands of remote communities and families are closer to a post office than they are to a bank or credit union, and the post office has remained in the poorer areas of the cities that the banks have been leaving. The federal government and Canada Post do not currently support re-creating the postal banking network, but it is an idea that should be considered for its ability to deliver an essential service to many underserved Canadians and Indigenous Peoples.

Expand Appropriate Financial Products at Banks and Credit Unions

We recommend that banks and credit unions be required to provide and to promote (i.e., market) financial products that will reduce the need for people to rely on payday loans. This includes access to savings accounts, small credit products, and overdraft protection.

For instance, many Canadians benefit from overdraft protection as it is an opportunity to borrow short-term funds for bridging an occasional gap between spending needs and income flows. As an essential banking service, all Canadians should have access to a minimum amount of short-term credit for this purpose. Such a requirement would pose no serious default risk for banks and credit unions since such loans are, on average, very small denomination, the customer already has a bank account, and the money deposited into the account will cover the overdraft loan. In addition to the low-cost accounts, banks and credit unions should be required by legislation to offer all customers a minimum amount of overdraft protection. Enhanced accessibility to mainstream banking services and an expansion of appropriate financial products on offer by banks and credit unions do not address payday lending issues directly, which brings us to another action choice.

Ban Payday Loans

As mainstream FIs step up their offering of better financial services and products for credit-constrained consumers, the role of payday lending can diminish. Moreover, Quebec, Newfoundland and Labrador, and many US states have effectively banned payday lending. There is no significant body of evidence that this ban has caused harm to people in those jurisdictions. Combined with the results presented in this book that payday lending can be harmful to some, we recommend the outright banning of payday loans. If all the banks and credit unions were to offer overdraft protection to all customers, then a ban on payday loans in their current form is a feasible companion policy.

Secondary Policy Recommendations

If an outright ban on payday lending is politically infeasible, we provide some secondary recommendations required to reduce the harm on those payday loan borrowers who find themselves trapped by this high-cost debt.

Design Loans from Fringe Financial Service Providers, Based on Solid Research, That Are More Appropriate for the Financial Needs of the Customer

We showed that problems with payday loans for consumers include the immediate balloon repayment and facing the high fees. For cash-strapped people this can disable their ability to repay the loan. In a sense, they have a long-term financial need that is not addressed by the short-term payday loan. For these people a payday loan might aggravate rather than alleviate their financial needs. To address this dimension of the payday lending problem, we recommend, akin to the recommendations from the United States Consumer Financial Protection Bureau, that payday lenders be required to restrict their loans to people with adequate credit reports or that they offer an installment loan rather than a balloon repayment loan.

We recommend that care be made in converting payday loans into installment loans. Three formats to replace it with installment loans have been tried, though there is not a lot of evidence to determine how well each one works. So a key component of this recommendation is that careful analysis be undertaken to gain a better understanding of the advantages and disadvantages of three potential formats.

- No payday loans in the current form are allowed, only installment loans, still at high rates, to customers who cannot get traditional loans or overdraft protection (Colorado model);
- Customers who take frequent payday loans are required to take the next loan as an installment loan with repayment spread over a longer period, and they are not allowed to take out other payday loans while the installment loan is outstanding. BC has adopted this model and Ontario is considering it.
- Payday loan customers are allowed the option to convert the loan into an installment loan before the maturity date.

Payday loan companies and some other lenders in Canada now offer high-cost installment loans at rates of 40–60% per annum, which is high but still within the Criminal Code limit. An installment option appears better for borrowers than the current payday loans model, but we don't know how it will affect the industry. The Colorado payday loan industry has contracted to a third of its former size. Canada's lower concentration of population outside a few cities would probably force closure of a large number of stores.

Rate Caps but No Size Caps

We have shown that fees greater than $15 on $100 borrowed provide unjustifiable excess profits to the larger firms and perhaps to all payday lenders. At an absolute minimum, we recommend capping the cost of the payday loans to no more than $15 per $100 borrowed for 14 days, or a maximum of 390% APR. This fee cap should be reviewed in a few years when the further concentration of the industry is likely to have reduced costs even more. We do not recommend a reduction in the maximum size allowed for a payday loan. That action will not produce any benefits and might even increase problems as borrowers try to borrow from more than one lender at a time.

Enhance Data Collection

Every province that allows payday loans should collect the statistical information that is at least as detailed as what British Columbia is collecting. Governments need to boost their data collection about the payday lending industry and customers to enable effective analysis. We need publicly available financial data on the financial results of the payday loan companies. Adequate data are required as well to undertake the analysis needed to ascertain the best installment loan format. Other regulated industries are required to provide these data to justify their pricing; there is no reason why payday lenders should be exempt.

Reference

Caskey, John P. 2010. *Payday Lending: New Research and the Big Question.* Working Papers, No. 10–32, Federal Reserve Bank of Philadelphia, Philadelphia.

Sample of Websites of Organizations Offering, Regulating, or Concerned About Payday Lending

Government Regulators

Canada

Financial Consumer Agency of Canada https://www.canada.ca/en/financial-consumer-agency.html
Office of Consumer Affairs www.ic.gc.ca/consumer

Provincial and Territorial Consumer Affairs Offices

Consumer Protection British Columbia https://www.consumerprotectionbc.ca/
Service Alberta, Consumer Contact Centre www.servicealberta.ca
Consumer Credit Division, Financial and Consumer Affairs Authority of Saskatchewan www.fcaa.gov.sk.ca
Consumer Protection Office, Manitoba http://www.gov.mb.ca/cca/cpo/
Consumer Protection Ontario https://www.ontario.ca/page/consumer-protection-ontario
Office de la protection du consommateur/Consumer Protection Quebec http://www.opc.gouv.qc.ca/en/contact/consumer/
Financial and Consumer Services Commission (New Brunswick) http://www.fcnb.ca/FinancialConsumer.html

J. Buckland et al. (eds.), *Payday Lending in Canada in a Global Context*,
https://doi.org/10.1007/978-3-319-71213-0

Service Nova Scotia https://novascotia.ca/sns/
Service NL (Newfoundland & Labrador) www.gs.gov.nl.ca/index.html
Consumer Services, Department of Environment, Labour and Justice (Prince Edward Island) www.gov.pe.ca/consumerservices/
Consumer Affairs, Department of Municipal and Community Affairs (Northwest Territories) http://www.maca.gov.nt.ca/?page_id=504
Consumer Affairs, Department of Community and Government Services (Nunavut) www.gov.nu.ca/english/
Consumer Services, Department of Community Services (Yukon) www.community.gov.yk.ca/consumer/index.html

United States

Consumer Financial Protection Bureau https://www.consumerfinance.gov/

United Kingdom

Financial Conduct Authority https://www.fca.org.uk/

Australia

Australian Securities and Investments Commission http://asic.gov.au/

Payday Lending Associations

Canada

Alternative Financial Services Providers Association http://www.payday-businessownersassociation.com/
Canadian Consumer Finance Association http://canadiancfa.com/

United States

Community Financial Services Association of America http://cfsaa.com/

Payday Lending Companies

Canada

Money Mart www.moneymart.ca
Cash Money www.cashmoney.ca
Cash4You www.cash4you.ca
Cashco Financial https://cashcofinancial.com/

United States

Advance America https://www.advanceamerica.net/

United Kingdom

The Money Shop https://www.themoneyshop.com/

Australia

Cash Converters http://www.cashconverters.com.au/

Civil Society Organizations Engaged with Payday Loan Regulations and Issues

Canada

ACORN Canada https://www.acorncanada.org/
Black Creek Financial Action Network http://cec.info.yorku.ca/bcfan/
Consumers' Association of Canada (Manitoba) Inc. http://cacmanitoba.ca/
Consumers Council of Canada http://www.consumerscouncil.com/
Momentum http://www.momentum.org/
Prosper Canada http://prospercanada.org/
SEED Winnipeg http://seedwinnipeg.ca/

United States

Center for Responsible Lending http://www.responsiblelending.org/
Pew Charitable Trust http://www.pewtrusts.org/en

United Kingdom

Community Investment Coalition http://responsiblefinance.org.uk/

Australia

Indigenous Consumer Assistance Network http://ican.org.au/

Index[1]

[1] Note: Page numbers followed by 'n' refer to notes.

J. Buckland et al. (eds.), *Payday Lending in Canada in a Global Context*,
https://doi.org/10.1007/978-3-319-71213-0

The manufacturer's authorised representative in the EU is Springer
Nature Customer Service Centre GmbH, Europaplatz 3, 69115 Heidelberg,
Germany. If you have any concerns regarding our products, please
contact ProductSafety@springernature.com

Printed and bound by CPI Group (UK) Ltd, Croydon, CR0 4YY
06/10/2026
02229006-0001